THE SPIRIT OF **SECULAR ART**

A HISTORY OF THE SACRAMENTAL ROOTS OF CONTEMPORARY ARTISTIC VALUES

ROBERT NELSON

MONASH University
ePress

ACKNOWLEDGEMENTS

This book was written with the assistance of an ARC Small Grant, which provided the time to write the initial draft, plus a Monash Small Grant, which afforded the invaluable and judicious assistance of Dr Cynthia Troup, who helped assemble the apparatus. In addition to this, I would like to acknowledge the formidable contribution of several readers who took time out to scrutinize the text and make prolific critical comment upon it. These include Professor Gary Bouma (Monash University), Dr Rex Butler (Queensland University), Associate Professor Domenico de Clario (Monash University), Geoffrey Dupree (artist, Monash University), Associate Professor Robert Gaston (La Trobe University), Dr M.A. Greenstein (Boulder and Los Angeles) Professor Kevin Hart (University of Notre Dame), Professor Bill Kent (Monash University), Sister Emeritus Professor Margaret Manion (University of Melbourne), Associate Professor Anne Marsh (Monash University), Dr Christopher Marshall (University of Melbourne), Dr Adrian Martin (Monash University), Dr Constant Mews (Monash University), Dr Luke Morgan (Monash University), Dr Eva and Dr Peter Nelson (my parents), Dr Polixeni Papapetrou (artist and my wife), Professor John Redmond (Monash University), Emeritus Professor Bernard Smith (University of Melbourne), Associate Professor Mark Wedig OP (Barry University, Miami).

— *Robert Nelson*

THE SPIRIT OF SECULAR ART

A HISTORY OF THE SACRAMENTAL ROOTS OF CONTEMPORARY ARTISTIC VALUES

CONTENTS

A NOTE ABOUT PAGINATION AND CHAPTER IDENTIFICATION

Page numbers in this book do not run consecutively across chapters. Instead, page numbering restarts on the first page of each chapter and is prefaced by the chapter number. Thus 01.1 is chapter one, page one; 01.2 is chapter one, page two; 02.1 is chapter two, page one; 02.2 is chapter two, page two; and so on.

As page numbering restarts at the beginning of each chapter, page numbers are not listed in the Table of Contents

This system, in which page numbering is self-contained within each chapter, allows the publisher, Monash University ePress, to publish individual chapters online.

CHAPTER 1

SECULAR SACRAMENTS AND THE PRESTIGE OF ART

Robert Nelson

Like many old words with new meanings, prestige indicates something archaic in contemporary values. Prestige is a kind of magical esteem. It is used to describe expensive cars and property and other consumer goods, normally suggesting a value which does not derive purely from the material qualities of the object or place. Something of a cultural nature has been cultivated which gives the car or house or fountain-pen an exclusive cachet, an aura of traditional desire and long-standing demand, a mysteriously authorized glamour which cannot be explained by engineering, mechanics or geography.

Art is quintessentially prestigious, and not just because its material basis is marginal, nor even because the artist has invested imagination in the outcome. It is true that the canvas and paint are cheap and the component of invention explains a great deal of the price of a painting. The artist's reputation, which is normally a good part of the prestige of the work, hinges on all the contributions of an artist's career; and the work fetching a high price is understood to distil those creative qualities. But none of this would happen if art itself were not prestigious, if the artwork had not been institutionalized as a site in which you are charmed by a peculiarly artistic spell. Art, in short, has a spiritual element. When you look at art, you are not just looking at the work of one artist but a hallowed plane of signifiers, established in western consciousness from who knows what ancestral times. One artist—by dint of superior imagination or sincerity—may be able to satisfy the spiritual expectations of buyers more than another; and this may explain a local difference in prices. But the larger structure within which the connoisseur discriminates is underpinned by ancient spiritual values.

Prestige in this book is not exactly the quality that makes one painting more valuable than another. In a popular sense, 'prestige' refers to meaningful glamour.[1] It is the quality that makes art distinctive among other commodities in a bourgeois economy. This book asserts that the inherited magic of art is based on anterior belief systems. Art is intrinsically cultish. All artistic things, except the prestige of art, can be empirically explained by examining style, iconography and patronage. What cannot be so readily explained is the reliance of all art—pre-eminently secular art—on religious intuitions which are carried forward from archaic times. There is a sacramental basis for the prestige of art, and this book provides a history of that foundation.

In matching art and the sacramental, we appear to be dealing with diametrically opposed ideas. Since the advent of modernism, art has been understood as freedom of expression, the untrammeled exercise of imagination, invention and experiment. Art means defying the conventions of the past and forging new visions. The concept of sacrament, on the other hand, is deeply institutional; it is stipulated in venerable authorities, based on age-old beliefs and practices rather than individual creativity. Nothing, on first glance, could be more remote from the liberality of art than the codified blessings of the sacramental. From the beginnings of a recognizable avant garde in the nineteenth century, art has been antithetical to religious observation. Notions like worship have long been discredited as uncritical, theocratically fostering in people an unquestioning submission to an order of absolute supremacy. The indoctrination required to induce in people the need to worship is itself felt to be repugnant in a culture based on the reasoned challenge to all spiritual assumptions and especially institutional faith.[2]

There is undeniably a cultish background to premodern art; but it is a popular misconception that the breakthrough of modernism involves the transcendence of religious institutions. First, secular art has a tradition long anterior to modernism. Second, there is a question of when and how the religious preconditions of art receded and the dependence on cultish ritual became inconspicuous. This book argues that those cultish contingencies were never abandoned: they were translated into secular enthusiasms, enthusiasms that paradoxically depend on the backdrop of arcane spirituality which they seem to transcend.

Most aspects of religious consciousness—right down to the sacramental—are preserved by a form of cultural abstraction in secular art. The process is a regular historical change by which art has seduced the religious, abducted its prestige and thrived on its spiritual assumptions. Art as we know it today could not have occurred without a sacred backdrop. Structures of a sacramental kind created the very preconditions of prestige in secular art and installed certain assumptions within it. Secularization in art does not simply mean abjuring religion. It means *abstracting* the sacred; it means commuting certain rituals—which, from epoch to epoch, have become historically exhausted—to a synthetic and autonomous spirituality which we call art. In this way, the sacramental element in art did not suddenly vanish but was transformed into secular guises of immense authority and influence, to the point that they are essential in the very definition of art. For two millennia, art has been eluding a liturgical role of one kind or another to achieve that freedom and autonomy which are axiomatic in art today. The sacramental status from the past is not dispensed with: it *goes somewhere*, whence it crucially informs the essence of art as an especially meaningful commodity. The sacramental component of art lies dormant and hidden in secular production; but it is all the more deeply embedded in the definition of art for its magic combination of spiritual prestige and philosophical evasiveness.

* * *

In my role as an art critic for a broadsheet, I see a large number of contemporary exhibitions in a variety of media, many of which reveal a strange persistence of motifs that I have come to understand in sacramental terms. They all occur in circumstances that have no religious pretensions. An example is a video performance by Christian Thompson,[3] an Indigenous artist based in Melbourne. In a screen divided into four quarters, the artist's father is shown grooming his children, who are grown up men (Thompson himself and his brother). Juxtaposed to these sequences, the artist's brother is shown again, only this time grooming his own child's hair. The action in each case is gentle and touching. But the ritual of grooming was not always so intimate, the artist explains. In the days when his father was in the army, the family had to line up for its hair to be chastened. Now, it seems, the parental disciplinary roles have softened. A new ritual is constructed—the art work—in which the regimental pain of strict mornings before school is exorcized. The video stages the generational handing down of a necessary and ancient ritual belonging to childhood; but the gist of the combing action is morally mollified: the acceptance of passivity is now recast in favour of tenderness. By rehearsing the memory of father-and-son grooming (now almost absurd on account of Thompson's maturity and the father's middle age) the scenes recall the harsher times and recover from them the fondness that underlay the paternal order. The sacramental combing transforms the memory of discipline into affection.

The motif of exorcizing past psychological hurt—or expiating it on behalf of society—recurs in performative contemporary art genres and also extends to traditional media. Another Indigenous artist, Clinton Nain, recently gave a performance at the opening of his exhibition of paintings (*a e i o u*) in Melbourne.[4] Nain painted 33 pictures containing the five vowels. Little else is included in the field beyond these vociferous letters. One picture has a little white fence around its border, a series of picket and rail, resembling crosses in an old graveyard. The rest of the enclosure is consumed by the letterforms denoting the five pure components of speech.

The works are not cheerful and the discourse hardly celebrates the elements of phonology. The pictures are mostly in deep browns and bitumen as if expressing the demoralizing gloom of learning a language imposed upon you. With dark colours, relentless bossy capitals and grim imagery, the paintings fiercely juxtapose the lessons with the sad Aboriginal reception of European education, someone else's idea of language, represented by abstract codes of spelling. Nain sometimes includes the target in his pictures, which seems to double as the head of a person. Sinister connotations abound, reinforced by the titles. A black heart which is empty inside bears the title 'they have dispossessed you'.

Against this history of displacement and stolen children, the triumphal linguistic system of European writing does not seem so glorious and universal. As Nain rehearses his primary school education, the repetition of "a e i o u" throughout the pictures acquires a poignant and reverberating timbre. It comes as a shock to realize that the pure vowels are the sounds of the scream and the howl. The baleful tone of the primal cry is shown at its most distilled by the five abstract analytical letters. Remembering the atrocities of white rule over Aboriginal communities is cause enough for prolonged wailing; and it seems a haunting paradox that the score for this mournful cry is provided by such a cerebral code for voiced sound. The rational spelling-based system, having abstracted the vowel sounds from their couch of consonants, leaves you with the pure agony of a voice that rises from the lung without the symbolic punctuation of language.

The rationale for sounds being divided into voiced and unvoiced categories is all for the sake of writing; the system works in any language, including the 'ethnographic' languages, which are being effaced as we speak. So, with Nain's show, the spectator has some relearning to do. Our teachers tried to instruct us in primary school; but we could not really understand things at that age and the principles slip past our memory as a blur. The memory of early lessons is disempowering, because the material is both basic and abstract, something mystifying for the small children but also for philologists and lexicographers.

Nain takes us back to the blackboard, where we can also passively imagine a teacher explaining to children that Australia was discovered in 1770 or a bit earlier by the Dutch or Portuguese. One of Nain's paintings looks like a blackboard, with nothing but emptiness. The dark void is inscribed with letters that look a bit like chalk on the blackboard: 'what Australia looked like before colonization'. We would not make that mistake now. The media sees the centre of Australia as a land over-full of abuse and wrecked lives. Nain almost seems to shriek at those circumstances too, since sometimes he places his "a e i o u" out of order, as if the pupil's mind is chroming, unable to fit the letters into alphabetical order. It is heart-rending stuff.

So is the sequence of salty ground under a blue sky that leads to a graveyard and the gallows. The history of subjecting Aborigines to white conventions—right down to the forbidding principles of orthography—is harrowing. Indigenous people were killed with bullets and books; and the art of painting expresses it in Nain's hands. But by enacting aspects of the hurt, the confronting content becomes available to language and feeling and can be dealt with; it contributes to a larger consciousness in which the psyche can embrace its failings. This condition of invoking horror for the sake not of transcendence but psychological negotiation, is an element of what can be recognized as the sacramental. The deeper origins of this sacramental element which surfaces in contemporary art such as Nain's remain to be investigated.

* * *

It has a necessary history. Alongside some further examples of contemporary art, the epochs discussed in the chapters which follow reveal a series of historical changes from sacred to secular which roughly coincide with the growing sophistication of art and the public recognition of art as an independent consumable. In each case, there is a four-stage process, by which sculpture and painting (a) draw from an archaic sacramental order to express religious processes, (b) detach themselves from liturgical incumbencies and celebrate their autonomy, (c) appropriate the language of the former religious order by subsuming its prestige in an aesthetic refreshment and (d) achieve new spiritual glamour for the miracle of converting a conventional and ritual-bound spirituality to a more universal expression of the human spirit. These are, so to speak, the 'moments' at which sculpture and painting become Art in the sense commonly understood today: autonomous things, charged with cultural meaning, intensity and prestige.

In no epoch did the move from sacred to secular entail the abandonment of spirituality in favour of formal or materialist qualities. On the contrary, the awareness of a spiritual ambition is if anything heightened with the advent of secularization. Whereas in archaic times the spiritual content was a kind of default—the necessary substance to be taken for granted in the mission of religious art—the more sophisticated secular art which overtakes it is strenuously preoccupied with its claims to spiritual powers, for they are no longer inherent in the artistic mission. Art is no longer attached to ritual. If it is to deliver the prestige and claim spiritually efficacy, it must devote special efforts to the artificial task of achieving it. Art does not possess an inherently innocent magic.[5] The peculiar immaterial qualities sought in art derive from religious motifs manipulated by successive generations, and historically evolving in a way which is integral to artistic tradition. This is the great self-consciousness of art which lies at the core of artistic prestige in a bourgeois economy and which creates Art in the sense commonly understood today.

In spite of the increasingly secular character of the western world, all western art has something sacramental about it. This is not a case of art *retaining* the spiritual, as if art were somehow a more conservative institution holding out with heroic tenacity against the onslaught of atheist materialism. The sacramental element in art is strategic. It is cultivated as an essential component of secularization, because the value of art in a secular context depends on the prestige of poetically rearranging the sacramental roots of artistic expression. The sacramental element is not a hardy left-over, an enduring relic which nobly survives in the production of newer artists. More often than not, the secular rearrangements of the sacramental roots of art depend on the new art rejecting tradition. There is little question of artworks somehow carrying an ancestral spirituality which is preserved inside them like a ruin abiding in barbarous times. Artworks actively and structurally exploit a sacramental tradition for their sense of spiritual value; they may even unscrupulously reconstrue religious ideas to flatter their own secular purposes. It may be that artworks paradoxically act as the nostalgic repository of spirituality in a world which has fewer and fewer sacramental vessels, but this guardianship of holy ideas does not proceed from piety for a religious past so much as an inherent reliance on the outdated privileges of the sacramental.

* * *

But what does this mean, the sacramental? In this text, 'sacrament' does not necessarily mean 'the sacraments' in the technical Christian sense. At the same time, however, it is necessary to acknowledge the perception that Christians have a kind of copyright on the term 'sacrament'. They (and they alone) have used it with specific meanings which, for centuries, were defined and debated in rich and earnest tracts. Perhaps the agreed meanings in Christian theology should rightfully prevail. There is a tradition—a Christian tradition—which has conferred so much meaning on the term that it would be naïve and reckless to ignore its historical basis and construct a new version in some kind of theoretical purity. But for all our debt to the Christian theology which massively cultivated the term over many centuries, there are two historical reasons which let us use the term with licence.

First, there is a history of the term anterior to Christianity. When Christians first used the word 'sacrament', they were translating the Greek 'mystery' (*mysterion*). Up to that time, the Latin word (*sacramentum*) had meant a pledge or oath, often used in the context of allegiance among military personnel. The classical Latin word carries a sense of ritual, but rather by way of duty; it is not pre-eminently religious but rather mechanistic, spiritually neutral and colourless as a psychological process and carrying only vague relations with the divine. The more spiritual usage of the Latin word therefore owes everything to the Greek concept for which the Romans required a translation in their indigenous language. In ancient Greek, mystery (*mysterion*) was used to characterize religious actions well before Christ.[6] Pagan cults all had their mysteries. The concept of mystery was neither confined to the Christian cult nor subsequently the exclusive property of the Church.[7] And of course today, mystery—unlike sacrament—is hardly bound by theological definitions; it is a word in very common usage with wide acceptations, running from the unexplained to the unfathomable to the divine.

Second, Christians themselves admit a category of human gestures with divine associations which have to be acknowledged as sacramental, even though they are clearly not 'the sacraments' of the Church. One such gesture cited by theologians is the washing of feet, with its biblical precedent of Christ's insistence on bathing Peter's feet. As with Thompson's grooming of the family's hair, this is not a sacrament in the strict sense but fits into another category of holy practices, a plain and humble action in which a sacred secret inheres, 'the sacramental' or a sacrament in the broader sense.[8] This is the meaning intended throughout the following chapters. The strictly Christian definition of the sacraments encourages a mechanistic conception of the sacred and limits the richness of holy offices. Furthermore, the restriction in meaning of 'sacrament' to the seven sacraments (baptism, confirmation, penitence, eucharist, marriage, ordination and last unction) is in danger of chauvinism. It excludes the sacramental in spiritual traditions which do not involve Christ.[9]

There is a risk that the archaic concept of 'sacrament'—overwritten, as it is, with Christian dogma—is not particularly useful. Perhaps mystery would be a better word. But the great value in the idea of the sacramental (which is not so strongly conveyed by the term mystery) is the ritual expression of spiritual elevation by means of the sensual. The sacraments in all traditions involve the body.[10] A gesture is performed of a corporal nature: one is washed or sparged or anointed or given to eat or drink; and the sensory experience in the body is an integral part of the ceremony.

Why the body? Initially, the involvement of the body may seem at variance with the exclusively spiritual aspirations of the religion. Some theologians (like the Jesuit Christian Pesch whose formidable volumes on the sacraments gather Catholic wisdom on the theme from the premodern period) have a bland and mechanistic explanation for the involvement of the corporal in the spiritual. As sin is normally committed through the body, so the spiritual medicine against sin should be taken through the body.[11] Pesch finds it appropriate that the supremacy of the spiritual over the carnal should be inverted when it comes to certain rituals of spiritual rectification. In fact, he sees something poetic in the address to the corporal for the failings of the spiritual.

There are two problems with this traditional explanation of the corporality of the sacraments. First, it seems rather limiting to see the sacraments as spiritual medicine. Penitence can easily be seen that way (for it directly relates to a failure of spiritual health) but other sacraments, such as baptism, are not such a good fit.[12] Baptism is clearly a rite of initiation, a stamp by which a person is deemed to belong to the cult. Medicines are not prescribed for a sense of belonging. Nor does it seem appropriate to consider the spiritual medicine prophylactic: the rite of initiation, regardless of the agency of the Holy Ghost, is not an inoculation against sin but a sign of entry into the cult. Second, there is no logic in the argument that the body is the appropriate site for correction—if indeed that is all that sacraments are—when all sin is committed in the mind and can only be chastened in the mind. To direct attention to the body (simply because the body is an instrument of sin) is perverse. The traditional explanation for the corporality of the sacraments is far from satisfactory.

But it would be still more unsatisfactory to imagine that the involvement of the body is incidental, or for an effect of sheer spectacle. It seems more apt to see the body as performing a function in the rites, namely to symbolize the access of the institutional to the personal.[13] Through contact with a sacramental gesture, the body becomes a kind of metaphoric opening to a person's innermost privacy. Through the sacrament this most intimate zone is infiltrated by an outside institutional agency. The sacraments stage an encounter between body and institution; the body takes on an institutional influence and the institution enjoys access to the body. It is an exchange in which various messages concerning influence and ownership are induced to flow in the most pervasive measure.

Physicality is not the only element of a sacrament. In all traditions, the workings of the spirit are intangible and abstract. They need to be enacted on a physical level to have any persuasiveness or immediacy; but not every action which is the physical means to a spiritual end is a sacrament. A sacrament has to involve a corporal intervention, because the body represents the preserve of a person's individuality, which is in some sense given over to the institution in the ceremony. A sacrament is performed with your body, not someone else's body, because the spiritual end is not general but absolutely concerned with you as an individual; and a part of you, as it were, is resigned in the ritual. In the sacrament, your body is submitted as a symbol of your personal acceptance of the spiritual institution.

Theologians have often argued that the purpose of a sacrament is not to sanctify things but to sanctify people.[14] In this, the sacraments distinguish themselves from consecration, the ritual by which ecclesiastical objects are established as holy and suitable for spiritual purposes. This is also physical; a priest performs certain actions while calling upon a superior spirit with appropriate traditional invocations. The spirit is engaged and the object is hallowed. Just as there is no corporal intervention, so there is no specific individual at the end of it who receives a blessing. The ritual is rather more general than a sacrament, pertaining to a scheme of institutional objects which do not directly relate to the sensory and those personal feelings which follow from it.

The centrepiece of the sacraments—sanctifying people—is also what distinguishes sacrament from sacrifice. A sacrifice is for expressing thankfulness or atonement, for making up to God, a form of ingratiation. Its scope is not to sanctify people, as with a sacrament, but to seek absolution by means of proffering a thing of value, a thing or being for which one has affection but which one will nevertheless resign to God as a victim.

The distinction is valuable but somewhat subtle. All the Christian sacraments derive their force from Christ's sacrifice.[15] They sanctify people but by invoking the agency of a sacrifice; they have a directly dependent relationship on a sacrifice and, in the Christian conspectus, they can never escape the haunting shade of the cross. It seems confusing to say that the purposes of sacrament and sacrifice are different when one of them presupposes the other, when one of them assumes all its efficacy from the other and is signally invoked for each rehearsal. It may be true that a sacrament is for sanctifying people while a sacrifice relates primarily to people's relationship to God; but if a good relationship to God is not a sign of blessedness, what is? The sacrifice is made to God in the belief that God's wrath will be appeased and consequently the person making the sacrifice—or the people on whose behalf the sacrifice is made—will ascend to a higher level of grace in God's eyes than before. It is therefore artificial to maintain that the sacrifice cannot confer a certain sanctity on people.

Finally, one of the sacraments, indeed the sacrament *par excellence*—the eucharist—has traditionally been called a sacrifice as well as a sacrament.[16] In holy communion, members of the congregation eat a wafer and drink wine in order to participate in Christ's sacrifice on the cross and thereby receive the grace issuing from it. The death of Christ is figuratively re-staged for each communicator who eats the body and blood of Christ in the form of the consecrated elements of bread and wine.

There is a useful distinction to be made between sacrifice and sacrament, but it lies in a different direction. A sacramental order is an abstraction of a sacrificial order. In a sacrament, you do not perform a sacrifice but appeal to an anterior sacrifice for obtaining the grace which can be drawn from it. A sacrifice has happened long ago; it is remembered in pious references and may even be re-enacted in a symbolic form (as with the eucharist), a ritual of physical gestures which mystically takes part in the sacrifice that it recalls. Of the Christian sacraments, the eucharist is clearly the example which most directly reflects and embodies the original sacrifice.[17] But its relation to the original sacrifice, already abstracted by the very process of representation, is further abstracted by its context amid the other sacraments. It is not an autonomous ritual but a celebration which belongs to a sacramental order, in a ceremonial sense analogous to baptism, marriage or ordination, even though, in a structural sense, those other sacraments seem to have nothing to do with the altar. Unlike the eucharist, the other sacraments are far from the bloody terms of sacrifice, even though they conduct the virtues of the sacrifice to the soul of the participant. In confirmation, for instance, the recalling of the crucifixion seems utterly remote, even if it remains the sacrificial backdrop which confers upon the ceremony the ultimate efficacy. In bundling together the rituals of very differing proximity to the altar, the religion draws away from the reality of sacrifice and abstracts its meaning on a more universal plane of signs.[18]

To enjoy the power of the blood but not the substance, to move from the lamb on the altar to a chain of blessed signifiers, some of which lack even a corpuscle of sacrificial immediacy: these are the workings of the sacramental order. What makes it all religious is the metaphysical faculty for a symbolic object or process to ascend to spiritual virtue. It is no accident that sacrament owes so much to the Greek conception of mystery. There is a mystery in the recalling of the sacrifice—however remote—which does not immediately surface in the original sacrifice. The abstraction becomes the vessel of mystery. A sacramental action is not mysterious because it mechanically mimics an earlier sacrificial event but because it enshrines the spiritual justification of the sacrifice while removing it from the local circumstances in which it took place. The sacrament makes the sacrifice transferable and lifts it onto a supposedly universal plane, stripped of the contingencies of the original event.

In spite of the abstraction which structurally underlies the sacramental order, there is nothing less abstract than a sacrament. The sacrament is staged in a demonstrative fashion. It involves the tangible and sensory intervention of actions in or upon your body. So the sacraments are both abstract and immediate: they happen in a direct contact with your body but their meaning is exalted by virtue of mystically relaying the powers of an earlier sacrifice. This paradoxical dual nature of the sacramental order first creates the motif of a spiritualized corporality which is the fundamental paradigm of art. To appreciate the relevance of the sacramental to the development of self-conscious art in western culture is to trace the genealogy of spirit. For autonomous art stands in the same relation to sacrament as sacrament stands in relation to sacrifice.

Before art became an institution of autonomous visual objects in galleries, there was already a paradigm of a spiritual uplifting through codified physical actions. This paradigm is the mysterious enactment of sacramental rites which are both corporal and abstract, corporal in their means and abstract in their agency. The preconditions of art did not have to be invented by artists. They were already established before artists were invited to contribute to the definition of the sacred and ages before anyone might have considered that art contains something mysterious in its own right.

But paradoxically, art has largely gained its contemporary status on account of being identified with the spiritual. Even people of a materialistic cast of mind—like me, I will admit—allow that art expresses a spirit. Often their idea of the spirit is empirical, as when art is taken as translating the social or intellectual character (or 'spirit') of an epoch or group. It may be unnecessary to ascribe to art a spirit of an animating kind, but it is very hard to talk about art without conceding that it involves the clinching of key attitudes which characterize the psyche of a given culture. And to that extent, art lays claim to the transcendental, for it is not merely a material object nor even a confection of codes but a symbol of deeper qualities, often cryptic and fugitive but fundamentally reflecting what is widely understood as a spirit.

To this spiritual charter, art adds the mystique of the aesthetic experience. To behold an art work is not merely to 'read' the spirit which is recorded within but to have the spirit impress itself upon you with demonstrative physicality. The visual qualities register on a profoundly sensual level. And so the artwork becomes visionary not just for showing certain key topics of belief in a community but for staging them with credible representational bodies, gestures, spaces and inventions. The work has prestige by a dual commitment of corporality and abstraction. It is esteemed by its success in evoking presence (corporality) and the simultaneous withdrawal from the direct circumstances of the objects portrayed. This paradox accounts for much of the potency of art.

No matter how accurately drawn, a painting is always a painting. It is never the motif which it depicts; it is always at one remove, abstracted from the particular thing which it figures, and lifted to that lofty general status of art, a universal window capable of reflecting all other visible objects. We are so used to art that we often forget what an abstraction it is in itself. When you look at a tree in a picture, even when painted in a naturalistic manner, you do not hear the wind in the leaves; you do not get your feet muddy when approaching it or feel the water shake itself on your shoulders when you stand underneath it. The great realm of sensory interconnectedness in nature and life is artfully undone by centuries of picturing in which only certain salient visual features are isolated for translation and expression on the two-dimensional plane.

Although there are structural parallels between art and sacrament which are by no means coincidental, the two phenomena are very distinct. The purpose of this book is not to argue that art is a *de facto* sacrament. On the contrary, it seems fair to assume that art as we know it today is by and large secular. But secular vision, as it expresses itself through the prestige of art, is predicated upon a series of underlying sacramental structures which derive from art's archaic relationship with religious ritual. Some consciousness of this oblique spirituality is commonly assumed but never explained. It belongs to artistic subjectivity to guard its spiritual connotations jealously. For two millennia, art has had a dependent relationship on archaic mysteries and has profited by preserving an uncanny silence in the matter of its peculiar spirituality. This text is an attempt to explain the development of secular art in its continuing dependence on the prestige of the sacramental order which it has historically overtaken.

* * *

This is by no means the first attempt to explore the sacred substrate of secular art. The most famous and influential study is Walter Benjamin's essay *The Work of Art in the Age of Mechanical Reproduction*. This short but seminal text from 1931 describes how photographic reproduction emptied the artwork of its aura, devaluing its air of 'here and now' that is the property of authentically unique works.[19] For Benjamin, there is a major difference between works that are created uniquely at one time—as once-off products—and those that can be churned out any number of times. The unique works reveal a link between once-offness and permanence or lasting duration (*Einmaligkeit und Dauer*) just as the editable or photographic works create a link between transitoriness and repeatability (*Flüchtigkeit und Wiederholbarkeit*).[20] For the artwork, this distinction marks the demolition of the aura (*die Zertrümmerung der Aura*).

For Benjamin, the uniqueness of construction is synonymous with the aura of an artwork. Benjamin does not seem to contemplate that some unique works have no discernable aura, much less that reproduced works are the subject of aesthetic veneration (like the *Caprichos* of Goya, which are celebrated as much as his paintings). For Benjamin, the interpretation of an artwork may change over time but not the understanding of the aura, which is relatively absolute, because predicated exclusively on whether or not the work is unique. The example of a statue of Venus is given. Among the Greeks, the work was interpreted as divine and a core ingredient of the cult, whereas in the middle ages the same statue is regarded as an abomination. But for all that, the unifying feature for both was its singularity, in other words its aura (*ihre Einzigkeit, mit anderem Wort: ihre Aura*).[21]

For our argument, the significant and extraordinary part is not that Benjamin connects the aura with uniqueness but with cultish origins, the contextual integration of art in tradition. He explains that in early times, artworks originated in the service of ritual, first magical and then religious. "It is significant that the existence of the work of art with reference to its aura is never entirely separated from its ritual function."[22] For Benjamin, "This ritualistic basis, however remote, is still recognizable as secularized ritual even in the most profane forms of the cult of beauty." However, it is also doomed. "The secular cult of beauty, developed during the Renaissance and prevailing for three centuries, clearly showed this ritualistic basis in its decline and the first deep crisis which befell it." The crisis is completed by photography.

Benjamin proposed a powerful theory which announces the transformation of the ritual function of art to a secular aesthetic, an economy of appreciation which is independent of belief. Benjamin observed this change shrewdly, but his underlying motive throughout the analysis is to explain how reproductive technologies discredit the aura gained by unique-state artworks. Alas, because of limiting the auratic to the uniquely crafted, the theory reveals a mechanistic understanding of the aura.

Benjamin first identified the discourse and brilliantly gave it a name: the aura. His contribution to this field of aesthetic inquiry is immense. But there is a problem in his analysis, which reaches into the very definition of aura. For Benjamin, as noted, the aura is absolutely connected with once-offness, which in turn is expressed in ritual: "the unique value of the 'authentic' work of art has its basis in ritual, the location of its original use value." But in a footnote, the word aura is defined as the unique appearance of something remote.[23] Though enticing and perhaps evocative, this is also a remarkably physical construct of near and far.[24] Something remote is unapproachable (*Unnahbare*) which is the salient feature of the iconic image in the cult (*eine Hauptqualität des Kultbildes*).[25]

And so, when Benjamin contemplates the agency of secularization, it is seen in terms of declining once-offness. As the cultishness of the image is secularized, the once-offness is progressively enfeebled. The uniqueness becomes a value enjoyed by collectors who adore authenticity; but this aside, "the function of the concept of the authentic in art appreciation remains unequivocal"; and with "the secularization of art, the authenticity of art replaces the value of the cult".[26]

The way that Benjamin sets up the ritualistic basis of art declining into "secularized ritual even in the most profane forms of the cult of beauty"[27] is problematic. What is this secularized ritual? The cult of beauty existed in religious times—notably Greek antiquity—and corroborates the holy portraiture of divinity. The movement from ritual toward the secular is not explained by Benjamin's writing; further, it is hard to see how it occurred under the explanation that he offers. Mechanical reproduction indeed progressively overtakes unique works; and this arises in the same period, broadly, as secularization. But there is no historically causal relation between them; if anything, the two phenomena have a common cause in the obvious escalating materialism from the Renaissance to the current epoch.

Benjamin is to art history what Freud is to psychology. He puts the subjective experience on a material plane, dispelling romantic projections and sentiment in favour of dialectical method. And like Freud, Benjamin nevertheless tackles the matter of deepest emotional charge, because at the heart of aesthetic appreciation you might detect the aura in the same way that a person has a soul. For Benjamin the agency of the aura can be traced from a role in religious practice to commercial or political manifestations.[28] But the case is confused. On the one hand, ritual is turned into a secular form of the sacred; on the other hand, it loses its aura and is a desacralized form of exhibitable exchange value.

The language that Benjamin invented is sharp and has retained its currency. But the story of what happened to the sacred (and indeed what the sacred agency is) remains inscrutable in his writing. Sometimes, you feel that the opposite point can be made with the same terms. For example: "When the age of mechanical reproduction separated art from its basis in the cult, the semblance of its autonomy disappeared forever." It seems more plausible to argue that the artwork, having lost its dependency upon holy institutions, has now been liberated and has therefore won its autonomy in aesthetic terms (if not exactly in market terms).

Benjamin left more questions than answers. How much mechanical reproduction interfered with the auratic remains a puzzle and is by no means solved with Benjamin's assertion. To this, we can add: what parts of the sacred make themselves available to the secular and survive and in what forms? What is the theology of art that Benjamin referred to? The doctrine of art for art's sake is a new aesthetic theology, he says.[29] Is the theology only art for art's sake? That sounds very unlike the kind of theology that was practiced with such diligence for two millennia in western ecclesiastical and academic tradition. How does art achieve credibility if it lacks an aura? How does the aura survive (*pace* photography) if there is no cultish basis for the art, which is apparently the precondition of the aura? Secular art is quite prolifically devoted to one-off production, as with painting and drawing. So where do such media manage to get their aura or can they never escape being conceived photographically, once photography was invented? Do they therefore lack an aura entirely and in perpetuity?

Who decides what is an aura, which works have it—on what grounds and in what measures—and which works do not have it? Benjamin's terms are brilliant but I sometimes fear that they have survived for 75 years partly because they are so vague. They accommodate many interpretations, which writers have found convenient; because the conundrum that he uncovered acquired in his writings the air of critical authority. At one point, Benjamin comes close to explaining the debt to the sacred owed by the secular, when he talks about the parasitic existence of art in relation to ritual; however, the discourse is how technological reproducibility emancipates art from such a parasitic condition.[30] It is not really an explanation of how secular art borrows or colonizes or transforms the sacred.

Since Benjamin, many writers have followed with learned studies of the sacred and its rapports with the secular, especially in recent times. Up to a point, these studies concern the larger question of the status of art and what the sacred gives—in some form—to the secular. The literature is rich. Two texts by Hans Belting approach the theme through the idea of image anthropology[31] and special reference should also be made to Arthur Danto's (1997; 2003) works concerning the philosophy of art and art history. Of particular relevance to the later chapters in the present book is James Elkins (2004; 1997), whose study of religion in relation to contemporary art is useful and imaginative; and the studies of David Morgan (2005; 1999) also explore the field with contemporary acuteness. Mark C. Taylor (1992; 1984) has contributed two texts of signal relevance to the connexion between art and religion, and the monumental book by David Freedberg (1989) elucidates many of the processes by which pictures elicit a response which might answer the auratic. But none of these studies solves the riddles left by Benjamin, least of all by plumbing the depths of sacred traditions and comparing their sacramental agency with the calibre of contemporary art. The link between sacrifice, sacrament and art—at least to my knowledge—has never been explored.

It seems a curious time to explore sacrifice as the origin of certain types of aesthetic agency. As we will see, individual artists themselves, like Clinton Nain, have no difficulty invoking the cruel blow of a punishing order in which the individual finds redemptive awareness. But art historians, like theologians, are no longer so sure that they want to go there. Even the religions with the greatest possible historical interest in the matter are not keen to acknowledge or preserve the abstraction of sacrifice as the basis of sacraments. For example, contemporary discussion of the sacraments in a land as Catholic as Brazil reveals an unmistakable shyness in relation to the bloody origins of the key sacrament, holy communion. In an official exegesis of the eucharist for the National Conference of Brazilian Bishops, the word 'sacrifice' is not used.[32] This beautiful Portuguese text by José Ariovaldo da Silva, a Professor of Liturgy at the Franciscan Theological Institute in Petrópolis, explains the historical movement of the eucharist in a way that I find warm in personal terms but coy in terms of cultural history. Da Silva describes how the eucharist in the first millennium is understood primarily as a celebration, recalling Christ's death and resurrection, to be sure, but bringing to the ingathering the real presence of Christ. Da Silva goes on to show how in the second millennium, the service became intellectually abstracted, remote from the oration, and detached from the real presence of Jesus. During this period, it was also studied, held up as an academic object, a thing, reified, further rending its efficacy in directly affecting the soul. Furthermore, a prevailing individualism dictated the terms of divine contact, displacing the great communitarian devotional sway of the previous millennium. This gave a privilege to learned people who were able to understand the Latin incantations.

In contrast to this, Da Silva says, the Constitution promulgated by the Holy Council of Vatican II restores the mystery of faith which was always installed in the eucharist during the first millennium. It is rescued with the real presence of Christ throughout the celebration; and so the communitarian transportative agency of the rite is also recovered from ancient times. But it is notable that, unlike Da Silva's exegesis, the Constitution of Vatican II uses the word 'sacrifice' to describe the eucharist—just as Franzelin and Pesch had done around 1900—in full acknowledgement of the sanguine origins of the sacrament. Perhaps for reasons of a new decorum, this bloody source is somewhat sanitized. And I feel that it is possibly the same with art. We do not really have a heart to uncover the archaic basis of our most aesthetically pure productions, with their aspirations of beauty, sensitivity and spiritual salvation. But with so much contemporary art obliquely approaching the theme, now is the time to encounter the story behind the history.

* * *

The method followed in this book neither adds historical information nor increases the body of knowledge in the archive. The text does not find out new facts about the priesthood, the household or the workshop; it does not discover new contracts or social ties between sacred or secular institutions and artists. In one sense, it retells a story which archaeologists and art historians already know, resting on a history of styles, subject matter and patronage which is the stuff of any good university survey of western art history. What the book identifies within that received history, however, is not well known; indeed, the very 'commonness' of knowledge about the standard chronological art history discourages curiosity about the deeper relationships between spirit and art which have been fostered within it. In seeking the shape and substance of the changing relationship between art and spirit, this text does not run to the esoteric borders of knowledge but confronts the traditional mainstream art history in order to uncover its spiritual assumptions.

While restaging a more or less canonical art history, interspersed with evidence of the contemporary urgency of the themes, this text examines the spiritual implications of cultural and artistic progress. There would be numerous other ways of telling the history of art, emphasizing many of the ideologies, social themes and practices, particularly dwelling on the people and objects excluded by the canonical history of western progress. Just as there were political reasons for establishing the canon, so there are political reasons for challenging it and presenting alternative material. This book, however, is not intended to replace the canon nor even to propose historical or geographical areas in which the canon is deficient. It is not revisionist in its art-historical subject matter but radical in its interpretation of the spiritual calibre of art in the western canon.

In places, the text presents unorthodox links between the cultural and the technical, perhaps modestly increasing the scope of the standard art-historical narrative. An example might be the interpretation of the changing conventions for framing pictures in the Renaissance, or the linking the technique of transparent glazes in baroque oil painting with metaphors in contemporaneous poetry; in other periods, the relations between art and media or popular culture may even contest the dominant paradigms of art history. The purpose of such discussions is not to contribute a novel slant for its own sake but to chase a single insight through material that we already know all too well.

The single theme is the re-spiritualizing of art, the induction of sacramental status upon art in the very process of art becoming secular. The information already lies to hand: it calls only for a candid expression. This book proceeds from a feeling that there are obvious things which need to be said about art and spirituality which, for understandable reasons, have either been unrecognized or suppressed. To understand the spiritual dynamic of secular art it is necessary to acknowledge a number of features of artistic production and appreciation which are unflattering and even distasteful from either a spiritual or artistic point of view. First, while art is initially heavily patronized by religious institutions, it historically pulls away from them. Second, art is highly dependent on the spiritual privileges of institutional faith which, in some sense, it forsakes.

Hence there is a kind of inbuilt duplicity in secular art, a kind of pretension in arrogating spiritual status to itself while disavowing the premises which, to a large extent, it relies upon for its prestige. In many ways, therefore, this is a story which suits no one. It is melancholy for the pious and confronting for the unreligious.

Art is a reluctant servant of religion, anxious and ambitious for its freedom. When it wins a degree of autonomy, however, it craves spiritual power. Every step that it takes toward spiritual autonomy marks a further stage in the abstraction of religious principles. Art is therefore never entirely secular. Its secularity is asymptotic, for the conservative nature of its prestige is structural. Art finally disappoints most radical sentiments and even its most adventurous manifestations menace the hope for a materialist intellectual autonomy which is free of spiritual conceits. Art is the bitterest pill for the radical avant garde which enthusiastically cultivated new visual languages since the nineteenth century and contributed the striking formal redefinition by which art is often understood to have reached the pinnacle of intellectual independence.

Art historians, by and large, have not shown themselves to be eager to explore these home truths. But the evidence is in almost every history of western art from the first chapters. Let us reread the basic story-line with a special curiosity for the spiritual afterlife of secular art.

ENDNOTES

1 The Latin term (normally given as the plural *praestigiae*) meant trickery and juggling, deceptions, legerdemain; its origins refer to the physical or technical motifs of tying, grabbing, holding, drawing together (*stringo*). These motifs have nothing to do with the phonologically similar concepts of pre-eminence or superiority (*praestantia*) or the verb for surpassing (*praesto*) which, coincidentally, the term prestige relates to today.

2 However, the sacraments were not extensively theorized by theologians until the period of early modernism. Although central to dogma, they seem to have resisted systematic explanation and to have remained with the contemporary understanding of mystery. Sacraments have been practiced continuously but they exist more on a practical level (almost corporal) than a theoretical level. As the Jesuit theologian Christian Pesch has noted: "Ex hac enim disciplina arcani intellegitur, cur Patres de sacramentis satis parce loquantur, et ubi loquuntur, non raro verbis obscurioribus utantur; cur integros tractatus de sacramentis non ediderint, sed res singulas, in quantum necessarium erat, explanaverint." ["From this learning, the arcane reasons can be understood for why the Fathers spoke little enough about the sacraments, and where they do speak, they use obscure words, why they did not publish an entire or comprehensive tract but only explained individual things in so far as it was necessary."] See Pesch (1908, 1:37). This convenient text in two volumes, published in the year of Georges Braque's *Grand nu*, faithfully gathers the wisdom of scores of Catholic authors and serves as a summary of the sacramental tradition to the date of its publication. For this reason, I have drawn upon the authoritative and well-argued account in developing the view of sacraments for comparison to the agency of art.

3 *Army Brats*, Shrine of Remembrance, Melbourne, November 2006 – January 2007.

4 Clinton Nain, 'a e i o u', nellie castan gallery, 12 River St, South Yarra, until May – June 2006; some of the paragraphs here are grafted from my review "Agonized voice of scream and howl" in *The Age* (Nelson 2006).

5 Though we sometimes spontaneously use the word 'magic' in art appreciation, the term is quaint and familiar—rather like 'fabulous', which is abstracted from the fabled—and is slightly foreign to the institutional promotion of artefacts that I seek to explain. It is perhaps telling that as an oriental

word, the term is not indigenous to Hellenic tradition. In Greek, magic (μαγεια) is a loan word, which somehow lacks authority. It is sometimes qualified with its origins, as in Plato's phrase "the magic of Zoroaster": *Alcibiades* 1.122a. Already in antiquity, the concept has enough currency to enjoy an adjectival form (μαγευτικος), as given in Plato *Politicus* 280e, and to function as a verb (μαγευω), as in Euripides *Iphigenia on Tauris* 1338. The personal noun is much associated with the Persian tribe, the Magians, as in Herodotus *The Histories* 1.101 or 7.37; but the associations readily shade into vulgarity, with meanings of 'charlatan' or 'impostor', as in Sophocles *Oedipus the King* 387, or Euripides *Orestes* 1498. Of course, the personal noun was redeemed by Christian tradition in the *magi* or wise men from the East. In nearly all of these senses, magic is diametrically opposed to 'mystery', which preserved impeccable hallowed status until the term 'mystification' was coined in the modern age.

6 It is difficult to find an instance of the word in Greek (μυστηριον) which is not solemn and religiously grave. The word is used most often in the plural (τα μυστηρια) and carries an awesome onus of secrecy in ritual. The mysteries of Demeter at Eleusis were especially famous and revered in antiquity. See the word in the tragedians Aeschylus *Fragments* 479; Sophocles *Fragments* 804; Euripides *Suppliants* 173, and the comic playwright Aristophanes *Frogs* 887. The mysteries are in a sense abstracted by literary means on the tragic stage, as Chapter 2 of the present study examines.

7 Parallels between sacramental systems were noted in antiquity and were not viewed with inclusive spirit in patrological literature, even though the religion was grafted into Graeco-Roman culture along syncretic lines. Rather, affinities with heathen religion were viewed with horror by the Church Fathers, such as Tertullian: "Diabolus ipsas res sacramentorum divinorum in idolorum mysteriis aemulatur". ["The devil mimics these very things of the holy sacraments in the mysteries of the idols".] See *Praescript* 40 in *Patrologiae Cursus Completus* (Migne 1844–64, 2.51). It is notable in this sentence that the connotations of *mysterium* and *sacramentum* are different. The Greek term trades in the pagan but the Latin does not. Tertullian would never have substituted the two words in the sentence. Meanwhile, scholars at the end of the nineteenth century became more systematic in comparative studies of religion and implicitly noted the affinities between diverse sacramental traditions of the Mediterranean. This was in keeping with the glamour of the learned mystical cults of Florentine Humanism: see Wind (1980). See also Anrich (1894); Cumont (1902); Dieterich (1903); Hepding (1903); and Koch (1900). A certain anxiety resulted on the part of some Christian theologians, who sought to deny the parallels on doctrinal grounds, suggesting that parallels were in name only. Thus: "Nam sacramenta christianorum sunt ritus quidam sacri, quibus homo cum Christo, persona illa historica, de cuius vita, morte, resurrectione evangelia referunt, spiritualiter coniungitur eiusque meritorum et satisfactionum particeps fit. Nihil tale vel simile in mysteriis genitilium. Unde etsi nomina saepe sunt similia similesque ritus, res tamen his nominibus significata et his ritibus repraesentata toto caelo est diversa." ["Because the sacraments of Christians are a kind of sacred rite, in which a person is spiritually conjoined with Christ—that historical person to whose life, death and resurrection the Gospels refer—and becomes a participant in his worth and fulfilment. There is nothing similar in the mysteries of the gentiles. Thus, even if the names are often similar and by similar rites, the thing signified by the words and represented by those rites is poles apart".] See Pesch (1908, 1:3).

8 Christian tradition separates the two concepts of 'sacrament' and 'sacramental', the former referring to the canonical ritual and the latter to the spiritual quality that arises in pious but uncodified gestures. Thus the washing of feet (archetypically by the Magdalen) is sacramental but not a sacrament. Christian Pesch refers to the judgement of St Bernard that it is a sacred sign but only sacramental in a general sense: "Itaque lotio pedum erat Bernardo sacramentum, quia, ut ipse explicat, est sacrum signum, sive sacrum secretum, seu sacramentum latiore sensu vel sacramentale" ["Thus the washing of feet was a sacrament for Bernard, because, as he explains himself, it is a sacred sign or a sacred secret or a sacrament in the broader sense, or the sacramental"] Pesch (1908, 1:39).

9 Even Jewish sacraments are considered by Pesch in a somewhat begrudging spirit to be true sacraments, being aligned with legalistic reasoning. They may be denied sanctifying agency: "Imprimis igitur certum est sacramenta veteris legis non contulisse gratiam sanctificantem." ["First it is certain that the sacraments of the old law do not bring with them sanctifying grace."] As a lower-order religious institution, they appear somewhat limited to 'dirty work': "sacramenta veteris legis conferebant sanctificationem legalem seu '*sanctificabant ad munditiam carnis*', ut loquitur apostolus ... Ergo quia rationem sacramentorum ex iis diiudicare convenit ... dicendum est sacramenta omnia aliquem sanctificationem conferre, legalem quidem, si ad ordinem legis mosaicae ... pertineant." ["the sacraments of the old law confer a legal sanctification or 'they sanctify toward the cleansing of the flesh', as the Apostle says... And so because the reason for the sacraments can be judged by such... it is necessary to say that all sacraments confer some legal sanctification, if they belong to the order of Mosaic law."] See Pesch (1908, 1:8). Through the Council of Trent, the distinction between Jewish and Christian traditions pertaining to 'sacrament' was dogmatically affirmed: "s.q.d. novae legis sacramenta a sacramentis antiquae legis non differre ... A.S." ["If someone says that the sacraments of the new law do not differ from those of the old law, it is anathema."] See Denziger (1932, 727).

10 Attempts to abstract the sacraments away from the body toward greater spiritual purity were long resisted by orthodoxy. Thus "Lutherus ... docet sacramenta non aliud esse nisi signa mere theoretica, quae ut efficiant quae significant, sola fide suscipientium fieri." ["Luther teaches that the sacraments are nothing other than a merely theoretical sign which, to render what they signify, only works on the faith of the participant."] See Pesch (1908, 1:46).

11 "Quia homo corporalibus maxime allicitur ad peccatum, per corporalia quoque medicinam spiritualem applicari convenit" ["because man is most of all drawn to sin through the bodily things, it is also appropriate to apply spiritual medicine through bodily things"] Pesch (1908, 1:1). This brings to mind Thomas Aquinas (*Summa Theologiae* 3.61.a1.): "sic igitur per sacramentorum institutionem homo convenienter suae naturae eruditur per sensibilia, humilatur se corporalibus subiectum cognoscens, dum sibi per corporalia subvenitur; raeservatur etiam a noxiis actionibus per salubria exercitia sacramentorum." ["thus it occurs that by the institution of the sacraments, man can conveniently be improved in his nature through the senses, be humbled in recognizing how he is subject to things of the body when he is seduced by things of the body; for he is insulated from evil actions by the healing exercise of the sacraments."]

12 There are many ways to categorize sacraments, according to whether or not they are repeated for an individual and whether they are related to a stage of life. See Pesch (1908, 1:44), the section titled "de sacramentis vivorum et mortuorum". Baptism does seem clearly a sacrament of character, that is, "signum spirituale animae indelebiliter impressum, quod maneat, etiamsi gratia et fides amittantur" ["a spiritual sign indelibly stamped on the soul, which remains and even brings grace and faith"]. And further: "Hac qualitate homo configuratur Christo. Sancti enim Patres characterem describunt ut 'affinitatem ad Christum', ut 'sigillum, quo ab angelis cognoscamur pertinentes ad familiam' Christi, ut 'conformitatem ad Christum', Dominum nostrum" ["In this quality, the human approaches Christ. Because the Holy Fathers described the character (or stamp) as 'an affinity with Christ', as 'a seal, by which we are recognized by the angels as belonging to the family' of Christ, as 'conformity with Christ', our Lord"] (Pesch (1908, 1:79–81).

13 Even in canonical interpretation of the sacraments, a peculiar sympathy was imagined to exist between the communicator's body and the body of Christ, which is the *fons et origo* of the prestige of the body in Christian cosmology. This enjoys maximum force in holy communion. See Franzelin (1899, 304): "haec tamen mystica unitas carnis nostrae cum carne Christi suam pleniorem consummationem et velut sacramentalem consecrationem accipit per coniunctionem glorificati corporis et sanguinis eius cum ipsis corporibus nostris, in qua coniunctione celebrantur nuptiae Agni cum sponsa sua Ecclesia adhuc peregrinante in membris singulis, quae iucundiores et plenioris unitionis solum celebrabuntur in patria ... Sic igitur ex sacramentali coniunctione oritur peculiaris illa affinitas, qua Christus sponsus

considerat carnem digne manducantium carnem eius et bibentium sanguinem eius speciali titulo ut carnem suam. Et propterea conformat carnem nostram carni suae incorruptibili ac glorificatae." ["this mystical union of our flesh with the flesh of Christ receives its fullest consummation, and indeed a sacramental consecration, by the conjunction of His glorified body and blood with our own bodies, in which conjunction the wedding is celebrated between the Lamb and his spouse the Church, till then wandering in its separate parts, which are more happily celebrated in a fuller union only in Heaven. Thus it occurs that from the sacramental marriage, that peculiar affinity arises by which Christ the husband considered eating the flesh worthy of his flesh and drinking his blood the special quality of his flesh. And for that reason, our flesh conforms to his incorruptible and glorified flesh."]

14 Thus: "non quamlibet rem sacram sed principaliter sanctificationem hominis significant, idque non theoretice sed practice seu efficienter." ["It does not signify some kind of sacred thing but principally the sanctification of people, thus not theoretically but in practice and toward an effect."] See Pesch (1908, 1:5).

15 As noted in Pesch (1908, 1:3): "Nam sacramenta christianorum sunt ritus quidam sacri, quibus homo cum Christo, persona illa historica, de cuius vita, morte, resurrectione evangelia referunt, spiritualiter coniungitur eiusque meritorum et satisfactionum particeps fit." ["Because the sacraments of Christians are a kind of sacred rite, in which a person is spiritually conjoined with Christ, that historical person to whose life, death and resurrection the Gospels refer, and becomes a participant in his worth and fulfilment."] Christ is considered the author of the sacraments: "Christus est auctor sacramentorum, quatenus passione sua virtutem eorum meruit" ["Christ is the author of the sacraments, in that he granted their virtue by his passion"] (Pesch (1908, 1:86).

16 See Pesch (1908, 1:250: "itaque sanctissima eucharistia consideranda est ut sacramentum et ut sacrificium." Note as well the section "De sacrificio, speciatim de sacrificio eucharistiae" ["Thus the holy eucharist is to be considered as both a sacrament and a sacrifice"], in Franzelin (1899, 307 ff).

17 Hence the incomparable prestige of the eucharist in the Catholic faith, as the principal sacrament. See Pesch (1908, 33: "quia autem septem sacramenta non sunt omnia inter se paria ... Ita interna dignitate omnibus praestat eucharistia, ad quam propterea alia sacramenta tamquam radii ad solem referri possunt. Paenitentia vero sub hoc respectu est infimum sacramentum." ["the seven sacraments are not all equal among themselves... because for its internal dignity the eucharist rises above all the others; and for that reason, all the other sacraments refer to it as do the rays to the sun. Penitence in this respect is the least of the sacraments."] The centrality of holy communion is revealed in the phrases by which it implicitly comprehends the other sacraments on account of its substantiality (read corporeality): "Immo non raro vocatur simplicter sacramentum per excellentiam, quia omnium sacramentorum est excellentissimum; est enim sacramentum quia signum gratiae, est excellentior omnibus sacramentis, quia est ipsa gratia substantialis" ["So quite frequently it is called the sacrament par excellence, as it is among all sacraments the most excellent; as a sign of grace it is a sacrament excelling the others, because it is substantial grace"] (Pesch (1908, 1:251).

18 Sacraments are always referred to in semiotic terms, even in the most generous definitions; "Praeterea sacramentum dicitur signum alicuius rei sacrae et latentis" ["a sacrament is said to be a sign of some sacred or latent thing"]. See Pesch (1908, 1:5). Perhaps here Pesch is echoing Augustine (*Epistulae* 138.7.): "signa, cum ad res divinas pertinent, sacramenta appellantur" ["signs which belong to divine things are called sacraments"].

19 "Die Umstände, in die das Produkt der technischen Reproduktion des Kunstwerks gebracht werden kann, mögen im übrigen den Bestand des Kunstwerks unangetastet lassen—sie entwerten auf alle Fälle sein Hier und Jetzt" (Benjamin 1931, ch. II: 13). A good analysis of the implications of Benjamin's ideas in the Australian context can be seen in Butler (2002, 501–518).

20 "Und unverkennbar unterscheidet sich die Reproduktion, wie illustrierte Zeitung und Wochenschau sie in Bereitschaft halten, vom Bilde. Einmaligkeit und Dauer sind in diesem so eng verschränkt wie

Flüchtigkeit und Wiederholbarkeit in jener. Die Entschälung des Gegenstandes aus seiner Hülle, die Zertrümmerung der Aura, ist die Signatur einer Wahrnehmung, deren »Sinn für das Gleichartige in der Welt« so gewachsen ist, daß sie es mittels der Reproduktion auch dem Einmaligen abgewinnt" (Benjamin 1931, ch. III: 15).

21 "Die Einzigkeit des Kunstwerks ist identisch mit seinem Eingebettetsein in den Zusammenhang der Tradition. Diese Tradition selber ist freilich etwas durchaus Lebendiges, etwas außerordentlich Wandelbares. Eine antike Venusstatue zum Beispiel stand in einem anderen Traditionszusammenhange bei den Griechen, die sie zum Gegenstand des Kultus machten, als bei den mittelalterlichen Klerikern, die einen unheilvollen Abgottin ihr erblickten. Was aber beiden in gleicher Weise entgegentrat, war ihre Einzigkeit, mit anderem Wort: ihre Aura" (Benjamin 1931, ch. IV: 16).

22 "Die ursprüngliche Art der Einbettung des Kunstwerks in den Traditionszusammenhang fand ihren Ausdruck im Kult. Die ältesten Kunstwerke sind, wie wir wissen, im Dienst eines Rituals entstanden, zuersteines magischen, dann eines religiösen. Es ist nun von entscheidender Bedeutung, daß diese auratische Daseinsweise des Kunstwerks niemals durchaus von seiner Ritualfunktion sich löst" (Benjamin 1931, ch. IV: 16).

23 "Die Definition der Aura als »einmalige Erscheinung einer Ferne, so nah sie sein mag«..." (Benjamin 1931, ch. IV: 16, footnote 7).

24 "stellt nichts anderes dar als die Formulierung des Kultwertes des Kunstwerks in Kategorien der raumzeitlichen Wahrnehmung" (Benjamin 1931, ch. IV: 16).

25 "Ferne ist das Gegenteil von Nähe. Das wesentlich Ferne ist das Unnahbare. In der Tat ist Unnahbarkeit eine Hauptqualität des Kultbildes. Es bleibt seiner Natur nach »Ferne, so nah es sein mag«. Die Nähe, die man seiner Materie abzugewinnen vermag, tut der Ferne nicht Abbruch, die es nach seiner Erscheinung bewahrt" (Benjamin 1931, ch. IV: 16.

26 "Unbeschadet dessen bleibt die Funktion des Begriffes des Authentischen in der Kunstbetrachtung eindeutig, mit der Säkularisierung der Kunst tritt die Authentizität an die Stelle des Kultwertes" (Benjamin 1931, ch. IV: 16, footnote 8).

27 "Der einzigartige Wert des »echten« Kunstwerks hat seine Fundierung im Ritual, in dem es seinen originären und ersten Gebrauchswert hatte. Diese mag so vermittelt sein sie will, sie ist auch noch in den profansten Formen des Schönheitsdienstes als säkularisiertes Ritual erkennbar" (Benjamin 1931, ch. IV: 16–17).

28 "Von der photographischen Platte zum Beispiel ist eine Vielheit von Abzügen möglich; die Frage nach dem echten Abzug hat keinen Sinn. In dem Augenblick aber, da der Maßstab der Echtheit an der Kunstproduktion versagt, hat sich auch die gesamte Funktion der Kunst umgewälzt. An die Stelle ihrer Fundierung aufs Ritual tritt ihre Fundierung auf eine andere Praxis: nämlich ihre Fundierung auf Politik" (Benjamin 1931, ch. IV: 18.

29 "Der profane Schönheitsdienst, der sich mit der Renaissance herausbildet, um für drei Jahrhunderte in Geltung zu bleiben, läßt nach Ablauf dieser Frist bei der ersten schweren Erschütterung, von der er betroffen wurde, jene Fundamente deutlicher kennen. Als nämlich mit dem Aufkommen des ersten wirklich revolutionären Reproduktionsmittels, der Photographie (gleichzeitig mit dem Anbruch des Sozialismus), die Kunst das Nahen der Krise spürte, dienach weiteren hundert Jahren unverkennbar geworden ist, reagierte sie mit der Lehre vom *l'art pour l'art*, die eine Theologie der Kunst ist. Aus ihr ist dann weiterhin geradezu eine negative Theologie in Gestalt der Idee einer »reinen« Kunst hervorgegangen, die nicht nur jede soziale Funktion, sondern auch jede Bestimmung durch einen gegenständlichen Vorwurf ablehnt" (Benjamin 1931, ch. IV: 17).

30 "die technische Reproduzierbarkeit des Kunstwerkes emanzipiert dieses zum erstenmal in der Weltgeschichte von seinem parasitären Dasein am Ritual" (Benjamin 1931, ch. IV: 17).

31 *Art History After Modernism* (Belting 2003) and, with special reference to Chapter 2 in the present study, *Likeness and Presence: A History of the Image Before the Era of Art* (Belting 1994). See also Belting 1987.

32 "A Reforma 'Eucarística' do Concílio Vaticano II Vista dentro do contexto histórico geral da liturgia", documents of CNBB, Conferência nacional dos bisbos do Brasil, http://www.cnbb.org.br/documento_geral/02AREFORMA_EUCARISTICA.doc.

REFERENCES

Anrich, G. 1894. *Das antike Mysterienwesen in seinem Einfluss auf das Christentum*. Goettingen: Vandenhoeck & Ruprecht.

Aquinas, T. *Summa Theologiae* 3.61.a1. Rome: Forzani et S. Giovanni Bardi. 1927 edn.

Augustine. *Epistulae* 138.7.

Belting, H. 2003. *Art History After Modernism*, translated by Saltzwedel, Caroline; Cohen; Mitch; Northcott, Kenneth. Chicago: University of Chicago Press.

Belting, H. 1994. *Likeness and Presence: A History of the Image Before the era of Art*, translated by Jephcott, Edmund. Chicago: University of Chicago Press.

Belting, H. 1987. *The End of the History of Art?* translated by Wood, Christopher S. Chicago: University of Chicago Press.

Benjamin, W. 1931. *The Work of Art in the Age of Mechanical Reproduction*. [*Das Kunstwerk im Zeitalter seiner technischen Reproduzierbarkeit*]. Suhrkamp Verlag, Frankfurt am Main, 1981 edn.

Butler, R. 2002. "Bright shadows: Art, Aboriginality, and aura". *The South Atlantic Quarterly* 101 (3) Summer: 501–518.

Cumont, F. 1902. *Les mystères de Mithra*. Originally Paris; Brussels: H. Lamertin. 1913 edn.

Danto, A. 2003. *The Abuse of Beauty: Aesthetics and the Concept of Art*. Chicago: Open Court.

Danto, A. 1997. *After the End of Art: Contemporary Art and the Pale of History*. Princeton, New Jersey: Princeton University Press.

Denziger, H. 1932. *Enchiridion symbolorum*. 18th edn. Fribourg: Herder & Co.

Dieterich, A. 1903. *Eine Mithrasliturgie*. Leipzig: B. G. Teubner.

Elkins, J. 2004. *On the Strange Place of Religion in Contemporary Art*: New York: Routledge.

Elkins, J. 1997. *The Object Stares Back: On the Nature of Seeing*. San Diego: Harcourt Brace.

Franzelin, J. 1899. *De ss. Eucharistiae sacramento et sacrificio*. Rome. S.C. de Propaganda Fide.

Freedberg, D. 1992. *Disfiguring: Art, Architecture, Religion*. Chicago: University of Chicago Press.

Freedberg, D. 1989. *The Power of Images: Studies in the History and Theory of Response*. Chicago: University of Chicago Press.

Hepding, H. 1903. *Attis, seine Mythen und sein Kult*. Giessen. In *Religionsgeschichtliche Versuche*, vol. 1, by Dieterich, A.; Wuensch, R. Giessen: Ricker.

Koch, H. 1900. *Pseudo-Dionysius Areopagita in seinen Beziehungen zum Neuplatonismus und Mysterienwesen*. Mainz: [Publisher unknown].

Migne, J. P. 1844–64. *Patrologiae Cursus Completus. Series Latina*. Paris: Garnier.

Morgan, D. 2005. *The Sacred Gaze: Religious Visual Culture in Theory and Practice*. Berkeley: University of California Press.

Morgan, D. 1999. *Visual Piety: A History and Theory of Popular Religious Images*. Berkeley: University of California Press.

Nelson, R. 2006. "Agonized voice of scream and howl". *The Age*. 31 May: p. 24.

Pesch, C. 1908. *De sacramentis, praelectiones dogmaticae*. Fribourg: Herder & Co.

da Silva, J. A. 2005. "A reforma 'Eucarística' do Concílio Vaticano II, vista dentro do contexto histórico geral da liturgia". National Conference of Brazilian Bishops. São Paulo.

Taylor, M. C. 1992. *Disfiguring: Art, Architecture, Religion*. Chicago: University of Chicago Press.

Taylor, M. C. 1984. *Erring: A Postmodern A/Theology*. Chicago: University of Chicago Press.

Wind, E. 1980. *Pagan Mysteries in the Renaissance*. Oxford: Oxford University Press (first published Faber & Faber, 1958).

Cite this chapter as: Nelson, Robert. 'Secular sacraments and the prestige of art'. *The Spirit of Secular Art: A History of the Sacramental Roots of Contemporary Artistic Values*. Melbourne: Monash University ePress. pp. 1.1–1.20. DOI: 10.2104/ssa07001.

CHAPTER 2

MORTAL THEATRE

Robert Nelson

In contemporary performative art, which is often presented as video or DVD, rituals of death and sacrifice are not unusual.[1] An example is the Australian artist Catherine Bell, whose works reckon with loss and killing in dubiously redemptive ways. In one of her works, the artist gathers snow on a Parisian rooftop. She packs this around her belly with a fond and tender action. As this is completed to form a mound in the shape of a pregnant woman's tummy, the bundle is brought inside. We next witness the artist taking herself into the basement of the building and slowly and painfully dissolving the icy lump. This is not just an allegory of a termination or an aborted love-affair that takes the still-fecund artist perilously closer to looming infertility: it is a sacramental evocation of another tragic event (or nameless scores of fatalities *in utero*) in order to overcome their sadness.

Heavily concerned with ritual, Bell explores in other works the connections between the redundancy of contemporary western ritual and social aberrations such as infanticide.[2] This relationship has been reinforced by anthropological study outlining an empirical link between social crisis in tribal communities and the performance of cathartic rituals to alleviate tension and offer psychological relief. As in ancient times, her work is about emotions in a cathartic dynamic.

The obsessive collection of newspaper articles that outline the heinous crimes involving women and children, in most cases their own children, luridly draws attention to some primal urge to kill one's child that Freud adumbrated in his psychoanalytical interpretation of the legendary Oedipal story. Bell juxtaposes two groups of women: mothers who under desperate circumstances kill their children and another group of women desperate to have children who perform bizarre and unexplainable acts, sometimes violent, neurotic or—drawing upon the professional vocabulary that historically stigmatizes the womb—hysterical. In spite of its erotic overtones, her work *Making a baby* explores, through monthly ritual, certain morbid feelings during pregnancy. She bakes a cake in the shape of a baby and invites public interaction to cut and devour. The cake tins were designed for baking celebration-cakes for Christening and baby showers that have a perverse destiny of being destroyed and consumed.

In her *Special delivery*, Bell bakes and ices a baby cake every day for the duration of the exhibition. The remains of the baby are placed on perspex shelves, covered by lace food canopies attached to the wall at stomach height to suggest a line-up of pregnant bellies. This domed shaped device, used to keep flies and other pests away from the food has forensic implications in this context. It not only protects the identity of the mangled remains but metaphorically expresses the melancholy state of phantom pregnancy and miscarriage. These tragic outcomes of foetal loss have been known to trigger the crimes that Bell has uncovered in her research. The cake project introduces text written in icing. Subverting the function of the space left bare to print the usual merry sentiments or infant's name, this cake collects disturbing headlines and criminal details. The viewer is enticed to cut and eat the cake but may be repulsed by the narrative. Those participating are reminded of their stomachs (the wrong tract) and, as if by a perverse sacramental induction, re-enact the crime. The remains of the day are placed under their lace-covered shrine. The sugary text is salvaged as epitaph and clue. Nine cakes were baked in total and nine shelves positioned in waiting to encrypt their mutilated offerings under the protruding lacy bulges.

Death itself, let alone the morbid thoughts that seem to invoke death in miniature, becomes strangely proprietorial in ritual. Rituals enable us to own death, even when we seek most vehemently to disown it, to distance ourselves from its inevitable triumph and dominion. What strikes us as morbid has a paradoxical allure, because the miniaturizing of death in the morbid fantasy enables a degree of tenure in the face of mortality. There are ancient, dare I say archetypical, motifs in this. They are traceable to the font of western reason, where grim frameworks and obscure spiritual practices lurk among the sparkling temples of dialectic.

* * *

Two thousand years of poetic nostalgia for antiquity have distanced us from the spiritual basis of Greek art and design. In their origins, the art and architecture of that skeptical and sophisticated people were liturgical. They were steeped in solemn rituals involving all the elements of religion that ever compelled belief. These comprise worship of both an inspired and a formulaic kind: the demonstration of goodwill to the gods by means of incantation and reverent offering, banquets and intoxicated music and dance, the appeasing of deities through sacrifice, heroic enactments of tragic episodes which communicate the potency of divinity and the pathos of mortal supplication, the evocation of a higher order beyond mortal taint, an immaculate condition of heavenly euphoria which is only enjoyed by the blessed, and from which mortals are alienated through inherent baseness.

It is not poetic nostalgia alone that clouds our view of the deeper religious character of Greek art and design: it is the Greeks themselves in their apparent devotion to reason. Greek design, for example, seems to enshrine the discipline of dialectic, arguing the place of each member with a weighty sense of importance and majesty. In its almost obsessive articulation of parts, Greek architecture is intellectual, chaste and abstract. Like Greek design, Greek art from the archaic to late-classical periods is defined by symmetries and balance, a sense of order which is impervious to emotional transport. Greek art and design are free of capricious inventions or irrational fancies. The temples and statues are removed from the domain of passion and contention, even if they figure warfare; they are beyond the emotional contingencies of personality or private inflexion, either in their making or their subject matter. Stylistically and iconographically they carry no signs of furious or prophetic artistic genius. Particularly in architecture, the physical members are structured with a rigid ethos of division of parts which perfectly parallels—in a synthetic plastic medium—the habit of analysis with which the philosophical mind orders all phenomena in the great matrix of scientific intelligence.

Logic, restraint and intellectual deliberateness are striking in any Greek temple. The architecture is systematic and rigorous. Each part has a kind of inevitable multiplicity about it which consistently reinforces the presence of the whole. A column typically not only has three parts (capital, shaft and base) but each of those three parts can be further divided into separate parts. The whole thing is riddled with definition. The same can be said of all members in classical architecture and the ornament which attends them with expressive accents. The entablature with its several courses and registers, the articulation of triglyphs and metopes and so on all speak of the argumentative rigor of an intellectual system. Never was architecture so 'straight' in its conformity with an intellectual canon. The canon expresses the argument of stresses and support which belong to engineering. There is never a horizontal which has the character of a vertical or *vice versa*: each action has its proper figurative sign. It would not be hard to interpret Greek architecture as an allegory of logic, a triumph of reason over the spiritual.

The same can be said of Greek ceramics, with their emphatic distinctions of foot, belly, shoulder, neck and lip, their regular horizontal articulation by means of borders, the dedication of the flattest parts to figuration and narrative, appropriately consigning the denser and more abstract repetitive patterns to the tighter spaces in which the curvature changes sense from positive to negative. Like the architecture, the ceramics have both a complexity of forms, a disciplined tightness in their placement. Like the architecture, their unity of shape is an allegory of control: the well-separated parts contribute to an overall shape of solemn circumscription and elegance. The combination of complicated parts and forceful whole not only argues for a sense of co-ordination but endows the object with an imperiously serene presence.

Reason, analysis, logic, control and order. Even the corporeal element of Greek sculpture seems to demonstrate the priority of the intellectual over the spiritual. From the archaic to the classical period, Greek sculptors moved from severe blocky standing figures, with weight carried equally by both legs in static poses and with schematized knees, chest, mouth, hair and so on, to figures of naturalistic rendering, with weight distributed through spine and legs according to a specific muscular action. The success of this naturalism depended on drawing skills, that art of working out 'what is there' when you observe the knee (say), how the parts not only have a separate identity but in what way they connect to one another in an organic whole. The skill of perceptual drawing that underwrites the accuracy and poetic poise of Greek sculpture is intensely intellectual: it is about recognition of individual elements in a larger whole; it is the appreciation of the proportions between these elements, their neighbours and the whole. As in contemporary science, these constructs proceed from analysis and trial; they involve the comparison of a conjecture and a reality and ultimately propose something which is falisifiable by critical examination.[3]

If we were so disposed, it would be easy to interpret the whole of Greek art and design by such intellectual preoccupations. As the abstraction of Greek language testifies from an early date, the penetration of logical thought was undoubtedly present at all levels of Greek consciousness, and probably nothing in Greek art and design was ever achieved without philosophical and technical rigor. But this is surely not the total story. Greek art may be all these things; but it is more than that. In particular, as you approach the whole motivation of Greek art and culture, headier forces dominate.

In addition to being impressively intellectual, Greek art is also compellingly erotic. Throughout Greek art, bodies are sensual, captured in a kind of lusty potential even when still. Greek sculpture and vase painting reveal adoration for the flesh, the love of flexing thighs, curving flanks, the shape of a breast beneath a *chiton* or male genitalia peeping out from under a skirt. And of course, total nudity is common for the heroic presentation of men from archaic times, reaching to women in the later classical epoch. The celebration of the carnal causes the most beautiful technical refinements. In order to show just how gorgeously the shoulder-blade is articulated, the sculptor's modelling registers all the movements from bone to muscle, relishing all the tender spots and their organic relation with the skin. Though often possessing a kind of expressive austerity—especially in the impassive faces—the naturalism of classical Greek sculpture is ravishing in its subtle devotion to each inflexion in the flesh.[4]

Greek vase painting testifies to the openness of artists to represent overtly sexual practices, from courtship to love-making. These representations are not merely signs for the sexual act—like naughty graffiti—but are nicely developed line drawings, showing elegant bodies and draperies with a certain sensual conviction. They have a lyrical appeal, an artistic element that unites the erotic scenes with ornamental borders and the occasional piece of furniture. Stylistically, the vases are restrained and disciplined, for they follow an ethos of limited means, employing relatively simple frieze-like compositions without perspectival or tonal depth. But within those clear and tasteful parameters, the imagery argues psychological transport. It is not uncommon to find music and dancing on the vases, dynamic rhythms of bodies with heads flung back to the enchanted tones of the *kythera*. Not infrequently, the chaste styles of Greek vase painting belie a kind of emotional fury (*mania*) in which the reveller or comast experiences those conditions for which our words are still tellingly Greek, euphoria and ecstasy.

It is natural that these dimensions of Greek art and culture should be interpreted as hedonistic and without a convincing spiritual charter. Where the Greeks are not intellectual, they are lustful, abandoning themselves to the orgies of carnal delight. This view is strongly reinforced by the superficial reading of Greek mythology, according to which the gods were motivated by little which is edifying. The gods are prolific fornicators who, when not spending their energies in the irresponsible abuse of mortals, consume their libido in spiteful machinations against one another, usually also involving the unscrupulous manipulation of humans. The promiscuous gods of Olympus are so far from a spiritual condition that they connive pettily and seek adulterous unions with hapless victims whom they have no intention of ever rescuing when the momentary privileges of divine intercourse are exhausted. The gods seem ethically debased, competitive, vengeful and sly.

Critics of Greek culture would readily agree that there is a mythological basis to Greek art, but they would faintly begrudge this backdrop the title of religious piety. The Greeks undoubtedly inherited a consciousness richly informed by traditional stories; their artistic vision was therefore suffused with narratives of a coherent and authoritative kind, from which artists would draw and seldom depart.[5] And certainly, the Greeks cannot be stripped of the religion proper to them, for the institutionality of their beliefs was made manifest in the patronage of the temples. These were enormous and expensive, indeed by today's standards they were fabulously extravagant given the relatively scanty population of the Greek peninsula, the islands and the colonies.

While there is a meaningful distinction to be made between myth and religion, it is technical. Myth is an inherited body of stories which have authority but no author; religion is the organized context for having a rapport with the divine.[6] No definition of religion could exclude Greek spiritual practice, nor could Greek religion be denied the quality of piety. Sure, the gods were hedonistic and possessed of unfettered erotic impulses; but their flagrant randiness is an expression of their potency. Some of the female gods are without sexual appetite (such as Artemis or Athena) but, as befits the patriarchal order of Greek culture, the female deities are inferior to their male counterparts and their lack of sexual inclination matches their lesser authority and slighter prowess in all other respects.

For the Greeks, the free expression of libidinous energy equated with perfection. A god is not a lesser being for exercising this faculty but demonstrates the ability freely to enjoy pleasure. The gods experience bliss in its most complete forms; their perpetual access to orgasmic delight is far from shameless but a sign of their supremacy. Thus the gods are unabashedly sensual; their consumption of food and drink in the proverbial nectar and ambrosia is another dimension of divine privilege under a superintending order of destiny. The gods have all enviable attributes—including immortality—and all imaginable pleasures belong to them in an almost archetypical way.

The revelry with which the Greeks worshipped the gods proceeds from these assumptions. What may seem an unholy carousal to puritanical eyes is the logical expression of a sharing in the god whose divinity is steeped in voluptuous transport. The means of approaching a deity in ancient Greece were not limited to prayer (for, depending on the epoch, prayer was possibly confined to invocations of a rhetorical temper) but more compulsively involved rituals pertaining to the physical and psychological character of the god. Worship as a kind of standardized beseeching is not much in evidence, though there is a rich iconographic tradition of votive offerings and, especially in early times, there were definitely acts of sacrifice which were held to propitiate an enterprise. The participation in feasts, music and inspired dances—though apparently merely hedonistic—delivered the comast from the incumbencies of daily life and brought him or her to a sacred and sublime state, a being-in-the-god (*enthousiasmos*) which gives us our word enthusiasm. Though seized only momentarily in the rapture of harmonious sounds and dance with head flung backward, the condition of euphoria allowed ravishing contact with the life which the god leads in perpetuity. The dancing seen in Greek vase painting testifies to a corporal ritual of definite spiritual significance. Through the mania of dance and musical incantation, one could reach a sensual rapport with a god.

Greek sculpture contains a dual aspiration which embodies this transport. From the classical period, almost any sculpture of Apollo or Hermes or Aphrodite is extraordinarily sexy in its evocation of the carnal, but the face is aloof, impassive, emotionless. We sometimes imagine this rather chilly expressionless perfection in technical terms, as if the sculptors were simply not up to figuring the passions. But even so, it fits with the image and role of Hellenic godhead. The deity is entirely satisfied and no expenditure of zeal is necessary on the god's part to contact the infinite pleasure that matches his or her eternal life. The god is self-sufficient, not exactly narcissistic but assured of universal admiration.[7] Not a muscle in the face is ever caused by local contingencies to be stressed. The god is expressionless because, in some sense, he or she represents the consummation of all desirable expression and has nothing to express but the wholeness of his or her being. Godhead in Greece is the freedom of desire being constantly and serenely gratified; and therefore desire is forever stabilized beyond the point of consummation.

Direct access to this grace is impossible. You will never enter their heavenly abode. Your abjection as a mortal must be overcome by ritualistic experiences in order to capture so much as a glimpse of the remote condition of the gods. And this depends on the god. A celebration for Dionysos would not be appropriate for Athena. The classical period undoubtedly inherited protocols from remote centuries, prescribing by unwritten but traditional formulae the appropriate rhythms, mood and level of solemnity for the relevant god. Heady banquets were by no means the appropriate gesture for the more sober among the gods. And so it is that the differences among the gods balances the ecstatic with the grave. An overarching sense of majesty prevails and subsumes even the wildest frolicking, making the protagonists seem vulnerable, fluttering in sensual display for the benefit of the god, an act of 'giving over' to the god.

But the abjectness of mortals and the sublimity of gods are not the whole story. Somewhere between them are heroes, mortal to be sure (unless by exceptional and late dispensation, as with Herakles) but aspiring to the nobility of the gods in their great actions, brave temper and aristocratic privileges. Greek art devotes much attention to the heroes, as does Greek literature and, though apparently artificial or literary in a chivalrous genre, the heroes are central to the beliefs and practices of Greek religion. Like the gods, the heroes are represented in classical times with impassive faces; they are sexy, charismatic and they enjoy a kind of eternity by means of their fame. But there is one outstanding difference: the heroes are nearly all tragic. And in their inevitable demise you find the key motif of the religion: sacrifice.

The blood sacrifice of humans at the altar is exceedingly archaic, probably predating the development of the Homeric poems; but traces of it are present in the myths, as with Iphigenia and Polyxene.[8] The idea of a priest slitting the throat of a human victim at a ceremony devoted to the occasion was deleted from the delicate canons of Greek religious practice and would have been entirely obliterated from memory had it not been for theatrical reworkings of myth in Greek literature. But the motif of sacrifice is nevertheless carried forward in numerous artistic representations which once had religious status.

Greek tragedy is read today in the context of today's drama, from Shakespeare to Beckett to Joanna Murray-Smith, intellectual and poetic, to be sure, but circumscribed by a humanist understanding of the autonomy of the play as an art work. The origins of tragedy in Greece were less artistic than ritualistic and would have been as near to sacramental as anything else in Greek culture. Initially tragedies were not performed in theatres in urban contexts for people's recreation or entertainment. They were first a part of festivals which drew people from towns—rather like pilgrims—to a religious event.[9] In the drama, a hero is brought down. The play ritually stages the necessary killing of the hero. All spectators know the outcome before the play begins. There are no surprises. A chorus (literally dancers) chants the verities of the catastrophe on a more general plane. The rehearsal of the hero's death is a kind of aesthetic abstraction of the killing which took place in ancient times. The repeat performance attempts to relive the immediacy of the trauma so that the spectators can share in the fear; they can subsequently recognize a divine order and can experience a reconciliation with its omnipotence.

The public suffers during this spectacle. There is anxiety, terror and bitterness, the grief of seeing one's affection for a charismatic figure rudely cancelled by fate. Through the pain felt as a spectator, a psychological subjugation is tendered toward destiny: not only is the hero given up but a superior interest must be accepted. An almost erotic transference of respect takes place, as the heroic mortal is punished and the hand of godhead must be revered. The efficacious aspect of this process was noted and discussed by Aristotle who used the term purgation (*katharsis*) to describe the result of the tragedy. But the cleansing that he had in mind was of a mechanical kind. The mind would be cleared by entertaining fear, as if—like an enema—the thought of something terrible would chase out the impure thoughts that accrue in a chaotic unholy life. Greek tragedy is more than that. The experience could also be described as a salutary humbling. It reconciles the public with its impotence, the victimhood of mortality, that vulnerability by which the hero submits in an exemplary killing.

It is not that Aristotle is wrong but simply that the ritual element has a role which is not completely exhausted by his definition. You go to the theatre and relive the death of a hero; and witnessing the killing of the hero induces a bitter submission in your mind, not exactly a humiliation but an absolute deference to the divine order that enforces your mortality. There is certainly a sacramental element in the sacrifice. But because the drama is an artificial re-creation and not a mere catechism, it belongs to an aesthetic realm in which the wits of the poet are magically exercised in brilliant labours of lyrical evocation. As Greek literary culture evolved in the fifth century BC, the presence of the poet's artifice reaches impressive heights and prepares the way for the modern world to see the drama as a more or less autonomous art form, with certain residual object lessons from a body of myth with suitably grave topics of psychological agonies.

From our perspective in the modern world, Greek drama is the perfect antecedent to our own. The tragedy is offset by the comedy—both impeccably Greek words, like the very words drama and theatre—so that the key preoccupation can be identified with a creative exploitation of narratives, no matter what they are about, provided they grip the audience with suspense, eloquence and ingenuity. Admittedly scholars and theorists have always been ready to concede that there is an awesome dimension to tragedy. But the manipulation of ancient myths tends to be construed as a kind of working with necessary cultural givens, perhaps analogous to the way in which Renaissance painters were constrained to paint the Virgin when in fact they had equal interest in painting Venus in a passionate embrace with Mars. Instead of being the spiritual basis of the tradition, the mythical content is sometimes understood as little but a pretext for creative expression, perhaps a condiment to the genius of an author, a way of steeping the dramatic content in the sublime, a dark tremendousness which satisfies all the earnestness of a deep and poetic genre. In its origins, Greek theatre is more than that. It is profoundly religious.

Greek sculpture is similar. As sculptors gain in skills and personal reputation, their work is increasingly easy to categorize as pure art, perhaps even the purer for dwelling on a godlike form. The ideal body of the Greeks seems absolutely hermetic and aloof from expressive concerns other than its artistic completeness. It is as if art sought utter perfection and therefore resorted to a representation of the heroic nude as the most total expression of nature's perfection, the only appropriate subject matter for art. The goddesses on the east pediment of the Parthenon, the Lapiths in the metopes of the same temple, the Hermes with the infant Dionysos of Praxiteles, and gracious works such as the *Apollo Belvedere* seem to bear this out.[10] Far from the narrative immediacy of the myths and the consequent specificity of emotional expression and gesture, these figures hold themselves with a kind of lofty disdain for the world in front of them. The congruence of the lofty style and haughty subject matter is in itself one of the marvels of art history and virtually defines the concept of the 'classical'. But it is not the style which requires the ideal but the ideal which requires the style.[11] That ideal is divinity, a height of being, a sublimity, the consciousness of which had been fostered for centuries before any satisfactory incarnation in marble.

Grace, beauty, equipoise, harmony: these virtues are surely human and artistic; but there is a prior claim on their agency. The copyright, so to speak, is held by the gods, those infinitely superior beings in every sense, whose disposition allows even intoxication, fornicating and killing to be undertaken with enchantment. For their every movement in whatever dire action is fatally appealing, forever valorizing the contempt which they are privileged to bestow upon mortals. Throughout all of Hellenic culture, the Greeks never lost sight of the Olympian proprietorship of the human, and especially the charismatic figure of the hero. But the way in which Greek sculpture refers to the archetype of perfection is not immutable. Just as it develops through several stages from the sixth to the fifth and fourth centuries BC toward the high classical style—moving from static and stylized bodies to accurately drawn nimble bodies—so the art of sculpture in the succeeding centuries exceeds the humility of its classical aspirations. The great inversion of western spirituality begins with the Greeks; for Hellenic culture indeed sees the exigencies of art overtake the worship of the gods.

Beauty and perfection as autonomous artistic conceits had a certain immanence in sculptural production from the time—let us say the fifth century BC—when the ideal human form was confidently embodied in figures with free and subtle movements. But in the Hellenistic period (by the third century BC), the divine recedes to a series of illustrious cues, no longer the governing rationale for the work but the authoritative and academic pretext for a brilliant sculptural conception and execution. Certain works retain the sublime tenor of a god-fearing past (such as the awesome *Nike of Samothrace*) but, by and large, the high religiousness of the classical period declines in favor of an artistic spectacle for its own sake.[12] Often, they are contrived with overwhelming sophistication, repudiating the simplicity of classical statuary and engaging the most extravagant compositional and expressive resources.

Sculptures such as the *Crouching Aphrodite*, the *Sleeping Hermaphrodite* or the *Aphrodite Kallipygos* are sensational displays of an artistic intuition, a personal infatuated vision of a sculptor. They are artistically autonomous spectacles which bear witness to the domestication of divinity in later Hellenism: to the greater worldliness of the period and a wholesale weakening of the ritual significance of ancient myth.[13] We call her the *Crouching Aphrodite* but there is little evidence that she is even Aphrodite. She could be any beauty, wringing out her hair in a lovely coquettish tilt of the head, very self-conscious and aware of catching the incidental glance, cute in her knowledge of being looked at. Why a goddess at all? Why not a young woman at a pool? And indeed the sculpture would be well placed at the poolside of a wealthy bourgeois townhouse such as we know better from the culture of imperial Rome.

Sculptures such as the *Sleeping Hermaphrodite* are also delicious essays on the evocation of domestic phenomena, the hot night spent lying bare in bed and twisting restlessly, charged with a youthful eroticism and needing all the sexual gratification which the form invites by reciprocation from the spectator. In one sense, there is a simple continuity with the classical tradition of the eroticized immortal, inspiring a breathtaking reverence for an ideal gift of beauty and sexual prowess. But as beautiful and sexy as such figures are, their eroticism is not so self-contained, not so remote or high-born. The figures direct attention toward us and consequently seem dependent on our interest in them; they seem to require an engagement with us, seem to be on the point of inviting our participation in a gorgeous intercourse. Although dwelling in this erotic immediacy, the works are by no means frivolous but they no longer signal the detachment and reserve of the impassive Olympians of the classical period.

Hellenistic sculpture—and we assume painting—appears to have been prolific in appealing to a similar poetic interest and possessing a similarly vague spiritual calibre.[14] The guidance of the work is no longer pre-eminently religious: the imperatives are all aesthetic, involving a canon of taste which balances the seduction of a naked figure with a level of dignity proper to the ideal. In this decorous matter of inspiration and judgement, the artist functions as an individual, no doubt earning a reputation for courageous steps taken in both technique and accomplished transgressions of previous limits. Art begins its tussle with decorum, endlessly inspiring for the artist and fascinating for the public.

Other works notoriously deal with the tragic emotions, masterpieces such as the *Laocoon* group and the *Apollo and Marsyas*.[15] More than any sculptures before them, the narrative figure groups of the Hellenistic age bear the fear and pity which are the passions moved by tragedy and sanctioned by Aristotle's *Poetics*. Not only are the works formidably emotive but they stage the hero's decline with memorable immediacy. Pain and the anxiety of knowing one's grueling doom are represented with sensational acuteness by tense muscles, facial contortion, swollen veins and compositional stress. But through the excellence of this life-like performative element, the works transcend the dread of their subject matter. They are an artistic *tour de force* of sensory engagement. That is the one quality which tragedy does not require in bestowing upon the hero's death the ritual values of sacrifice.

In the heroic scheme of tragedy, the terrible end of the hero stands for a result, a necessary spending of human life for the consummation of divine desire. The suffering is sacred; it is ultimately elevating on account of 'heroizing' the acceptance of mortality. For a killing to qualify as a sacrifice, the sense of resignation must be installed in the victim, a dignified form of passivity, a knowledge that the fate which one must undergo is inevitable and, even though wretched and bitter, almost seductively harmonious. The *Laocoon* group and the *Apollo and Marsyas* qualify as tragedy in every sense except this: they are more about an atrocious process of killing than a result in which the energies resolve themselves in divine serenity. The sensational immediacy of the deaths deflects the consciousness of an awesome spiritual justice. The *Laocoon* group and the *Apollo and Marsyas* are about timing rather than the timeless: the sculpture registers the momentary affections rather than the eternal—and repeatable—yielding of life to divine might. The sculptures are bound to their physical symptoms. The interest is pathological. And beyond this iconographic emphasis, the dominant visual characteristics are stylistic, as the spectator is overwhelmed by the technical ambition of rendering the physiognomic gestures and the momentary spasms of agony.

Hellenistic sculpture is the first example in western art of the transition from a religious art of emotive simplicity but spiritual complexity to an autonomous art of emotive ambition but liturgical emptiness. It is the secularization of art but with all the privileges of the sacred miraculously retained, rolled over, appropriated. The transition in art occurs under the auspices of a religion, ostensibly the same theography that inspired the development of art from archaic to classical times.[16] But the age was no longer religious. It was interested in some religious ideas and signs but the enthusiasm had shifted from the hallowed engagement with local myths and deities to worldly abstractions, allegories, personifications, a kind of signifying allegorical machinery analogous to the new world order that blew the arrogant trumpet of empire across the Mediterranean and beyond.

Sculptures were dedicated to powerful forces like Victory (*Nike*) and emphasized the might of the mightiest gods, especially Zeus, in conveying the inevitability of destiny, or the fate of the world which had, co-incidentally, bestowed all power upon the rulers of enormous lands. Gone was the local devotion to the deity whose shrine was poignantly remembered in conjunction with certain actions that took place in the vicinity. Certainly Greek myth had always enjoyed a kind of universality. The deeds of the god Dionysos at Naxos were known throughout the Greek world, not just in Naxos. But the demands of religion in the Hellenistic age discouraged the awareness of the local roots of myths. The later cults instead celebrated the universal embrace of a superintending destiny which somehow valorized the authority of worldly potentates.

Both classical and Hellenistic art have a certain solemnity and grace; but the religious element in the classical yields to a secular element in the Hellenistic. From a culture of holiness, we move to a culture of glory. The discreet and tender worship of godly perfection gives way to the forceful show of grandeur, magnificence, prowess, and the invincible power as a thing in itself, an abstraction which gratifies the arrogance of ambition. The sculptures on the Altar of Zeus at Pergamon are the ultimate expression of this pride.[17] With muscular extravagance, the gods displace the order of giants as if famous warriors deriding their vanquished foes. From the classical plinth of divinely self-contained glamour, the gods have descended to a kind of allegory of magnificence, entirely suitable for attachment to the pre-eminence of the despots of Pergamon.

Like the art of the classical period in the lesser genres (especially vase painting), Hellenistic monumental sculpture presents a bewildering variety of emotional conditions, all somewhat tied to the cult of the gods. To match the bawdy scenes of Greek vase painting, there are flagrantly erotic manifestations such as the *Aphrodite Kallipygos*, a kind of ancient strip-tease in which the woman—if she is not the goddess imputed by the title—draws aside the long *chiton* to reveal her bottom and thighs, all the while looking over her shoulder to survey with narcissistic delight the attractiveness of her contours. To match the classical heroic character of narratives on the Parthenon and elsewhere, there are tragedies a-plenty in Hellenistic sculpture. Then there is always a stock of static deities standing around in civic uprightness, populating venerated locations, or stoic representations of the dead in cemeteries for pious commemoration. And finally, to match the scenes of bathing, education and the receipt of athletic prizes in Greek vase painting, Hellenistic sculpture monumentalizes wrestlers, rhetors or a boy taking a thorn out of his foot. In one sense, nothing changed between classical and Hellenistic. All sculptures have an excellence in technique which is the envy of subsequent ages. But classical and Hellenistic have a different inflexion. Whether driven by political bombast or bourgeois domestic intimacy, the art of the Hellenistic period is precocious, show-offy, arty, sensational. Hellenistic art is awesome as art rather than awesome as subject matter. If the subject matter in Hellenistic art is awesome, it is nevertheless executed in such an exaggerated way that the meaning of the work is somehow hijacked from contemplation of the event, and invested in the fabulous imagination and skill of the artist.[18]

In this promotion of art at the expense of the spiritual inspiration which initially caused its development, the post-classical epoch foretells the conceit of art for art's sake, that paradigm associated, above all, with modern art. It is further advanced in Roman times when Greek production continues through the so-called Roman copies of Greek originals. Once Rome enjoyed hegemony over the Mediterranean, the Greeks had already developed the modern concept of art as commodity, an object produced by artists, sold at a market price and enjoyed as a prestige object in a civic or domestic context. Somewhere within this status as art-object is the ancient objective: to be 'of' the god or to enact a divine event. But that is almost a precondition, like a dead metaphor. Sure the sculpture deals with the gods or some other vaguely ceremonial matter, such as wrestling. It is subject matter for art. It is not art for the subject matter. The priority is the condition of being an object of aesthetic admiration. To that end, art engages the most sumptuous concepts, reaching to divinity. The divine is a resource to be exploited for its repertoire of glamorous themes and legendary, beautiful bodies. The divine survives by means of its exploitation by the secular.

Rome consolidates these attitudes. Secular authority had reached impressive heights of legal and administrative principle: armies, markets and entertainments functioned efficiently by due bureaucratic reason, and domestic life was greatly enriched by relative economic prosperity. In this thoroughly materialist climate, art flourished as a wonderful condiment of Greek culture, pointing to that world of erotic license, music and philosophy which Romans cultivated as the basis of an ideal education. And so the demand for ideal figures was met—still pre-eminently by Greek artists—by reworking the masterpieces of Hellenistic sculpture in variants of considerable charm and historical prestige. Roman patronage explains how Greek sculpture, with whatever originality, came to fill up the museums of Europe and America with that superb proliferation of august and imaginative figures.

The Romans no doubt sought Greek art for spiritual sophistication but, ironically, their indigenous traditions of portrait sculpture were infinitely more steeped in family piety. Perhaps uncritically, the Romans bought Greek sophistication in an indivisible item which today would be identified as art. Even more than the worldly Hellenistic upper class, the Roman patricians would have felt tremendous awe for mythical antiquity. Five hundred years separated them from classical Athens: the legends of Phidias and Myron and so on had enviable cachet but the myths to which they appealed were unimaginably anterior. The myths embodied an authority which the Romans could only latch onto with diligent scholarly and poetic labors, as in the work of Virgil. The Romans were the first neo-classicists. They could never quite see their touching portrait heads—based on the deceased family members and set upon tiny domestic altars—as great art. Having bought Greek sophistication, the Romans must have construed those morbid relics as part of a naive tradition belonging to a relatively uninformed *priscitas*, a reverence which is old enough to seem out-of-date but not ancient enough to reach to universal claims for divinity. That was the preserve of the Greek patrimony.

For many centuries, comprising the Hellenistic and Roman periods, Graeco-Roman art achieved its peculiar spookiness, its special claim to spiritual values which, in different guises, it has retained to the present time. One speaks of 'art for art's sake' but this is not quite the point. Art is not intrinsically vested with such prestige, as if by being totally autonomous it is utterly spiritual. Art in the bourgeois economy derives its peculiar prestige from a three stage contact with earlier traditions. First, it seems to subsume the spiritual calibre of an anterior religious epoch. All intuitions of Aphrodite or Hermes are deposited in this work, say, and our understanding of them is somehow updated by the sculptor's imagination and sympathetic powers of identifying with the divine. Second, the sculpture apparently transcends the narrative context in which the myths were told: it potentially stands in a neutral space, suitable either for a temple or a domestic garden, either for leisure or worship, as if it would not matter which. And third, by means of confidently projecting powerful metaphors of beauty, grace and charm upon the divine figure, the work seems to inherit the qualities formerly imputed only to godhead, that high self-sufficiency, the sublimely inscrutable mind of the god, the lofty aura of Olympian inspiration and immortality.

In the Graeco-Roman period, art had all the privileges of religion but none of its responsibilities. It could draw upon all the sacred names and physical attributes that ever attracted reverence but it would ultimately owe nothing to a priestly function. Art and liturgy parted company; but in the parting, art took the liturgical trappings and gravity with it. Art incorporated these pretensions into its own aesthetic order of grace and immortality; it incorporated the illustrious knowledge of myth and insight into the psychology of the gods, a thaumaturgical power beginning with that magic to make the object 'come alive', as ancient writers often say very nearly happened.

From the Graeco-Roman period, art began its ascent as a spiritual entity in its own right, apparently no more dependent on myth for its subject matter than myth was dependent on art for its fame. In all events, art was quite free of a priesthood which would define objects for liturgical ends, as in the ornament of temples. Judging by the more domestic scale and appeal of the works, patronage came from elsewhere; yet the aspiration of high-minded bourgeois collectors and even state authorities was nevertheless for something illustrious, the sum of art, the most brilliant conception and the most 'divine' execution. In these circumstances the sacred is of course used for secular ends. The more interesting consequence is that the secular is accorded a sacred character. It is the modern role of art. A new spirituality arises which is 'artificial', perhaps in the best postmodern sense of the word. It takes a cult of worship, abstracts it in aesthetic terms, retains its glamour and projects—through synthetic magical means—a route to immortality.

The key element in this argument is the abduction of an anterior sacred order into a secular form of sophistication which reinterprets the holy as divine entertainment. But if this is so, what should be said of the religious calibre of the new secular form, this new sophisticated synthetic prestige which parallels so much of the sacred and aspires so much to its powers? Is it entirely bogus, pretentious and deserving of contempt? That seems unfair. The art which survives testifies to belief of a kind, for it is extraordinarily well-conceived in artistic terms and is technically consummate. It is hard to see something so rich in its own integrity as mere posturing. Somewhere deep within the secular appropriation of the sacred there is a slight but new sacramental function.

Hellenistic or Graeco-Roman sculpture may not relay the sublime indifference of the gods or the passing of heroes in a particularly sacred way. However the sacrifice that it does relay is, ironically, the passing of a spiritual order. To look at a Hellenistic or Graeco-Roman image of divinity involves the melancholy awareness that simple belief in a deity is no longer possible. Each sculpture of the later period is a kind of nostalgic hymn to its counterparts of an earlier period, a wistful acknowledgement that former cults were closer to a spiritual identification with the gods. All neo-classicism is like that. It is a restaging of a famous artistic attainment which was rightly or wrongly destined to collapse, which was unsustainable in a world so irretrievably changed. To relive the experience of a now-unpossessable worship is painful. Sure, the belief is no longer current, but it still enjoys credibility on account of once having been accorded such an artistic embodiment. The naïve belief has evaporated but its artistic vestiges are poignant. Your admiration for the artistic evocations of gods and heroes promotes the legitimacy of the lost spirituality. The former conventions of reverence are more than a superb lullaby; they resonate with consciousness which cannot be properly reinvoked. You grope for the lost contact in the re-creation, only to realize all the more poignantly the loss of each and every precondition for its survival.

Art begins to find its own sacraments. They are built upon a spiritual tradition, but rather than simply reproducing that tradition and hoping to achieve an identical sacramental virtue, the new sacraments are a dirge for the loss of the old sacraments. It is not just that everything is second hand—as the very concept of tradition encourages us to consider—but that everything is inverted. And far from recovering the former spiritual beliefs, the new artistic gestures are somehow anachronistic and therefore highlight the unavailability of the prestigious earlier consciousness. The new art, however sophisticated in technical terms, is melancholy, bitter-sweet, and divinely pathetic in an artistic way. A new glory is invented: the paean to a past of supposedly superior spiritual values. It is the first manifestation of a neo-sacramental order, proffering a form of grace for the present by mourning the sacrifices of time. In gross terms, the neo-sacramental order of art is art history, that knowledge of unrecoverable practices past, which were destined to be forfeited by progress toward the present. Progress, both social and artistic, displaces the past in the same way that the Olympians displaced the Giants. You live your consciousness on account of it; everything that you are and think is the result of what has occurred before you. Simultaneously, this life-giving and life-defining passage of time is also what kills the things of the past. It is sad beyond all hopes that the future might bring redemption.

The neo-sacramental order may seem weak when compared to the compelling forces of ancient ritual—the almost sexual identification with divinity and the serene expression of Olympian self-sufficiency in the classical period. There is no direct contact with divinity by means of swooning riotous dancing, no grief-bound witnessing of greatness of soul in the tragic confronting of mortality, no trust in the rhythms of festivals and performances that left their sublime erotic residue in art. But Greek religious practice had never been efficacious in the sense of leading to redemption or eternal life. It had only ever promised people a bitter-sweet reconciliation with mortality, a heroism of reckoning, a spiritual majesty to live a short life with the full awareness of never sharing anything godly—beyond ecstatic or orgasmic moments—but the feeling of inferiority relative to the gods. Thus, the sacramental rites were modest in their scope, and anything of an artistic character in the neo-spiritual periods was not necessarily vastly inferior in its effect.

When art lost its direct connection to the rituals of the temple it did not lose any glamour in the public imagination but, on the contrary, gained prestige as a surviving route to ancient spiritual virtue. In addition, it gained a new power of embodying in its very re-creations the melancholy dying of earlier stages of art history, remote periods in which art functioned in a more directly worshipful manner. This becomes a monumental blueprint for the ascent of art in its role of replacing a religious order. Much that happened in the modern world is foreshadowed by Graeco-Roman art, not just the stylistic basis of western artistic progress and the famous canon of beauty but the spiritual positioning of its meaning.

ENDNOTES

1 Australian performance art has a history embracing aspects of the spiritual: see Marsh (1993), especially chapter 3, Body art, shamanism and Western ritual, 96–140.

2 *The Raw and the Cooked*, Blindside, Melbourne, 17 November – 3 December 2005, an exhibition which included Stephen Garrett, Pip Haydon and Victor Meertens as well as Catherine Bell. Some paragraphs in the text have been grafted from my writings in the catalogue.

3 See Hacking (1992, 29–64). In this influential article, Hacking argues that the unity of modern science lies in scientific practice rather than theory. He has characterized modern science in terms of the 'robust stability' of experimental, laboratory practice.

4 See Stewart (1997), especially Stewart's discussion of the choice of medium for sculpture as integral to the meaning and connotations of the resultant figures, in "Tooling the Body," 43–60.

5 See Boardman (2002).

6 See the discussion of specific myths closely linked with religious practices in Graf (1993, 101–120).

7 "Against those in contemporary society who might debate the very existence and reality of the gods, the tragedians and artists reply most emphatically that they are present in our midst, but stand eternally outside the laws that govern human behavior" (Tarn Steiner 2001, 95). Steiner reads the expression of Greek statues closely, concurrently with literary sources on images. See also Spivey (1996, 173–186), for a socio-cultural perspective on the particular eroticism of Aphrodite as a motif and subject.

8 For a discussion of the two traditions concerning the sacrifice of Iphigeneia and Polyxena, and their consequences for reading or 'decoding' images in Greek art, see Woodford (2003, 4–9). Woodford's book is a detailed study of different ways in which painters, sculptors and other artists engaged with the heritage of narratives in classical Greece.

9 See Wiles (1997) on the simultaneously religious and political logics of theatrical space for Greek tragedy.

10 The goddesses (perhaps Hestia, Dione, and Aphrodite) from the east pediment of the Parthenon, ca. 438–432 BC, marble, British Museum, London; Lapith and centaur, metope from the Parthenon, ca. 438–432 BC, marble, British Museum, London; *Hermes and Dionysos*, ca. 340 BC, marble, Archaeological Museum, Olympia; *Apollo Belvedere*, 2nd century AD, marble, Vatican Museums, Rome.

11 For poetic and philosophical comments on the concept of the classical centred on Greek sculpture, see, as published for the first time in English, the reflections of Kantorowicz (1992, 123–135) in "The Concept of the Classical and Classicism," fragments brought together as the final chapter in her work *The Inner Nature of Greek Art*. See also Focillon (1948).

12 *Nike of Samothrace*, ca. 190 BC, marble, Louvre, Paris.

13 *Crouching Aphrodite*, 2nd century AD, Roman copy, marble, British Museum, London; *Sleeping Hermaphrodite*, Roman copy after an original from the 2nd century BC, marble, Louvre, Paris; *Aphrodite Kallipygos*, Roman copy after an original from the 2nd century BC, marble, Museo Archeologico Nazionale, Naples.

14 For a study of our problems in evaluating Greek spirituality, see Veyne (1983).

15 Agesandros, Athenodoros and Polydoros, *Laocoon and his Two Sons*, 1st century AD, marble, Vatican Museums, Rome; *The Hanging Marsyas* (from a 3-figure group depicting the flaying of Marsyas), Roman copy after an original from the 3rd century BC, marble, Louvre, Paris. See Weis (1992).

16 Robertson (1993, 67) cites the statue of Athena for the library at Pergamon (2nd century BC, marble, Staatliche Museen, Berlin) as "an example of one kind of statue with a religious affiliation which could hardly have been made before the Hellenistic period: the adaptation of a classical cult-figure (originally designed to be approached down the long darkness of a temple-cella) to a totally different setting and purpose."

17 The Altar of Zeus from Pergamon (reconstructed), ca. 175 BC, marble, Staatliche Museen, Berlin.

18 "The world's first art histories were written in the Hellenistic period, and traced a linear development of constant innovation along a trail blazed by a canon of great artists towards ever better representations ... These art histories established the influential idea of ancient art as an autonomous cultural phenomenon" (Smith 2002, 69). Smith's article is a stimulating overview of the use of images in the modern discipline of ancient history.

REFERENCES

Boardman, J. 2002. *The Archaeology of Nostalgia: How the Greeks re-created their Mythical Past.* London: Thames & Hudson.

Focillon, H. 1948/1989. *The Life of Forms in Art*, translated by Hogan C. B.; Kubler. G. New York: [Publisher unknown].

Graf, F. 1993. "Myth, Sanctuary, and Festival". In *Greek Mythology: An Introduction*, translated by. Marier, T. London: Johns Hopkins University Press.

Hacking, I. 1992. "The Self-Vindication of the Laboratory Sciences". In *Science as Practice and Culture*, edited by Pickering, A. Chicago: University of Chicago Press. 29–64.

Kantorowicz, G. 1992. *The Inner Nature of Greek Art*, translated by Benson, J. L. New York: New Rochelle. 123–135.

Marsh, A. 1993. *Body and Self: Performance Art in Australia 1969–92.* Melbourne: Oxford University Press.

Robertson, M. 1993. "What is 'Hellenistic' about 'Hellenistic' Art?" In *Hellenistic History and Culture*, edited by Green, P. Hellenistic History and Culture, 9. Berkeley: University of California Press.

Smith, R. R. R. 2002. "The Use of Images: Visual History and Ancient History". In *Classics in Progress: Essays on Ancient Greece and Rome*, edited by Wiseman, T. P. Oxford: Oxford University Press.

Spivey, N. 1996. "Revealing Aphrodite". In *Understanding Greek Sculpture: Ancient Meanings, Modern Readings.* New York: Thames & Hudson.

Stewart, A. F. 1997. *Art, Desire and the Body in Ancient Greece.* Cambridge: Cambridge University Press.

Tarn Steiner, D. 2001. *Images in Mind: Statues in Archaic and Classical Greek Literature and Thought.* Princeton, New Jersey: Princeton University Press.

Veyne, P. 1983. *Les Grecs ont-ils cru à leurs mythes?* Paris: Éditions du Seuil.

Weis, A. 1992. *The Hanging Marsyas and its Copies: Roman Innovations in a Hellenistic Sculptural Tradition.* Rome: Bretschneider.

Wiles, D. *Tragedy in Athens: Performance Space and Theatrical Meaning.* Cambridge: Cambridge University Press.

Woodford, S. 2003. *Images of Myths in Classical Antiquity.* Cambridge: Cambridge University Press.

Cite this chapter as: Nelson, Robert. 'Mortal theatre'. *The Spirit of Secular Art: A History of the Sacramental Roots of Contemporary Artistic Values.* Melbourne: Monash University ePress. pp. 2.1–2.15. DOI: 10.2104/ssa07002.

CHAPTER 3

BODY AND BLOOD

Robert Nelson

Sigalit Landau's *Barbed hula* is a video projection, presenting a female trunk gyrating slowly and blissfully by the beach. A hint of the performer's chin appears to be cast backwards, as if in euphoria, as the woman rolls a hula hoop around her midriff. As the camera concentrates on the torso, the gaze becomes disturbingly clinical, for you notice that the hula hoop is made from barbed wire and etches nasty weals into the flesh. Landau, an Israeli artist, performs nakedly, with the display of crutch adding to the sexual rhythm of the hips as they maintain the hoop in its cruel orbit. As the symbolic seat of arousal, the principal orifice gently revolves in masochistic rapture, only to inscribe small orifices around the belly, a proliferation of wounds that record the perverse penetration of the wire spikes into the soft skin.

This gruesome ornament is watched in slo-mo progress in an almost hypnotic way, as the rhythms of the dance make the stomach alternately tense and relaxed, apparently always soft and passive at the moment the hoop comes around to inflict its gouges. Only a strong sexual urge on the part of the performer could maintain the muscular pulse in defiance of the reflexive expectation of regular pain. As a voyeur, you fixate upon the horny spectacle with uncontrollable waves of marvel and horror. The barbed wire may be a symbol of brutal social division, the stuff of aggressive fences and insecure authority. A barbed-wire fence threatens to make lesions in your flesh if you attempt to penetrate beyond the boundary. Such motifs of reciprocal damage for transgressions across unfortunate barriers abound in Israel.

But the work is not a simple political allegory. It also invokes another famously barbed hoop, the crown of thorns, a motif of pitiless scorn and sarcasm. As with the violence of Christ's passion, there's a suggestion of sacrifice, expiation, perhaps redemption. The spectacle is convulsively erotic but also bizarrely grand in its reference to archaic rituals of atonement. What are these rituals and why do they retain such power in the artistic imagination?

* * *

Christianity distinguishes itself from earlier religions by the strict theological definition of its sacraments. While ancient Greek worship remains uncertain and inaccessible—almost allegorized by the role of their temples, entered by no one but priests—the Church has scripted explicit terms of religious practice, addressed to an obedient participating audience, with a strong sense of authority. For centuries, various Councils attended to the details of creed and participation with passionate debate and occasional warfare; the outcome was dogma, to be passed down a canonical chain of command among clerics, and zealously disseminated to laity. We do not lack knowledge and need not make cautious conjectures, for though there is a paucity of rich discursive texts concerning the sacraments, the deficit simply signals general knowledge of a practical kind, too obvious to merit the record. By the later middle ages, the sacraments were standardized at seven. These are baptism, confirmation, penitence, communion, marriage, ordination and extreme unction.

Pre-eminent among these, according to all sources, is holy communion or the eucharist, which is usually understood as the sacrament *par excellence*. Worshippers eat a wafer and, depending on the sect, drink wine. The elements of bread and wine have already been consecrated with an invocation of the Holy Ghost. The communicating members of the congregation file past a priest to take the offering. On one level, the ceremony simply follows the touching lines at the last supper in which Christ asks his disciples to take the wine as his blood and the bread as his body: "do this in remembrance of me".[1] But the ritual before the altar is much more than a mechanical mnemonic process or a sentimental gesture of not forgetting Jesus. It is a form of participation in his sacrifice on the cross.

The spiritual power of the communion rite has an elaborate theological explanation proceeding from the *Bible* itself. St Paul's famous letter to the *Hebrews* argues that Christ's sacrifice on the cross must be understood in the context of early sacrifices in ancient Jewish religion. According to implied archaic principles in the indigenous religion of Israel, man is guilty of sin and must expiate those sins before God, a wrathful God whose anger can only be assuaged by both sacrifice and future obedience. The efficacy of the sacrifice is measured according to the worth of the victim placed on the altar. A small sacrifice does not express much contrition or gratitude and therefore scarcely registers before God as a great act of remorse or thankfulness. A significant sacrifice, such as killing a sheep, makes decent amends and helps to convince God that his trust in you is not misplaced. Onto this archaic system, Paul grafts his view of Christ. Jesus, as only son of God, constitutes the supreme victim, the lamb of God, whose sacrificial blood has infinite redemptive power. The sacrifice of Christ on the cross makes all other sacrificial justifications redundant, for the ultimate sacrifice has already been enacted on behalf of anyone anywhere. In order to share the efficacy of this sacrifice it is only necessary to believe in the divinity of Christ, and to perform such rites as confer the redemptive power of Christ's crucifixion on the believer.[2]

In the ritual of holy communion, when the body and blood of Christ are offered to the congregation, the sacrificial killing of Jesus is figuratively restaged. Behind the abstract aesthetics of liturgy, the physical terms of sacrifice are emphatic: the altar, the body and the blood. To complete the ritual, of course, God is invoked; the killing (of God) is to assuage God, to have the power of expiating human abominations, provided that there is a genuine will for the participant to achieve grace in God's eyes. In the eucharist (a Greek word, meaning literally 'good grace') the worshipper not only admiringly remembers Jesus but figuratively shares the taste of his blood. The ceremony has a corporal dimension which replicates on a solemn and decorous level the shedding of blood and the other bodily torments suffered by Christ. In various epochs the wine has been felt as real blood passing down the throat, in accordance with the believer's heartfelt experience. The nails were driven into Christ's hands, and his flank was pierced in an awfully physical ordeal. Such a physicality is returned as the imagined blood is ingested by the faithful, and this bodily intervention by the sacred permits the spiritual virtue of sacrifice to be absorbed and directed toward the person's salvation.

In its tight theological argument of redemption through the sacrament of holy communion, Christianity might easily have developed into a religion with little need for visionary figurative art. Judaism, for example, had no great need of artistic inventions and, it might be argued, neither did the Eastern Orthodox Church. Indeed, in Eastern Christendom of the eighth and ninth centuries the case against religious images was moved with passion. Eventually the iconoclasts of

Byzantium were defeated, but the suspicion over images had been incipient in Hebraic tradition; and an underlying mistrust remained for centuries. It flared up in the northern Renaissance, and some antipathy toward images still survives in certain Christian communities today. The reasons for this strike at the very core of Christian spirituality.

Although officially pronounced an anathema by the Orthodox Church, iconoclasm in many ways represents the sacramental character of Christianity at its most jealous. The argument did not concern the validity of pictures as such, but only their use in the context of religious practice. Unfortunately, owing to the violence by which the heresy was obliterated, the texts of the iconoclasts do not survive and their reasoning has to be conjectured from its 'refutation' by Orthodox writers.[3] The iconoclasts did not object to image-making *per se* but to what they saw as the sanctioned abuse of image-making, namely the conceit that the image becomes a receptacle of holiness, that it enshrines some portion of the Holy Ghost. The iconoclasts were the first critics of the new spiritual promotion of art which had already evolved through the Church and was destined to continue in spectacular developments in the West. Iconoclasts could see that art was rising to a new authority, not merely in its material patronage—in the sense of so many illustrious walls and ceilings being plastered with handsome pictures—but in the assumed function of those pictures.[4]

In all the 'refutations' by iconophile Orthodox writers, images are described as holy images (*hagiai eikones*). Had images been conceived simply as earthly pictures of saintly figures, they might not have attracted such vehement challenge. But the title of holy images seemed absolutely to confer upon paintings, mosaics and sculptures the qualities which belong to the prototypes represented within them. For iconoclasts, Christ is holy but a picture of Christ is not holy, just a secular and fallible interpretation of divinity, absolutely not to be confused with the divine itself. Images made of earthly matter had deviously received the blessing of their subject matter. Thus, while a painting of a dog or a criminal is plainly not holy, a picture of a saint (though exactly the same in material terms) achieves the title uncritically and unreasonably. Mere matter cannot capriciously ascend to the realm of the spiritual. There must be a religious process for this to occur; the object so invested with the spiritual must be deeply sacramental. A priest cannot take the plank of wood with a picture upon it, wave a hand over it in a gesture of consecration, and assume that the Holy Ghost has infunded it, which is the unique privilege of God and God's supreme sacrifice. There is no authority for such a benediction, no text, no biblical archetype. It is a falsehood, a pretentious temerity that worldly people can pre-empt the judgement of God and effectively declare what is full of the Holy Ghost and what is not. Sacraments must be instituted by God.[5]

Iconoclasts considered that an object made of earthly matter can only be given the title of holy if analogous to the eucharist. When the elements of bread and wine effectively become body and blood, they are sanctified by a great mystery. The elements transcend their materiality by the direct agency of God. Thus it seemed outrageous to claim that a similarly sacramental result is achieved in the appreciation of an artificially coloured plank as holy.

The most powerful argument against the iconoclasts involved a comparison between religious images and the cross. Whether held above the altar; above the Church building, or around one's neck, the cross is a representation. It is not the real cross, the wood upon which Christ was crucified. For example, it might be made of metal or ivory. It is notional, just like a painting. But no Christian would ever deny the form of the cross the status of holiness. The cross is an image but is not a heresy. It directly participates in the mystery of Christ's sacrifice, and therefore the 'rehearsal' of the cross in the form of jewelry and architecture is liturgically legitimated. Iconoclasts would never have challenged the cross; undoubtedly they would have had their reasons along these lines: the cross, as chosen instrument of Christ's sacrifice, was instituted by God and can legitimately enjoy all sacramental status. Nevertheless, invoking the cross remained a worthy and compelling point against the iconoclasts: a material object (for argument's sake made of the same stuff as the metal that holds the dog's collar at the buckle or keeps the criminal in gaol) transcends its substance and is very easily accorded holiness. Tradition has approved a symbolic order that permits such objects to be richly endowed with belief, granting them a powerful function in the most pious devotion.

Rightly or wrongly, images in the Church were hallowed. They were conceived as possessing supernatural properties—holiness, in short—and were adopted into the inner framework of reverence which included the mysteries of the altar. Not only did they share with the altar the charismatic qualities of consecration, but they physically occupied the same spaces, creating scenic backdrops for the altar and even finding their way onto chalices used for dispensing the eucharist. No holy object would repudiate the spiritual ornament of images. The whole Church, its furniture and liturgical accoutrements would visually chant in the festive colours and forms of image-making; and this optical psalmody would freely penetrate the consciousness of the congregation with almost that sacredness by which the eucharist would penetrate the worshipper's body.

Christian images derive their primary power not from any stylistic grace but from a doctrinal function. This virtue is somehow axiomatic, analogous to the efficacy of Christ's sacrifice as rehearsed in holy communion. Regardless of its virtues by any other criteria, art achieves a religious value, a sublime credibility which is necessary in the liturgical context lest the context be devalued. Once art gets within the portals it must be worthy of the altar. It cannot lack spirituality; it must in principle live up to a divine mission, in order to enshrine the grace that is actively bestowed upon the congregation in holy communion.

To honor these high expectations, the styles of early Christian art maintained a rather severe adherence to traditional formulae. The Byzantine artist, for example, did not want to step outside a fairly narrow frame of reference for the drawing of figures. There were standardized methods, steadfastly turned away from the illusionism of antiquity, which made figures share a single emphasis, as if echoing one another in devout compliance with a single spirit. The sacramental character of image-making did not readily admit the idea of experiment with posture, anatomy or drapery, much less an enthusiastic appropriation of Hellenic pagan sophistication. There was no room to check the rightness of the schema for painting noses, for example, by comparing the noses as painted in the past with the noses on living people's faces. This exercise would have served only to weaken a traditional dedication: dedication to following the inspired patterns in which all blessings were invested, lifting the work from the material into the sacred realms.

Byzantine art is not consciously distorted or mismanaged for expressive ends. The list of deviations from Graeco-Roman naturalism is extensive. The noses are too long and thin; they proceed from strange gullies around the forehead, many features are represented by inscribed lines rather than the logical spilling of light over forms; the attitudes are stock still, heads angled on tilting necks, often with an undifferentiated inflexion; certain bones are ill-proportioned, feet dangle with downward-pointing toes when they might rest flat on the ground, and so on. Because these characteristics are found throughout Byzantine art, they do not communicate the peculiar intensity of a mood or moment; they are generic and therefore seem somewhat inexpressive, for insofar as they have an expression, they all seem to express much the same thing. Byzantine schemata evoke an overall religiousness rather than psychological or dramatic qualities specific to certain situations, actions, people or feelings. The art of painting is not guided by optical, anatomical or theatrical incumbencies. Its inspiration is entirely religious: it is to facilitate the veneration of the holies and to be sacred. To introduce spatial and tonal sophistication—not to mention dramatic poses—would lessen the integrity of the image as a sacramental elevation of matter to spirit (transubstantiation), authorized by strict codes in old traditions.

However, in Italy with Cavallini, Giotto, Duccio and the sculptors Nicola and his son Giovanni Pisano, the hallowed stiffness yields to new spatial conquests: figures in art seem to own their own bulk; their draperies move according to their bodies; their volumes are registered in logical tonal shifts, and space is constructed in a more illusionistic fashion. Perhaps the greatest discovery of the period circa 1300 is to have seen that technical achievements did not have a corrosive effect on the religious integrity of the image: the spiritual calibre of the more optically sophisticated renditions did not suffer. A well-drawn Virgin Mary is just as spiritually compelling as a dogmatically cramped one. In fact, once the mind begins to demand a degree of conformity to illusion, the stilted depictions of the past appear to lack a degree of conviction, as if they were just repetitions of stylistic prejudices, without a personal inspiration in the enthusiasm of the individual artist.

Art historians are forever pointing out the impressive strides taken by artists circa 1300. Paying special attention to Giotto—thanks largely to Vasari's systematic promotion of Florentines—art historians affirm parallels between visual art in Tuscany and the elegant new styles of verse (the *dolce stil novo*) in poets like Cavalcanti and Dante, which culminated in Dante's masterpiece *The Divine Comedy*, where the writer appropriately acknowledges Giotto's pre-eminence in painting. The volumes and spaces of the new painting are concerted, reasoned, innovative and, in their combination of clarity and ambition, point to the almost linear progress of Italian painting toward the Renaissance. All this is true, but perhaps the most remarkable achievement of the period was to redefine the holiness of the visual. Art historians sometimes leave the impression that the 'breakthroughs' of the proto-Renaissance point toward a renewed confidence in the intellect, and in the ascent of the critical spirit, the inquiring mind, the genius of logic and analysis at the expense of religious values based on firm belief, faith, acceptance and continuing profession of the systems of veneration of the past.[6] This view also contains some truth, but is misleading in certain respects. Although there is increasing esteem for analytical observation and conformity to appearances, there was no concomitant lessening in the dominance of religious values. Sure, religious values did change and, in particular, the power of the artist's original conception gained credibility relative to the received paradigms of the sacramental tradition.

In the past, a painting was holy because it dealt with holy subject matter and subscribed to a holy method. A style had been sanctioned by tradition, prescribing fairly tight formulae and imposing limits to licence. In their regularity and conformity, the visual formulae seemed to parallel the sacramental recitation of the mass which invoked the redemptive powers of sacrifice.

Moreover, on the symbolic level of method, the rather unquestioning rehearsal of stylistic tropes in Byzantine art accords with the liturgical submission to repetitive rhythms of devotion. With the new generation, however, pious confidence would imperceptibly withdraw from this predictable submission. The imagination and skill of the artist would be charged with the challenge of finding or redefining sacred visions rather than enacting once again those mannerisms which had already been ratified as the correct means for expressing devotion.

The rapidity of the change should not be overstated. The new generation emerged very slowly and was probably not initially conscious of a radical departure from Byzantine tradition.[7] Artists around 1300 did not conceive of themselves as revolutionaries and would not have understood the word *avant garde*, a retrospective honor which they can do without. Nevertheless, their painting and sculpture is significantly different from that of earlier Christian periods. It invites us to check the accuracy of things, where Byzantine art deflects this scrutiny in a kind of hallowed rhetoric of sombre elongation. The obsessive narrowing was for the sake of piety; it would have been almost a sacrilege to question it. Perhaps the new artists criticized this spiritually hermetic convention, perhaps not. They may have considered the older art stylistically lugubrious and actively rejected it, but perhaps not. They may simply have moved on to more adventurous reflections of the divine stories, as if moving on is the natural way to achieve distinction as a painter or sculptor, especially in a land nostalgic for classical antiquity. They were undoubtedly seduced by the promise of producing life-like images, representations so true to appearances that a person might mistake the painting for its prototype. This idea was proposed in the mid sixteenth century by Vasari, in his *Lives of the Most Eminent Painters, Sculptors, and Architects*; and later historians also leave us with this understanding.

In all events, the artists had the encouragement of their religious milieu. By all means, do not paint in the old Byzantine fashion. Work out how to construct more convincing illusionistic tableaux. Improve the consistency of your light; register correctly the habit of the drapery responding to gravity, the overlap of figures, the proportions of members, and the representation of emotion through close observation of facial gesture. In short, exploit the art of drawing to make the figures take on a credible air in a credible space. An idea of visual credibility must have prompted the developments. Truth had a dual referent. There was holy truth, enshrined absolutely in scripture, preached weekly in Church and supported by holy offices. But there was also the truth of things seen by the artist, of which neither priest nor text knew a great deal, but which promised enormous and persuasive powers when successfully translated by artistic skill.

Art and design work very happily with two masters. There is no necessary contradiction between the two systems of truth (axiomatic faith and empirical reason); it is just that the single truth seems to be available from two different sources. The charm of the 'Italian primitives', as they used to be called, lies in the ingenuousness with which they reconcile a pious emphasis of saintly gestures with an unmistakable ambition to improve their perspectives, to include more orthogonals for suggesting recession, to supply the floor with a quaint architecture of parapets, porches and courts (often looking like little booths) to make the scenes more believable, even if they seem naive to us. The effort would often extend to sophisticated renderings of two-dimensional textures, such as the veined patches of marble. The artist's imagination, sensibility and skill were on show. The ambition in vision and technique, over which artists competed for patronage and fame, were brought into the quest for sacred pictures. The art which did not demonstrate improvement in these qualities was consequently devalued.

What once had been the sign of reverent adherence to orthodoxy was now the sign of spiritual paralysis. What once would have seemed secular vanity was now recognized as congruent with the inspirational colour and brilliance of biblical narratives. After fulfilling a demand for the sacred through somewhat sclerotic formulae (however solemn and moving), art could become a kind of divine refreshment, a system of engagement of icons and narratives which would champion divinity through poetic sympathy, an artistic richness in illusionistic evocation of places, bodies and gestures. God was there, but in touching metaphors of inspiration. God no longer haunted the image in the sense of a sacramental repetition of holy refrains—echoing the invocations and transubstantive properties of body and blood—which best stood in pious stillness for veneration. The presence of God would rather be felt in the way in which the artist's imagination could compel your own imagination to see or envisage a personage or scene with believable rapture.

In this, the artwork gains yet further prestige. It moves from the province of altar boy to that of priest or even prophet. The visionary talents of the artist are a route to piety. From this, the power of invention is interpreted as a kind of substitute for sacramental processes, an inspirational labor which already translates spirit into material—almost internalizing within the artist the agency of the holy Ghost—and yields a religious transport. It is the greatest irony: in becoming more materialistic, the artwork is credited with greater spiritual powers. As the artwork becomes more sophisticated on an illusionistic level and divorces itself in stylistic terms from the repetitious sacramental service of the liturgy, it paradoxically gains mystical properties. The artist only has material, simple reason, mere physical or spatial observation; but, in the context of evoking the divine, these intellectual faculties gain the power of the mystical.

It is common to interpret the liberties of the proto-Renaissance as the first light of secular values displacing theocratic dogma and prejudice; but the artwork does not gain this new prestige by becoming 'autonomous' from a religious context. The new investments only take place because the sacramental character of images is already assumed, an assumption akin to the deepest mysteries of the altar and demonstrated in the austere and solemn mannerisms of Byzantine painting. The new art relies on this archaic importance but in addition gains all the new imaginative glamour—as it were, the artist's demonstrative intellectual and creative property—that the old art could never possess. Paradoxically, the new art only possesses this glamour by virtue of the old art forbearing from the claim to spiritual authorship. The old art creates all the expectations of a sacramental moment too great to be comprehended by lay consciousness; and, while assuming the grave backdrop of the more archaic art, the sweet new style seizes the holy powers that the old art discreetly left to liturgical traditions. The new art is then free to arrogate to its imaginative graces those powers of consecration which the old art left to the processes of holy tradition.

The transition from Byzantine to Italian proto-Renaissance can be compared to another signal step in the canonical histories of art, namely the art and architecture of the Middle Ages as they move into later Gothic. The transition is also gradual and should not be overstated.[8] There was no single invention, no great stride forward but a stepwise development of traditions. Beginning in northern France, severe Romanesque churches yielded to nimble and lofty Gothic ones; the hefty pier is divided into subtle flutes; the bastion-like walls are succeeded by air-filled networks of masonry and light transmitted through brilliantly colored illusionistic glass paintings; the fortified towers are replaced by soaring spires advertising their height with multiple pinnacles.

These achievements are a triumph of engineering—albeit through trial and error—and testify to the genius of practical and reasonable men, building up their knowledge of materials and construction technology, to say nothing of what today would be called project management. But the technical achievements are also a triumph of symbolic coherence; they are an unforgettable manifestation of belief and heavenly aspiration. Indeed, in the common keenness to remove the bulk from building materials and ascend to ethereal heights, the spindly architectural members often have a febrile and neurotic tenuousness. As technically brilliant as they are, the Gothic cathedrals stand as a monument to the material stretched by the spiritual.[9]

The sculpture adorning the Gothic cathedrals moves away by degrees from the columnar figures of Romanesque tradition. In the west, there was nothing so traumatic for artists as iconoclasm; and because of the general acceptance of images embellishing churches, the justification for art based on a sacramental character did not receive such attention. But Romanesque sculpture is sometimes as stiff as Byzantine painting and, especially in the formal parts of the Church such as the portals (definitely not the capitals or furniture which display individual fantasy and brilliance), it bears witness to the same solemn 'disclaimer' of individual authorship. Romanesque sculpture can demonstrate the same compliance with superintending repetitious structures—as in the rhythms of incantation—that denies the sculpted image a spatial agency of its own, and consequently denies the faculty of imagination in the artist. Yet as the Gothic epoch progresses, the character of the sculpture loses some of that God-fearing stasis; it asserts the skill of the sculptor in determining the vigor and personality of the sacred personage.[10]

As with the transition from Byzantine convention to the liberties of early Italian painting, the change from Romanesque to later Gothic involves a paradoxical dependence of the new art upon the styles that it superseded. Centuries of devotion in churches containing and supporting strictly 'disciplined', stone-like, elongated figures with pronounced mannerisms (such as the floppy feet already noted in Byzantine painting and mosaic) had built into the very concept of sculptural embellishment a sacred awe. This seemed to justify future sculptural inventions as equally holy. The knowledge of hallowed precedents created a backdrop of austere reverence, a dour sense of archaic liturgical gravity, which vouched for the sacramental character of the genre. Later sculptors would be able to profit from the sternness of Romanesque, its stark and frontal formality, its obedience to a superintending regimen, and its lack of interest in the spatial freedom of figures. They would, by degrees, make their own constructions of holy figures and bestow upon them the magic of life-like illusion. They thereby imparted a new glamour which, however, carried all the archaic connotations of piety formerly belonging to the stiff art whose place it had inherited. Sculpture in the north of Europe gained the double prestige that painting did in the Mediterranean: it enters a scene already rich in sacramental connotations, and also sets about creating the prestige of new illusionism: a faculty rich in mystique, and in effect the blessed gift of bestowing life upon the stone in the evocation of heavenly majesty.[11]

Parallels with the contemporaneous ascent of illusionism in early Italian painting are tempting. As in ancient Greece the growth in sophistication—both technical and scenographic—rides high on a former religious discipline whose pious earnestness it subsumes. Further, as more and more of the decision-making behind the appearance and composition of the artwork occurs under the authorship of the artist—rather than following the givens of a sacramental tradition—extra religious magic accrues to the artistic process. Far from seeming a step in the direction of the secular (which in one sense it is), the novel developments are interpreted as having a peculiar spiritual pregnancy, requisitioning something sacred from the archaic sacramental order and installing it in the imaginative gifts of the artist. From this point, the spiritual fortunes of art are secure for many centuries, offering unprecedented worldliness, empirical excellence, and mystical powers.

ENDNOTES

1 See Luke 22:19–20; 1 Cor. 11: 24–26. Moorhead's (1986, 1–18) discussion of change in the perception of images and their role in sixth-century Byzantium takes these lines as a point of departure.

2 Hebrews 9:15–10:22.

3 See the now classic discussion of the intellectual history of Orthodox discourse on images by Ladner (1953, 3–34). See also the article by Elsner (1988), which closely examines the discourse in terms of the iconographical theme of the Transfiguration of Christ. More recently, Barber (2002) conscientiously and very readably traces the trajectory of the theological debates prompted by iconoclasm.

4 Clearly shifts in the status of art were attended by shifts in the status of the artist. "In the course of almost 180 years of debate, Greek [iconophile] theologians produced a radical change in the language with which they framed the icon. In so doing, they raised the status of the work of art to that of theology and the status of the artist to that of the theologian" Barber (2002, 138).

5 Emphatic in Pesch (1908, 86): "Sacramenta, cum sint signa ad placitum et praeterea ipsa sua significatione effectus producant, qui illis signis nullo modo naturaliter causari possunt, *institutore indigent*, qui et eorum significationem determinet et cum significatione efficacitatem coniungat. Iam per se patet neminem posse ex innata sua potestate et ut causam principlaem physicam signa gratiae efficacia instituere *nisi solum Deum*". ["Because they are signs in principle and above all produce an effect by their very meaning, which cannot be caused naturally by signs of themselves, sacraments are in need of one who institutes them, who determines their sense and connects their effectiveness to their meaning. Thus it is self-evident that no one but God alone can institute the effective signs of grace by his or her inborn powers or even be their main physical cause."]

6 For a sustained critique of such 'conventional scholarly wisdom' about the Trecento, which traces the trajectory of this interpretive tradition to Giorgio Vasari (for example, through Bernard Berenson and Jacob Burckhardt), see Maginnis' (1997) monograph on Tuscan Trecento painting, *Painting in the Age of Giotto: A Historical Reevaluation.*

7 See Belting (1994, 370–376): as part of an account of the relationship between Duccio's painting and the *dolce stil nuovo*, Belting describes Duccio's profound empathy with the aims of the Byzantine icon painters. For a broad background to Byzantine influence on the art of the Medieval Christian West, before, during and after the fall of Constantinople, see the lavishly illustrated catalogue essay by Wixom (1997, 435–507).

8 The monograph by White (1993) remains a valuable survey of these transitions in Italy. As White affirms with reference to painting, "Apart from the extent to which even the greatest innovators still remain within conventions handed down from the immediate past, the degree to which their fellow artists were unmoved by what they did is as notable as their often very partial borrowings. This great, slow-moving current of conservatism must not be forgotten" (288).

9 "The Middle Ages are the civilization of vision, where the cathedral is the great book in stone, and is indeed the advertisement, the TV screen, the mystic comic strip that must narrate and explain everything, the nations of the earth, the arts and crafts, the days of the year, the seasons of sowing

and reaping, the mysteries of the faith, the episodes of sacred and profane history, and the lives of the saints…" This excess of narratives and significations relates to the cultural status of the cathedral as "a massive popular culture enterprise" (Eco 1986, 81–82). On the architectural development of the Gothic cathedral, see, for example, Wilson (1992).

10 See Williamson (1995), for a thoroughly documented survey and appraisal of monuments in Gothic sculpture throughout Europe.

11 On the especially sophisticated naturalism of sculpture under the patronage of the Burgundian court at Dijon at the turn of the fourteenth century, see Morand (1991).

REFERENCES

Barber, C. 2002. *Figure and Likeness: On the Limits of Representation in Byzantine Iconoclasm*. Princeton, New Jersey: Princeton University Press.

Belting, H. 1994. *Likeness and Presence: A History of the Image Before the era of Art,* translated by Jephcott, Edmund. Chicago: University of Chicago Press.

Eco, U. 1986. "Living in the New Middle Ages". In *Travels in Hyperreality: Essays*, translated by Weaver, W. San Diego: Harcourt Brace Jovanovich. 81–82.

Elsner, J. 1988. "Image and Iconoclasm in Byzantium". *Art History* 11: 471–491

Ladner, G. 1953. "The Concept of the Image in the Greek Fathers and the Byzantine Iconoclastic Controversy". *Dumbarton Oaks Papers* 7. Dumbarton Oaks.

Maginnis, H. B. J. 1997. *Painting in the Age of Giotto: A Historical Reevaluation*. University Park, Pennsylvania: Pennsylvania State University Press.

Moorhead, J. 1986. "Byzantine Iconoclasm as a Problem in Art History". *Parergon* n.s. 4: 1–18.

Morand, K. 1991. *Claus Sluter: Artist at the Court of Burgundy*. London: Austin.

Pesch, C. 1908. *De sacramentis, praelectiones dogmaticae*. Freiburg: Herder & Co.

Vasari, G. 1979 edn. *Lives of the Most Eminent Painters, Sculptors, and Architects*. New York: Abrams.

White, J. 1993. *Art and Architecture in Italy 1250–1400*, 3rd ed. New Haven and London: Pelican History of Art.

Williamson, P. 1995. *Gothic Sculpture 1140–1400*. New Haven: Yale University Press.

Wilson, C. 1992. *The Gothic Cathedral: The Architecture of the Great Church*, 2nd edn. London: Thames & Hudson.

Wixom, W. D. "Byzantine Art and the Latin West". In *The Glory of Byzantium: Art and Culture of the Middle Byzantine Era A.D. 843–1261*, edited by Evans, H. C.; Wixom, W. D. New York: The Metropolitan Museum of Art. 435–507.

Cite this chapter as: Nelson, Robert. 'Body and blood'. *The Spirit of Secular Art: A History of the Sacramental Roots of Contemporary Artistic Values*. Melbourne: Monash University ePress. pp. 3.1–3.10. DOI: 10.2104/ssa07003.

CHAPTER 4

THE AGONIES OF SPIRITUAL INVENTION

Robert Nelson

Why would a woman sew her thighs together, using a needle and thread? You have your suspicions: sexual perversity and perhaps shock value in the context of art. It could be as simple as a child doing something silly or painfully naughty in order to get noticed. You could have lots of theories. But because you have probably never met a woman who sews her thighs together, you do not really know the answer. It is an extreme act with an extremely uncertain motivation.

The performance, recorded and spectacularly monumentalized in large photographic images, is by Monika Tichacek.[1] You only see the outcome of the stitching and not the enactment; but in many cases, a ritualistic scenario is played out with another participant. The photographic language, with its morbid darkness and lighting from the sides, belongs to an erotic genre; and the women exercise their wits on cruelty for the sake of sado-masochistic pleasure. Sometimes, these rituals extend to eating one another. Mouths are bruised and garnished with thorns; face and shoulder are apparently gnawed away and a figure is seen in the act of devouring, like a proud lioness pawing lustfully over her kill. The work that stages this lurid anthropophagy reminds me of the animaliers of the nineteenth century.

Numerous bronze works by Barye and Fremiet and the earlier paintings by George Stubbs show helpless herbivores succumbing to the claw and fang of hungry cats. The genre develops a cruel aesthetic, in which the misery of the victim heightens the glee of the aggressor. It makes death perversely attractive. Cruelty is valorized as natural, as a part of instinct, an urge that the carnivore cannot suppress, any more than it can deny its hunger. But the sculptures of the early industrial period make you focus on the anguish of the horse or doe, which is presented as horribly beautiful.

The artists of the period were able to clinch an archaic sentiment in favour of the precious victim. The fiercest rush of adrenaline in the final moments is seen as sacred, related to the lamb of sacrifice, transcendental and paradoxically full of grace. But no sculptor or painter could ever disentangle the hallowed virtue from a base thrill, a ghastly joy in carnal conquest seized at its height in mortal penetration of the helpless desirable other by the predator. There is an erotic dimension that you recognize with inner perplexity, a troubling elation that sanctifies death with love.

Tichacek's photographs are absorbing and sensational, titillatingly theatrical in a crazy and eccentric vein. They make you think of Matthew Barney rather than Barye and Fremiet: they do not relate the world of the erotic to another sphere of spirit. For all that, the works are astonishingly stressful and seem somehow to threaten the decorous sublimation of ritual. The best sequences are those where circular holes have been cut in the stockings in ritual preparation for a stitch in the skin: the legs have then been threaded in a beautiful web that makes you think of cat's cradle (an innocent string-game that seven-year old girls adore), only riddled with pain.

In one photograph, a couple dances; but the woman with free legs hooks her foot in the elasticated mesh, which would send brutal shivers into the inner legs of the encumbered woman. In another sequence, a dominatrix figure attends the victim at the trunk of a tree. The young woman with sown thighs (presumably the artist) sits primly: for she could not easily alter her posture until the stitching is nipped. Meanwhile, the older woman lifts the younger woman's sequin dress with gnarled authority, making you expect that a final phase might unpick the infibulation and deliver the torment to her satisfaction. One of the images presents the legs like a gateway, with the cat's cradle connecting them in a symmetrical web, pinching the skin and drawing a series of graphic lozenges in the centre. The angular shape is vaginal in a crazy staggered fashion, dropping a bizarre ladder of abstract openings below the crutch toward the ground. Each tensile window beckons for some hideous maltreatment.

It is hard to unpick the meaning of these works. They could be nothing but a simple rehearsal of sado-masochistic pleasures. Or they could reach toward greater metaphoric or allegorical clout. There is potential for a powerful meaning. The dance with depravity strikes me as possibly more than narcissistic thighmanship. It belongs to a larger critique of the cultural reception of the body, in which the erotic is not seen in terms of ideal beauty but a highly customized subcultural organization of fantasy. This critique occurs in numerous performative works, mostly by women, such as the Australian group of artists, The Kingpins. In terms of cultural history, this is a critique of humanism.

As with Tichacek, the terms of this critique centre on the body. The body is no longer owned by culture (much less God) as an archetype, with its predictable biological function. It is inhabited by filthy thrills, possessed of unseasonal urges; and in the sense that the body represents life, you could say that it is constituted by outrageous desires: my body is inseparable from a psychological animus, intrinsically grotesque and perverse, that endows the flesh with its felt meaning. If I figure the body in art, it must come with the peculiar set of internalized social dynamics that make up my desire, this greater economy—as Freud called it—in which my libido and superego have constructed my ego in relation to the outside world. It makes no sense to segregate the visible flesh as some kind of passive vessel or vehicle or host to be understood as the machinery that carries the psyche. The very distinction of body and mind is a deplorable furphy that prevents the body from being understood as organically intimate with its own life, its energy, its will and desire. The psychological properties, as grotesque as they may appear alongside the objectified conventions of humanist body are celebrated in their lurid richness; and the lustful and adorable spectacle of the flesh (which had for so long been denied its subjectivity) may now be championed through the peculiar and aberrant charge that makes my body relate to another's.

Humanism, that high achievement of the Renaissance intellect, is now the subject of innumerable critiques of objectification, in art overt, surreptitious and even unconscious; and you could sometimes suspect that no avant garde art is made which is not a critique of the values of humanism. But before we can unravel the spiritual virtues of such critiques, we need to explore the spiritual calibre of humanism itself.

* * *

Art historians and religious enthusiasts have to explain to one another what they mean by humanism. There is sometimes little common ground in their usage. Among fundamentalists, the word is synonymous with a scornful atheism, the perverse idolization of mankind, the promotion of humans above God, indeed the arrogant displacement of God from the cosmos. Renaissance historians, on the other hand, use the word to talk about Christian people of great learning who admired antiquity, studied Latin and Greek texts, enjoyed an impressive curiosity for ancient myth and sought parallels between pagan philosophy and Biblical truth.[2]

The great artistic resource for this community was allegory. There had always been allegory; it was not a Renaissance invention (as the Greek word testifies) and could even be understood as eminently Biblical inasmuch as the parables are a literary trope of symbolic representation, akin to allegory. The parables are an ingenious method of making higher truths manifest to a relatively uneducated audience but—the prophet hopes—with such poetic magic that the deeper truths are also apprehended with greater pregnancy by the learned who can appreciate the subtle poetic reasons for the layered allusions and their pertinence to the ineffable. When Christ himself speaks in parables, who will contest the suitability of the genre for expressing the workings of providence? Allegory did not have a pagan copyright; it was apparently universal and very suitable, too, for expressing universal truths.

As a rambling but sophisticated philosophical system which reconciles sacred and secular wisdom, humanism forever engages allegory, because allegory is capable of converting dogma into speculation; it is apt for inviting poetic and philosophical inflexions into a pious domain, or for linking certain rigid ideas so that their greater complexity affords an enchanting open-endedness, far from the spiritual closure of dogma. With allegory happily marrying earthly matters to the higher realms, the poet could (a) enjoy a whole sensual world of imagery, (b) expect that it would be capable of extrapolation toward divinity and (c) consider that the imaginative and veiled shadow-boxing of the spiritual in the arena of the physical would prove supremely artistic. The poet can celebrate the heavy breath of the lover, the restless night spent thinking about the beautiful form of the object of desire; and not only can this relishing of lust be construed as an intellectual pilgrimage toward the divine but the poetic intermingling of candour and allusion could yield an artistic masterpiece.

The nineteenth-century historian of Italian literature Francesco De Sanctis says that Dante was Italy's first poet but Petrarch her first artist.[3] There would be several ways to interpret the remark, but something along the lines of allegory makes a useful point of departure. Both writers use allegory; but whereas Dante's allegories are self-evidently allegorical—and have a patently religious focus in the superintending divine order spelt out in the *Divine Comedy*—Petrarch's allegories are initially experienced as ingenuous emotional confession; for he writes about longing in such a sustained and preoccupied way that the allegorical conceit which subsumes all the poems to Laura is stylistically deflected. It is only through having the experience of desire evoked in an incantational obsessiveness that you later appreciate an ulterior energy. Petrarch does not delay the allegorical meaning in order to spend more time indulging in the emotion without religious interference; rather, he creates more free space around the emotional condition so that its link with the religious can be dramatized more fully. It is an inversion of the erotic paradigm by which the deferral of gratification heightens the pleasure: in Petrarch, the spiritual consummation is deferred to strengthen its infusion of your experience through so much sympathetic desire. In particular, the Christian sacrament of penitence can be drawn out with wonderful poetic effect in the extensions of the confessed desire.

The visual counterpart to the allegorical machinations of poets in the early Renaissance is more formal than iconographic. As already noted, painters and sculptors of the proto-Renaissance are absorbed in the labour of creating space around a motif; and this independence lets the motif enjoy a sensory life of its own, even as it is inevitably conscripted into a religious role with which it enjoys a marvellously convoluted relationship. The most memorable and seductive expression of this convolution is the style known as International Gothic, a visual ethos of great flamboyance in which lyrical pictures were configured in panels alongside the prolific use of ornament. In itself, the superabundance of decorative detail, protesting the festive elaborations of architectonic elements rather than the authority of the picture that it frames, can be interpreted as the deferral of dogmatic power.

In International Gothic, artists maintained the effort of the previous generation to create lifelike figures; but they conceived all illusionistic spaces within an independent ornamental regimen in the gilded frames. Instead of being held by an even cornice on all four sides, the picture is mounted within a Gothic arch, sometimes with smaller arches springing inside it and often rising on equally elaborate columns with barley-twist motifs and so on. To speak of the picture, singular, is misleading: there was often a whole typological complexity of images locking into architectural niches, oculi and plinths, all similarly ornamented and gilded. The ambitious structure of the frames did not contribute to the illusionistic spaces figured inside them; on the contrary, it created a rather rhapsodic teasing of the perspectival aspirations of each picture, and especially the larger ones whose attempts at rendering space were the more conspicuous. In aesthetic terms, the frames seem to act as a lyrical diversion, accenting the florid and sometimes languid compositions of International Gothic painting.

In symbolic terms, however, the reason for the frames was liturgical. Certainly the appearance of the frames (like that of the paintings) is graceful, refined and courtly, an air which has drawn some viewers to see the chivalrous style as foppish and frivolous, lacking all the gravity of the 'reformist' generation around 1300. This judgement is misguided. The complicated architectural schemes of International Gothic were for the sake of the liturgy. Most of the commonly published International Gothic paintings were configured along the lines of altarpieces, that is, church furniture at a most focal part of the celebrations. Although from a distance International Gothic altarpieces seem to constitute a pretty and seductive tickling of formerly severe religious iconography, the intricate festivity of their design is highly functional in a religious context. Sure there is a lightness and somewhat skipping rhythm in the visual texture of these highly permutated objects; but the spread of the architectural frame by the altar suggests a heavenly vision in which the clever little painted illusions are already in their place in heaven; an order greater than their little window attends them.

Artworks had always been commanded by architectural imperatives and, as often as not, the schemes into which pictures fitted were hieratic, defining the relative importance of each work and making each submit to an overarching order. In fact, artworks were seldom autonomous; they generally submitted to the terms of a larger design which, appropriately, would muster the individual energies of all of the spatial configuration within it and create a powerful whole. An example would be the sculpted figures in the portal of a Gothic cathedral. Their columnar direction would contribute to the energies of the doorway, to which they also contributed the symbolic ceremony of 'entry' as the textual human sentinels inviting a spiritual ingress to the word of God. And so it is, on a somewhat less august level, with any given painting in the picturesque regimes of International Gothic. The physical subscription, so to speak, of the painting to the architectural whole could be extrapolated to suggest the infallible co-operation of all earthly and celestial things to the greater harmonies of God. Architectural ornament is a language of agreements among minor details toward the most majestic, a reflection, then, of divine order.

By absorbing these architectural principles into the artwork itself, the work becomes a kind of allegory of heavenly will. The difference between the painting and the cathedral is scale and majesty: the painting lacks the tangible might and overpowering awe of the soaring piers and the expanse of the floor answered above by the spatial progression of column, window, clerestory, ribbed ceiling and so on, all striving upward with interpenetrating energies. The altarpiece is intimate, precious, adorable, cute. It is not a building but a painting. It is just that it retains within its essentially planar construction the architectural privilege of conscripting artworks into a greater totality, by analogy to the greater powers of God. The fact that this occurs in such a diminutive spatial ensemble intensifies the allegorical mission. Lesser pertains to greater. The Gothic cathedral was already dramatically great and its pertinence to an even greater order has a remoteness about it which quite matches the sublimity of the architecture. The altarpiece, on the other hand, is but a flourish, a gesture, a most pleasing token; but the great prestige of the altarpiece is its pertinence to God, in other senses no weaker than that of the mighty cathedral.

No one will compare a Gothic cathedral to an International Gothic altarpiece. The contrast is artificial, yet it is worth remembering that before the advent of International Gothic altarpieces, there was no very logical place for a painting in a Gothic church. Where would you hang it? The walls had been attenuated to such a degree that they were literally marginalized to the aisles, a dark area which hardly dignifies them. The whole nervous organic character of the church does not welcome square units propped up here or there; the upward thrust of the edifice repudiates the arbitrary rectangle of illusionistic space, promising a coherent sight 'through' the picture-plane. The cathedral directs the gaze 'beyond' the concerted definition of a rectangle, driving attention high up toward the stained glass windows with pointed arches or constellations of circles in the rose windows. The International Gothic altarpiece, on the other hand, institutes the picture in an architectural space of its own Gothic character, predicated on the plane and therefore sympathetic to the illusionistic spaces which it frames. The art now commands the ornament rather than the ornament commanding the art. It is a little church in its own right, a shrine within the church with architectonic presence. It goes without saying that the structural role of the frame bears no relation to the shafts, arches and buttresses of Gothic architecture. They are largely superfluous from an engineering point of view. They are assumed by the altarpiece for symbolic reasons.[4]

Although we must always affirm the integrity of the artwork as a whole (both painting and frame) the interest is in the status of the picture. By merely ornamental contrivances, the ensemble of frame and painting takes on the symbolic values of a house of worship. It is an honour conferred on the ensemble—not on the painting as such—but, on account of the obvious centrality of the picture, the prestige more readily passes to the painting than anything else. The painting provides the whole rationale for the frame. The dynamic between painting and frame works in a celebratory direction in favour of the painting. The hieratic relationship is obvious. Just as the frame contains the painting, the painting contains the holy personages and events. The medium of the saints is superior and is supported by appropriate supplication in the dancing and twisting of the frame.

Art is a stage on which mighty things are contracted to be performed on a small scale. It is not a modest charter. International Gothic altarpieces appear flighty and rarefied; but they are among the holiest thing in the Church—next to the altar itself—and, in their air of excessive gentility, they acquire a certain consecrated boastfulness. They are a sanctuary, a site of powerful spiritual investment, akin to the ancient arc of the covenant or any other noble piece of ecclesiastical furniture which was festively ornamented to enshrine the word in a figurative way. The spiritual achievement of International Gothic is to have taken solemn liturgical elements and absorbed them within an aesthetic, to have abstracted the independent sacramental status of both picture and ornament from their confinement to ritual and embodied them in a synthetic style of fastidious spatial hierarchies.

Pictures had never had this status. Miniature architecture was developed for them. It is allegorical architecture: it proposes that the images assembled within it are not merely isolated pictures of saints and holy episodes but a miniature heaven, a gorgeous gathering of holy things in divine unison. It is multiple stagecraft which enacts the sweetness of holy affinities and alludes, in its sumptuous fiddliness, to the universal harmonies of heaven. The painting 'happens' in a theatre rather than a frame; it is larded with connotations of a golden servitude, a world energetically celebrating God through worldly objecthood and, by its internal formal arguments, acquires some of the holiness of its painted content. So here again is the new ascendancy of the material to the spiritual: the stylistic agency to recreate by the altar the enchantment of heaven amounts to the ultimate sacramental prestige. But once again, this occurs through borrowing the vocabulary of a more austere liturgical artistic language—Gothic—in a period which had lost heart for its strenuous formal discipline. The credibility for the new International Gothic style derives from the old order whose liturgical gravity cannot be maintained; but the sacramental calibre of the new art—its ability to create an efficacious sanctified vision—is assumed to be greater because of its self-sufficiency, its allegorical lightness, its apparent freedom from a stony encompassing archaic grandeur.

Renaissance art and design, however, are normally placed by historians in the succeeding period in which the nervous Gothic cues were scrapped in favour of firmer classical roots. Profiting from the perspectival work by artists like Ambrogio Lorenzetti, the Renaissance proper also cultivated a powerful kind of drawing which placed all objects in a logical position, with an optically logical scale, given a fixed viewpoint.[5] The simultaneity of both changes is undoubtedly no coincidence and much has been made of the great spirit of reason resurfacing after a hiatus in the middle ages to dominate the art, design and literature of the Renaissance.

As with all the received paradigms of art history, there is some truth in it. But what the innovations take with them from the former spiritual predicates is often forgotten in the understandable focus on technical, formal, stylistic and even iconographic advances. Altarpieces, for example, did not cease to exist, even though very few remain in an International Gothic idiom, such as the *Adoration of the Magi* by Gentile da Fabriano of 1423.[6] It is the famous epoch in which Florentine sculptors, architects and painters—Ghiberti, Donatello, Brunelleschi, Masaccio—would clinch the classicizing enthusiasm of humanism, reflecting a neo-Roman climate in which the formal intricacies of Gothic were all but obsolete and sometimes even despised as dark and sinister, probably for chauvinistic reasons. But while the International Gothic frame ceases to be pursued on a stylistic level, its functional genius is maintained through a stylistic revetment of a classical nature. Instead of the delicate flutter of so many multiple pointed arches, innumerable crockets and pinnacles, the altarpiece would take on the trabeated form of classical architecture, all classical column, classical entablature and classical podium. An imposing example is the *Santo Zeno Altarpiece* by Mantegna of circa 1460. As in International Gothic altarpieces, the ensemble admits sophisticated typological arguments to ricochet between central images and their *predelle*, those little images in the lower zones, the structural part of the altarpiece whose architectural role is to form a base or stereobate for the taller pilastered zone above.[7]

The painting as temple or shrine is carried into the sixteenth century. Most aspects of the history of art are adequately told by looking at pictures and sculptures; but the symbolic and spiritual status of the objects is also revealed by their design, for this speaks clearly of a context of function. The vertical sides of the frame are presented as pilastered walls. The lower horizontal member is conceived as a base which runs underneath the two vertical sides and exceeds them by a small margin. The upper horizontal member is conceived as an entablature, a lintel which similarly runs past the vertical shafts beneath which figuratively support it, in the same way as the verticals rest upon the base below. All joins are right-angles. There are no mitres, which are the traditional way to resolve the encounter of horizontal and vertical in wooden construction. It is the language of the compressive, derived from construction in stone which is the medium of the whole of Graeco-Roman architecture. It is, however, neither the medium of painting nor of framing. The only reason for framing pictures in this way is to make of the flat surface a shrine, just as in International Gothic, but with the greater gravity and clout of the classical language of architecture, entailing heftier landmark status.[8]

Meanwhile, the framing method known today—consisting of four mouldings of uniform description joined by mitres—was used for a whole host of contexts. Most were secular, especially portraiture. But their use gradually spread and, by the middle of the century, the standard kind of frame known today (albeit with richer mouldings) supplanted the architectural shrines for sacred pictures destined for churches. The reasons for this take-over relate to the enthusiasms generated by the paintings themselves.

Since the epoch of *dolce stil novo*, painters had made significant steps toward greater accuracy in proportions, greater consistency of light, greater expression of volume, greater logic in the arrangement of space. The labour was undoubtedly intended to endow figures and their environment with a more believable value. Pictures form a more authoritative spectacle in their own right. The improvements in illusionism were clinched, as it were, by the invention of one-point perspective around the first quarter of the fifteenth century. Perspective is a systematic method for establishing the correct diminution in the size of objects according to their distance from the viewer. The process is neither spontaneous nor traditional but intellectual and scientific, concerned with optical logic. The recognition of one-point perspective invoked an imaginary grid in the artist's perception for charting orthogonals to a vanishing point, the spot where parallel lines in a motif appear to converge if taken to infinity. The implicit grid depends on consistency. There can be no distinctive accenting of horizontals or verticals, no privileging of one part over another. All lines in the grid must equally obey the same criteria for accurately mapping recession into space. This virtual grid is in no way acknowledged or flattered by a frame of compressive weights and different kinds of corners. It calls for even sides for all pictures.

Regular picture frames suited the pictures. If there was no conspicuously hieratic convention of large and small in the picture, why endow the frame with an architectural system of dynamic weights and stresses whose ornamental elaborations narrate the dependence of greater on lesser?

These allegories in design are somehow anachronistic. The use of polyptychs also declined, probably because comparisons between pictures in folding planes (and possibly of different site or scale or inconsistent spatial assumptions) seemed to countervail the illusionistic aspiration of each picture. One way or another, the regular frame prevails as does the perspectival rigour of the pictures within them.

From that time onward an altarpiece is never quite an altarpiece in the same way. Sure, they function as a backdrop for the celebration of mass and, on account of the simplicity of the plane devoted to a powerful illusion, sixteenth-century altarpieces have memorable presence. But it is no longer the presence of a shrine; it no longer has the connotations of a house of worship; it no longer miniaturizes through the allegory of ornament the relation between holies and heaven; it no longer figuratively intercedes on your behalf before the majesty of the almighty to produce an intimate theatre of episodic encounters. Later altarpieces are paintings which have a greater impact as paintings. The genre of painting is confident and self-sufficient; it boasts its own faculties of suggesting heavenly spaces and relations and does not need to subscribe to an archaic ornamental order to enact holiness. And, of course, the paintings are successfully holy. But part of their success as sacred images lies in the process of (a) stepping into the sacramental role of old altarpieces, (b) forswearing the ornamental context of the sacred tradition in which sacramental connotations were embedded and (c) appearing to have shed the materialistic appurtenances of the former archaic tradition and more appropriately addressing the spiritual through the primacy of vision.

The spiritual claims of painting would indeed move from the middle of the fifteenth century and extend to the furthest secular realms which could be reached by allegory. From the very moment when painters had an almost infallible perspectival technique, had perfected the rendering of volumes in light and had mastered anatomy and gesture, they paradoxically created scenes with incomprehensible iconography. The first notable case is Piero della Francesca, whose *Flagellation* escapes the interpretative consensus of any two Renaissance scholars in a given room.[9] The figures of men whipping Jesus are obviously enacting the Biblical episode as written. So is the gentleman sitting down, who must be Pontius Pilate, having authorized the punishments. The man closer to us with his back toward us need not be anyone very important. However, the three figures on the right hand side—apparently either implicated in the events or in some way reflecting them in a contemporary context—cannot be explained. No doubt it is allegorical; but the picture is intentionally mysterious. The soffit above Christ is illuminated by a supernatural light, and the picture is rich in ironies, such as the figure of a pagan god presiding pompously over the column around which Christ is tied. In an idiom of scientific clarity in the establishment of space, Piero has nevertheless installed a depth of speculation. Like the equally beautiful *Baptism*, his *Flagellation* has the air of being darkly encrypted by a slightly withdrawn personality.[10] There may not be a simple explanation for either picture. They are mysterious in content, even though limpid in their visual construction.

Toward the end of the fifteenth century the ambitions of Renaissance painting extend to allegories of secular subject matter. In particular, the paintings of Piero di Cosimo, Botticelli and Bellini present learned riddles which have for some time engaged the wits of scholars to supply interpretations. Even when advanced with erudition and confidence, all theories are somehow suspended by the paintings themselves and, sooner or later, lose the air of finality initially vaunted.

The paintings call for a learned hermeneutic response, and scholars have hardly shown vanity in accepting the invitation and attempting to derive sources in ancient literature for their purposeful juxtaposition of mythological figures. But their best attempts remain provisional, for the paintings are allegorical in a poetic way: they resist a single interpretation amid a plethora of possibilities; and this room for ambiguity, along with refined aesthetic nuances, creates their peculiarly pregnant inspiration.

Botticelli is the clearest example, because his work deals with love and therefore lends itself to Neo-Platonic interpretation. The voluptuous beauty of his women in sexually seductive poses and near or total nudity makes clear that his vision of love is erotic. But the subject matter is love in a functional allegorical sense as well; for the figures are identifiably Venus (as in the *Birth of Venus* and *Venus and Mars*) and Cupid (as in the *Primavera* or *Spring*).[11] The gentle painter has installed figures of Venus to tell stories in an oblique figurative way about the agency of love. The interpretations of art historians tend to converge in this; moreover, they favour a broadly neo-Platonic pattern, which emphasizes the role of sensual love in climbing toward intellectual and spiritual excellence, leading undoubtedly to God. The compositional thrust of the *Primavera*, for example, demonstrates this aspiration. A crude form of erotic energy rushes in from the right: the figure of Zephyr grabs the wood nymph Chloris who, in the encounter, emerges as the goddess of flowers, Flora. Thus the metamorphosis related in Ovid's *Fasti*.[12] Then, to the left, the goddess Venus (presumably) presides with vertical authority, dividing the composition with an air of equanimity. She gestures lightly toward the Three Graces who dance in a delicate but close and erotic manner. The central Grace is being shot by Cupid who flies above Venus. The beautiful dancing figure turns her head longingly at the final figure on the left, the god Mercury (a kind of god of communication) who, however, does not reciprocate but takes the energy, as it were, and gestures aloft with a rod—his attribute, the *caduceus*—and stirs the element of heaven. In this sequence, the force of raw passion and desire is transformed by grace under the guidance of a celestial Venus (for she has a star-spangled robe) to become an intellectual aspiration toward the godly.

Through such masterpieces, the art of painting gains inestimable prestige. The new glamour does not derive from usurping Christian belief. Art historians have generally been at pains to point out that there is no contradiction between the content of such pictures (nor indeed any of their possible neo-Latin sources) and Christian theology. On the contrary, the whole impetus of neo-Platonism was to reconcile Christian dogma and pagan spirituality, to find texts from antiquity—such as Plato but particularly Plotinus, much cultivated by the Florentine humanist Ficino—which had already abstracted, as it were, the carnal pantheon of gods to establish a core divinity analogous to the one true God. Philosophers, poets and painters were free to celebrate any of the pagan spiritual intuitions, within the parameters of confirming faith in Christ. The consequence of that celebration was to add to the earthly promotion of divinity, to provide new access to the mysteries, to enlarge the routes of mystical comprehension.[13] And, as the language used by philosophers, painters and poets was seductively rich (often centring around the spiritual value of beauty), the magic of the extended pathways was powerful. The imagination gained new spiritual gifts.

What Petrarch had done in the fourteenth century was to elaborate desire as a cue to ascend to holy awareness. What painters did toward the end of the fifteenth century was to identify

Christian theology in pagan spirituality, through a host of beautiful personifications and myths. For Petrarch, the perspective was rather cramped and at times contradictory: he wanted to allegorize the processes of sacred adoration through earthly desire; but he also needed to enact the process of contrition, thereby compromising his own allegorical privilege. In the mature Renaissance these anxieties were unnecessary. And because there was no need to agonize excessively over the theological justification of the erotic, the privileges could extend to painters. Artists now had the skills, too, to emulate the styles of antiquity; the work of architects and poets encouraged them; and their great proximity to the physical side of the ideal placed them in an enviable position for allegorizing the celestial ideal with any number of carnal nuances.

Despite intensive private patronage, the structure of the spiritual order did not change in the Renaissance. It was firmly based around the Church and the families who led the Church, none of whom had a concerted will to have the ancestral piety and privileges infiltrated by uncertain *arcana*. Most of Botticelli's paintings are religious in a fairly direct convention. Priests remained priests in the Renaissance; there was no backing down or weakening of canon law or any other administrative part of the church, just as there was no deviation from any of the traditional liturgical activities of the cult. If anything, the dominance of religious offices by family oligopolies reinforced the structural stability of the church by a close identification of ecclesiastical and temporal power.

And yet the religious discipline as represented in art seems to have been mollified by a new urbanity. Humanism made for an erudite culture: one wanted to be flattered by exorbitant scholarship, just as one wanted costly palaces with classical façades, *cassoni* with classical ornaments and priceless objects *all'antica*. In this ambience of historicist enthusiasm, paintings also had to be learned; they had to show not only a knowledge of ancient iconographies but an inspirational sophistication in manipulating the elements of classical subject matter toward philosophical arguments. The task was probably too ambitious for painters to cope with on their own. Art historians like to posit the agency of a 'humanist adviser', a thoroughly schooled poet who could suggest philosophical allegorical schemes for painters to borrow in informing compositions of their own imagination.

In this prestigious undertaking, a whole cosmology is envisaged and laid down for eternity, with the *imprimatur* of a Churchy family. Once the exclusive preserve of priests in a hallowed tradition, the devising of spiritual iconographies is now contrived by 'intellectuals', a humanist partnership of artist and poetic scholar, with a relatively high degree of doctrinal autonomy. Their relish of pagan gods as appropriate symbolic vessels of spiritual edification—no matter how consonant with Christian values—would not have been possible within the old structures of the Church. The praxis of the religion, the worship of God, remained steadfastly within the traditional dogmatic institution whose copyright on such matters no one would ever challenge from outside. But the most dynamic *theoria* was happening beyond the cloth, so to speak; for the theological insights concerning the deeper transference of divinity were in the province of poets and painters. In their hands, the innovative and inspirational speculations do not have the air of a severe theological discipline but a comely and inventive seduction.

Renaissance allegories appear to transcend dogmatic parameters, to go beyond worship toward contemplation, to take belief into the territory of philosophy. It seems more momentous than it really was. Religious self-referentiality seems to be challenged, to face an onslaught of parallel enthusiasms which take it away from dogma and so weaken its unquestioned hold on the imagination. Any religious idea could potentially be free to take on any doctrinal direction by the prophetic gifts of a humanist poet or painter. Unheard of-power! But there was one proviso, namely that whatever insights were furnished by these scholar-clairvoyants, it should be by way of supplementation—not challenge—with respect to all existing spiritual assumptions.

Artistic autonomy is not yet an imaginable condition. The innovations of allegorical artists lie within existing parameters; they are dependent on expectations of transcendence which were provided long since by the sacramental status of art. The most apparently radical art of the time trades upon Christian sacramental glory. It is a language of redemption and immortality. It represents and purveys an understanding of grace; and it does so with the magic of all of the best art at the time, an intimate sublimity which proceeds from the 'understanding brush' as it sympathetically pulls the paint around the exquisitely drawn volumes. The power of the radical subject matter seems to derive from a cache of exotic mysteries running somewhat independently of Christian rituals (which indeed they antedate); but the effect of those mysteries lies in their ability to connect to mysteries which are to a greater or lesser extent still believed. If the representations had been wholly free of Christian connotations, they would be fossils, conjectural specimens of archaeology. They are much more than that; they are animated by contemporaneous knowledge of Christian sacraments.

The Christian sacraments are all exploited in the new magic. If they had been totally ignored, there may have been an aesthetic thrill in by-passing Christian spiritual assumptions; but this would have been a form of witchcraft, a dark ratbaggery reacting resentfully against the hegemony of the Church. The tenor of all Renaissance allegories is harmonious and, with the exception of images such as those of Apollo and Marsyas, they are aesthetically cheerful. They have no axe to grind. Their content is authorized by Christian belief to whose imperatives they ultimately comply. Nevertheless, the glamour of art is greatly enhanced by the apparent audacity of the humanist cause. First, one replaces Jesus with Venus; second, one invests Venus with a Christian redemptive message by way of neo-Platonic allegory; and third, one draws new sacramental prowess from doing all this with the air of prophetic invention, of perceiving higher truth with independence, and hence achieving visionary status.

This is the paradigm which also underlies the wealth of Venetian art after Bellini, the allegorical work of Giorgione, Titian, the Bassani, Tintoretto and Veronese. The art of these masters also makes a historical claim to spiritual invention which, however, is wholly dependent on dominant Christian spiritual axioms for its vivacity and credibility. But with the generation of the High Renaissance, a whole level of force and conviction is added which makes the work of the earlier Renaissance seem modest.

Among the many achievements of the High Renaissance is the enviable establishment of art status. This was no mere ruse of careerists; it was a result of the self-consciousness expressed in artworks of almost megalomaniac ambitions. Admittedly, the artistic attainments are matched with almost equal ambition for fame and greatness, a yearning which today strikes us as somewhat shameless and embarrassing. Michelangelo's *Sistine Ceiling* of 1508–1512 is the earliest example of the superb, the almost arrogant pride of an artist in full mastery of unknown resources of the imagination, unknown confidence and expressive force.[14] The ceiling narrates with an air of declaration the creation of the world by God, as well as the first stories of mankind from *Genesis*; and, particularly in the representation of the virile-looking God the father, the painting takes on the potency of the creator-spirit. The visual emulation of God strikes us as singularly successful: Michelangelo is seen to be *doing the divine*, enacting sacred history with a fervid belief in its happening; and in the muscular power of the interventions in space with which his figures project the holy drama, the artist offers a properly sacramental rehearsal, sacramental inasmuch as an emphatically physical translation of divine energies which compels psychological involvement in its awesome majesty.[15]

Massive projects such as the *Sistine Ceiling* are not the only evidence of the High Renaissance enthusiasm for enacting magnificence. Smaller pictures, such as portraits, sometimes acquire an equal presence by faithfully reflecting the sense of assurance of the great. Look at the *Portrait of Pope Leo X* by Raphael.[16] The powerful Pope presides in an iconic frontal pose, flanked by a symmetrical entourage of two acolytes. The pictorial space is relatively shallow. Raphael proposes an alarming intimacy with the Pope, whose somewhat corpulent embrace of the materials on the table seems to fill up the picture. Behind him are two Cardinals, looking rather more shifty and ambitious than deferential or reverend. The Pope is not concerned about them. He knows that he embodies supreme authority: no one will challenge him and his every pronouncement on doctrine is infallible. Raphael demonstrates this certainty by showing the Pope in a relaxed and relatively informal pose and space. Of course the Pope remains the highest 'institution' in western Christendom and, merely by painting him in his cathedra and robes (which could not possibly have been substituted by casual clothes), a great deal of institutional authority is conveyed. But Raphael's approach begins a kind of de-institutionalizing process by which painting represents the inner character of a person. The focus on the institutional architecture declines and a new penetration of the person replaces it. The figure is scrutinzed as the painting insinuates the analytical gaze into people's carnal appearance, posture, gesture and habitual behaviour. That celebrated 'intellectual' or 'analytical' focus of the Renaissance genius is seen in *Leo III* with a kind of inverted pomposity. It candidly confesses the ambitious temper of the epoch in its very casualness.

The High Renaissance undoubtedly produced some duds but the keynote is set by masterpieces. In them there is nothing tentative or quaint, even when transferred from the aulic clarity of Florence to the intimacy and warmth of Venice. What Florentine artists could do by an aloof grandeur the Venetians would do with sanguine corporality. For centuries the art of the two towns has been compared, typically in favour of Florence by those who like discipline and chastity of form; whereas those who like the suggestion of slap-and-tickle normally hold their tongue but vouch for the ongoing affection for the Venetians by the attention they give to them and also, when artists, by their stylistic emulation.

Iconographically, the Venetians are closer to Botticelli than are the Florentine triumvirate of Leonardo, Michelangelo and Raphael. The Venetians enjoyed learned allegory and painted the pagan gods with the same kind of neo-Platonic richness which belonged to the Humanist tradition around the Medici, though perhaps somewhat simplified and earthy. Titian's painting of so-called *Sacred and Profane Love* is a checklist of virtues and vices which belong respectively with two female personifications (personifications of what one does not precisely know).[17] The two women sit on opposing sides of a classical well. One of them is clothed: she has a seductive look and, beside her legs on the well, there is a carved image of an unbridled horse; there is a ruined castle in the background and rabbits rooting around in the scrub. On the other side, the woman is naked; but instead of the ruined castle, there is a Church; the horse is replaced by a scene of chastisement and the plague of rabbits by husbandry. Clearly the nude woman is morally superior and is presumably related to the idea of naked truth. But the painting also deals with the erotic and is not so moralistic as to eliminate ambiguity. Both women are lovely and are painted with fulsome dignity; you know that Titian has enjoyed painting them and savouring whatever vices are contingent on whichever is the baser in his personal revaluation.

The privileges of painting are not merely to point out that such-and-such a god may procure a spiritual enlightenment when understood in a sublime way. It is to operate with whatever messages through the visual in such a seductive way that the viewer is drawn into the terms of the illusion—or even the paint itself—to try to divine the ultimate meaning. Ambiguity is not a thing in itself but it is a great commodity of the poetic. As a painter, you have to work within a basically shared understanding and reveal essential lineaments of an idea which are satisfactory on their own. But thereafter, the finer readings can be tickled this way and that; and in this teasing of the subject matter by the expression of its own sensuality, the painting gains an almost outrageous charm. So often in the works of Titian a beautiful woman represents an abstract virtue (as with the personifications above and numerous others such as Flora, even extending to sacred figures) but the sensual appeal which the painter captures spiritually hijacks the work.[18]

This is not quite like the divine sensuality of the Greeks whose perfection abides in a stony ideal, no matter how judiciously inflected with muscular gestures and the tensile erotic dynamic of bodies. Titian's eroticism is deliciously insidious: you never catch him painting goddesses but beautiful women; they all look like portraits, with the peculiar characteristics of the person often being repeated in paintings of incongruous thematic material. He has before him—not unlike Botticelli—his favourite beauty and paints her with a finely balanced and tasteful lewdness. You can tell that he wants to undress his women; he wants to peer more deeply into the cleavage and, in one celebrated picture, the *Bacchanale of the Andrians*, he actually inserts a piece of paper inside a buxom woman's bodice with his own signature on it.[19] When he paints women naked, he gives the impression that they want to make love or have just done so, as with the reclining—and presumably intoxicated—woman in the same picture.

But the ravishment of a Titian painting is not in the beauty of the model alone, nor even the venereal implications of the subject matter; and if it were only that it would probably be *Kitsch*. The high achievement is to have discovered a technique which internally celebrates the same sensuality, extending the voluptuous manner of painting to the umbrous landscape and ruddy sky. Titian only occasionally makes explicit gestures of love-making through the 'pornographic' interlacing of limbs. It is the quality of the painted flesh that makes almost all of his work so erotic. It is equally true of his male sitters in simple portraits. An example is the *Portrait of a Man* in the London National Gallery, sometimes known as a *Portrait of Ariosto*.[20]

The serene countenance turns toward us from a body oriented slightly away from us, with the foremost arm working its way across our access to the pictorial space and resting on the kind of ledge that was common in fifteenth-century painting. The features, the turning of the neck and the imposing sleeve are registered in an oblique light. You can intuit a light source in an unseen window not far away, that softest indoor source which illuminated the bulk of Venetian paintings and would inform the strongly directional lighting for the baroque. As the neck of the sitter passes into shadow, the turning of the surfaces on all axes is registered by several deliberate changes in colour. Tellingly enough, painters use temperature as a metaphor for chromatic relations; they speak of warm colours (in this case earth red, earth orange and earth yellow) passing into cool colours (earth green and earth blue). These transitions are subtle and at times rather disguised by an overall warmth installed in the flesh by warm glazes of siennas or other transparent oxides. But beneath them, the temperature of the flesh varies in finely controlled degrees.

Most of the movements in the temperature of the paint are explained as a logical drawing process, expressing the separate volumetric planes in the motif and their organic integrity. The colour, in other words, accompanies the correctness of the drawing, supplementing the perception of waxing and waning in light to match the different kinds of contour or the degree to which the surfaces move in a parallel or perpendicular direction with respect to the viewer. It would be possible to explain all transitions from a material point of view, if we were prepared to go through the steps in the drawing process, that is, the way in which the eye registers just how the planes of a motif are registered in illusionistic space. But this process, even if rooted in a logical regime of perceptual drawing, has highly sensual consequences and, following the genius of the metaphor of temperature, almost metaphysically moody corollaries.

The chromatic richness of Venetian painting expresses something about skin itself, especially the way in which it is intrinsically warm and yet passes into cold depending on exposure to the ambient elements. The skin has an organic relationship with a number of contingencies, like proximity to clothing or a source of heat. The skin will obviously be warmer if open to a pleasant radiance and will give up heat when left to the breezy emptiness. It is warmer if the muscles are active beneath the skin, cooler if they are idle. The colour of skin is altered by proximity to arteries or gristle or calluses. The hues of the skin relay a whole subcutaneous natural history. Similar things can be said about light. The glow which comes in directly from a window has a powerfully warming effect while reflected light might be stripped of the heat and simply illuminate surfaces in a cold manner. The combination of the warm and cool colours, when judiciously mastered, is an interpretation of the subtle dynamic between organism and the life-giving element of light.[21] So complicated are the variables of this dynamic that painters are generally imprudent to make rules about it. As a successful expression of living matter, it verges on the numinous.

Even though today physicists find it difficult to explain how light is simultaneously a particle and a wave phenomenon, we accept the view that it is a material phenomenon and, regardless of our embarrassments of finding the right language to say how it functions, that it has nothing supernatural or ghostly about it. But for past ages the opposite view was held, that light is a vivifying effulgence which obviously emanates from God and whose life-giving properties are a divine dispensation. Materialists though we be, it is hard to resist some thankful consciousness in the background that sunlight is intoxicatingly divine; and even in our industrial epoch Bataille will write a kind of heady hymn to the force of the sun, as if a neo-pagan nature-worshipper.[22]

To express this 'gift' of light, it is necessary to stage the encounter of the kindly element with the fragile and organic body which receives it. As if ultimately the reception of any god-sent largesse is always corporal, the physical boon is only committed to our understanding through feeling it—somewhat sacramentally—through the body. In Venetian painting, light does not merely appear to strike a hard surface, as in Piero della Francesca, but to penetrate a permeable surface. The skin is shown as somehow vulnerable to the light (just as it is vulnerable to cold) which can enter in subcutaneous degrees to share that agency of blood and muscle which also affects the tonality. Part of the effect, at least, is created by the shifting of chromatic tone which argues for the varying terms of the encounter between flesh and light, warming the flesh here and letting it transpire heat there and so on. But this joyful drama of the external element suffusing the inner substance is enacted by the paint in a further invention of technique to which the Venetians probably have a greater copyright than they do with chromatic modelling, which was immanent throughout the tradition and arguably developed in less sensual guises elsewhere.

The peculiarly beautiful penetration of light into the fabric of the skin is paralleled in the paint by using transparent glazes. Oil paint, which was invented in the north in the fifteenth century, enables layers to be floated over one another in thin glazes, using plenty of medium and very little paint.[23] If you have transparent colours, you can 'tint', as it were, the painted volumes without altering their definition. The technique of glazing is just that: to put colour over painted volumes which are already established beneath in order to make them warmer.

Normally, a figurative painter uses opaque colours to build up illusionstic forms. When the light encounters the opaque paint, some of it is absorbed and some is scattered. The reflected light may be animated by virtue of its combinations of colour; but it is not intrinsically luminous and does not compare with the glow of transmitted light. Glazing, on the other hand, allows the painter to let the light seep into a layer of transparent paint, to strike the opaque colour beneath it and then reflect back up through the transparent layer. The light which bounces back in this way is filtered by the glaze layer and consequently has the character of transmitted light rather than reflected light. The result is a gorgeous luminosity which in some way imitates the glow of real skin in natural light. Having developed the technique, painters would use it for all naturally radiant phenomena, some background buildings picking up the late sun, a pastoral landscape through a window caught by oblique afternoon light, a glittering belt or a shiny metal knob on the hilt of a sword. But when applied to skin, the technique is magically suited to expressing the interaction of light with the carnal; for it inherently mimics the 'breathing' of the skin, its reception of light and that sense of the membrane harbouring the light and casting it back to our eyes with the richness of its indefinable colours.

Venetian painters used glazes on all flesh: bony old men and beauties alike are kissed, as it were, with the radiant blessing of Venetian luminosity; for the handsomeness (and vulnerability) of skin is common to all sitters and models, regardless of the evenness of their complexion. If anything, the women of aristocratically paler countenance discourage the painter's inclination to infuse all painted flesh with a sumptuous depth of colour in the glazing. But a clever painter has resources in light oxides to cope with that ceramic calibre of skin too. In short, who would not have wanted to be painted in this style? There may be plenty of exaggeration in some of our sources, but when we read how the whole of European nobility was attracted to Venice in the hope of having their visages immortalized by Titian, Prince of Painters, we have a sign, at least, of a contemporary view of the painter's offering.

The painter offers a celebration which goes beyond the vanity of fame; for, in one sense, the sitter is only given what every other figure gets, namely the honour of his or her skin resembling everyone else's in real life and in real light. But the translation of what God does into the terms of what art does has a kind of sacramental status; there is a ritual of doing, a ceremonial incarnation of flesh in authoritative brushstrokes. The aesthetic re-enactments of form-making had never encroached so far upon the holiness of life, for it now deals with a corporal biological interchange with light. The Venetian painter did not register an 'ideal' in the sense of a perfect form—as of the fine-nosed Greeks—but an ineffable beauty about the warm-humoured organism which we share, regardless of the shape of our noses. Consider Titian's portrait of the nasally proud *Francis I*: he is still beautiful in the sensuality of his presence.[24] The Venetians have a portrait of the human whose physicality reaches beneath the epidermis; and it is universally glowing for all sitters. Beneath their brush, the flesh painted in warm light is celebrated in a way which parallels the consecration of matter for holy purposes.

The new offices of painting are secular; they do not proceed from liturgical incumbencies nor do they apply to sacred images more poignantly than to any private portrait commission. Nevertheless, they bring to all images an expression of great beauty and, in religious terms, a celebration of the most divine aspects of God's creation; for they attempt to clinch in a visible demonstration those physical things which are capable of spirit, whose agency seems to the pious much more than metaphoric but actually divine. It is as if secular technology proffers the consummation of all the sacred aspirations which anyone could have imagined attending the visual things of this world.

When Venetian painters devise cryptic subject matter analogous to Botticelli's, the presence of these techniques confers the most powerful mystique on the ideas; for there is an immanence in each personification, a magical trading of sacred elements, which gives to the whole allegory a kind of inspirational loftiness that goes with prophecy. In previous chapters, similar spiritual prestige has been ascribed to other secular techniques (which nevertheless ride upon prior hallowed authorities) but, by the High Renaissance in Venice, the difference reaches another order. With the technical genius of this period, the affinities with a spiritual order of worship are now installed deep within the language of painting itself. It is not a remote and abstract form of iconographic script-writing which provides the fateful links between the secular and the sacred; it is the vision of making itself. And it is in this broad area—let us call it the integrity of art as a visual expression—that we will find the future history of sacramental claims on behalf of secular production.

ENDNOTES

1 Monika Tichacek, *The shadowers*, Karen Woodbury Gallery, 4 Albert St, Richmond, Melbourne, 2003; some of the following text is grafted from my review "Don't try this at home" in *The Age* (Nelson 2003).

2 For art historical purposes, an important study of the creative interests of Renaissance humanists and their pertinence to Renaissance art see Cast (1988, 412–449). See also Trinkaus (1999, 667–684): from a much broader perspective, Trinkaus' review article provides concise reflections on major scholarly definitions of humanism and their relationship to the idea of the Renaissance.

3 "L'Italia ha avuto il suo poeta; ora ha il suo artista" (De Sanctis 1970, 255).

4 See Newberry et al. 1990). Premised on the interrelationship of frame design with architectural design and context, this catalogue demonstrates the precise distinctions that can be made between variations on the frame styles of Italian Gothic altarpieces: "But while Tuscan Gothic frames on the whole remained rather austere, as did Tuscan Gothic architecture, North Italian designers and carvers embraced the flamboyance of German and French architectural taste more wholeheartedly. Venetian artists and frame carvers were particularly sensitive to the florid Gothic style of local architecture and to the exoticism of Islamic design, familiar to them through the city's flourishing trade with the Near East" (Newberry et al. 1990: 18–19).

5 See, for example, Frugoni (1998, 36–78); Ambrogio Lorenzetti's intellectualism and his status as an innovator are principal themes in this survey.

6 Gentile da Fabriano, *Adoration of the Magi*, 1423, tempera on panel, Galleria degli Uffizi, Florence. For close studies in the history of Italian altarpieces and their functions see the authoritative collection of articles in Borsook and Superbi Gioffredi (1994).

7 Andrea Mantegna, *St Zeno Altarpiece,* ca. 1457–1459, tempera on panel, high altar of San Zeno, Verona. The originals of the three predella scenes of Christ's Passion are today held in the Musée des Beaux-Arts, Tours, and the Louvre, Paris. On the landmark status of this altarpiece in the history of Italian painting, see the exhibition catalogue by Martineau (1992, 109).

8 In fifteenth- and early sixteenth-century Tuscany, the frames of particular Gothic polyptychs were self-consciously classicized for reasons of religious and more broadly cultural prestige; see Troup (1998) and Hoeniger (1995, 101–126). Nonetheless, this change in frame-forms did not result in a new type of picture equatable with the modern easel painting; see Puttfarken (2000, 98).

9 Piero della Francesca, *Flagellation of Christ*, 1458–1460, tempera on panel, Galleria Nazionale delle Marche, Urbino. More recently, see Aronberg Lavin (2002, 96–97) for a concise summary and categorization of the art historical interpretations. This introduces the author's own interpretation centred on the humanist *topos* of consolation.

10 Piero della Francesca, *Baptism of Christ,* ca. 1455, tempera on panel, National Gallery, London. On the 'withdrawn' qualities of this image see Verdon (2002, 30–50), an essay which equates such qualities with religious gravity and specific pious contexts.

11 Sandro Botticelli, *Birth of Venus*, ca. 1485, tempera on canvas, Galleria degli Uffizi, Florence; *Venus and Mars*, ca. 1485, tempera and oil on panel, National Gallery, London; *Primavera*, ca. 1480–1481, tempera on panel, Galleria degli Uffizi, Florence.

12 Ovid 1959 *Fasti* 5.193–220.

13 In this vein, see for example the monographic study by Snow-Smith (1993), which methodically analyzes the *Primavera* as a work subtly conceived by Marsilio Ficino for the spiritual and philosophical initiation of the young Pierfrancesco de' Medici.

14 Michelangelo Buonarotti, ceiling including the *Creation of Adam*, 1508–1512, fresco, Sistine Chapel, Vatican.

15 See Barolsky (2003, 29–55). See also Nagel (2000), who focussed on the sacramental and theological impulses behind Michelangelo's bold experimentation in his figurative work.

16 Raffaello Sanzio, *Portrait of Pope Leo X with Cardinals Giulio de' Medici and Luigi de' Rossi*, ca. 1518–1519, oil on panel, Galleria degli Uffizi, Florence. To impressively convey the self-assurance of the portrait subject also required a certain self-assurance on the part of the artist: see West (2004, 163–164).

17 Tiziano Vecellio, *Sacred and Profane Love*, ca. 1514, oil on canvas, Galleria Borghese, Rome.

18 See Goffen (1997) for a closely considered argument of Titian's treatment of female beauty, and female subjects, throughout his career.

19 Tiziano Vecellio, *Bacchanale of the Andrians,* ca. 1523–1525, oil on canvas, Museo del Prado, Madrid.

20 Tiziano Vecellio, *Portrait of a Man (A Member of the Barbarigo Family; Ariosto)*, ca. 1510, oil on canvas, National Gallery, London.

21 See Hills (1999) for a multi-faceted consideration of the particular, potent relationships between effects of light and colour in the history of Venetian Renaissance art and cultural production.

22 See, for example, Bataille (1970, 79–86).

23 For background to the history of the painting materials and techniques in Venice see Dunkerton's (1999) contribution to the catalogue *Renaissance Venice and the North: Crosscurrents in the Time of Dürer, Bellini and Titian* (93–103).

24 Tiziano Vecellio, *Portrait of Francis I*, 1538–1539, oil on canvas, Louvre, Paris, the first of two portraits of the king painted by Titian.

REFERENCES

Aronberg Lavin, M. 2002. *Piero della Francesca.* London: Thames & Hudson.

Barolsky, P. 2003. "The Finger of God". In *Michelangelo and the Finger of God.* Athens, Georgia: University of Georgia, Georgia Museum. 29–55.

Bataille, G. 1970. "L'anus solaire". In *Œvres Complètes*, vol. 1, *Premiers Écrits 1922–1940.* Paris. 79–86.

Borsook, E.; Superbi Gioffredi, F., eds. 1994. *Italian Altarpieces 1250–1550.* Oxford: Clarendon Press.

Cast, D. 1988. "Humanism and Art". In *Renaissance Humanism*, vol. 3, *Humanism and the Disciplines*, edited by Rabil, A. J., Jr. Philadelphia: University of Pennsylvania Press. 412–449.

De Sanctis, F. 1970. *Storia della letteratura italiana*, edited by Lanza, M. T., 7th ed. Milan: Feltrinelli.

Dunkerton, J. 1999. "North and South: Painting Techniques in Venice". In *Renaissance Venice and the North: Crosscurrents in the Time of Dürer, Bellini and Titian*, edited by B. Aikema, B.; Brown, B. L. London: Thames & Hudson. 93–103. [Exhibition catalogue.]

Frugoni, C. 1998. *Pietro and Ambrogio Lorenzetti*, translated by Pelletti, L. Antella, Florence: Scala.

Goffen, R. 1997. *Titian's Women.* New Haven: Yale University Press.

Hills, P. 1999. *Venetian Colour: Marble, Mosaic, Painting and Glass 1250–1550.* New Haven: Yale University Press.

Hoeniger, C. 1995. "The Reframing of Gothic Altarpieces During the Renaissance". In *The Renovation of Paintings in Tuscany, 1250–1500.* Cambridge: Cambridge University Press. 101–126.

Martineau, J., ed. 1992. *Andrea Mantegna.* London: Royal Academy of Arts. [Exhibition catalogue.]

Nagel, A. 2000. *Michelangelo and the Reform of Art.* Cambridge: Cambridge University Press.

Nelson, R. 2003. "Don't Try This at Home". *The Age*, A3. 15 October, p. 7.

Newberry, T.; Bisacca, G.; Kanter, L. B. 1990. *Italian Renaissance Frames.* New York: Metropolitan Museum of Art. Distributed by H.N. Abrams, c1990.

Ovid. 1959. *Fasti 5.* Loeb classical library. English translation by Sir James Frazer. London; Cambridge, Mass.: Heinemann; Harvard University Press. 193–220.

Puttfarken, T. 2000. *The Discovery of Pictorial Composition: Theories of Visual Order in Painting 1400–1800.* New Haven: Yale University Press.

Snow-Smith, J. 1993. *The Primavera of Sandro Botticelli: A Neoplatonic Interpretation.* New York: Peter Lang Publishing.

Trinkaus, C. 1999. "Renaissance Ideas and the Idea of the Renaissance". In *Renaissance Transformations of Late Medieval Thought*, Variorum Collection Studies Series. Aldershot: Ashgate Publishing. 667–684.

Troup, C. 1998. *The Image as Body: Reflections on Language and Art Restoration through Neri di Bicci's Le Ricordanze 1453–75.* Melbourne: Monash Publications in History, Department of History, Monash University.

Verdon, T. 2002. "The Spiritual World of Piero's Art". In *The Cambridge Companion to Piero della Francesca*, edited by Wood, J. M. Cambridge: Cambridge University Press 30–50.

West, S. 2004. *Portraiture.* Oxford History of Art. Oxford: Oxford University Press.

Cite this chapter as: Nelson, Robert. 'The agonies of spiritual invention'. *The Spirit of Secular Art: A History of the Sacramental Roots of Contemporary Artistic Values.* Melbourne: Monash University ePress. pp. 4.1–4.18. DOI: 10.2104/ssa07004.

CHAPTER 5

SUBSTANCE AND SUBLIMITY

Robert Nelson

At first, the recent photographs of Vik Muniz, a Brazilian artist based in New York, look like drawings after old masters. Vistors to his exhibition in Chelsea[1] quickly recognize famous pictures from art history, like Caravaggio's *Narcissus* and Goya's *Saturn devouring his children*. The brownish drawing has no detail in the lights and a rather spotty treatment of shadow. With closer inspection, the method of construction is revealed. The image is assembled from masses of junk on a factory floor and photographed from 10 metres above. You identify the moment of realization by the rush of adrenaline that it gives you. For an instant, the eye flickers duck-rabbit style between seeing the picture and seeing the junk. You either behold an image like Delacroix's *Medea* or you descry a fridge, a suitcase, an automotive rear lens, a basket, a wheel, a fan, a lamp, some rope and heaps of old cans.

It is a fascinating encounter. The brain has to manage the gap as your consciousness oscillates between the image and the medium. You cannot apprehend both at the same time. Theoretically, the same would occur in a painting, where you are either aware of the illusionistic depiction or you see nothing but smears of colour on a canvas. But somehow the convention of painting takes care of the dichotomy and reconciles mark and image. The paint can either be a dab or a nose, and somehow your brain resolves their disparate nature in the instant of perception.

So there is something aesthetically dastardly about these giant pin-sharp prints of 2.3 x 1.8 metres. The photograph presupposes a performance, in which hundreds of pieces of industrial rubbish are placed on the luminous floor to make up the picture. The floor is treated as a canvas and the brush is made up of human arms and back, trolleys and crowbars. Watching the illusion give way to its components is an optical thrill. And it is paralleled by the freakish nature of the materials in relation to the image. The old masters are potentially desecrated by having their miraculous lineaments traced in industrial detritus; it is a kind of sacrilege to confound the perfect gestures with the dirty evidence of conspicuous waste.

But though apparently impious, the technique of Muniz also fulfills the grave and monitory character of the old masters. Whatever the illusion or fantasy, they are all turned to symbols of earthly failure and inevitable decrepitude. It is the same *vanitas* that haunts the prowess of the old masters. With optical and symbolic resonance on his side, Muniz has a heap of fun amid the garbage. The way he matches image and junk is wicked. In the *Minotaur* (from George Frederick Watts) Muniz manages to install a traffic light: stop/go. In Titian's *Sisyphus*, he places some particularly heavy things in the load that the hero carries for his punishment, like a piano.

This witty agreement is inverted parodically in Titian's *Icarus*, in which the artful new wings built by Daedalus are constituted from clapped-out heavy technologies like typewriters. For Rubens' *Bacchus astride a barrel*, Muniz finds a Texaco drum, as if petrol is the key drug of dependency in western society. But nor does Muniz neglect to provide the carousing revellers with a fridge and a bin. In Cranach's *Apollo and Diana*, the loin cloth looks as if a piece of fire-hose. And in the melancholy but virile *Mars* by Velazquez, Muniz garnishes the loins with a cloth drawn from Pepsi cans. The flank of the warrior-god is made from an automotive front-fender.

The jokes pile up with the junk. Every piece of visual notation is also an annotation, a conceptual footnote concerning the foibles of western culture, both high and low. You gaze at the field of trash like Oedipus solving the mortal riddle of the Sphinx. The rusty items that build the illusion were once the pride of progress and marketing; and now that their destiny is fulfilled in the scrap pile, they have life enough for just one further illusion. The refuse is destined for recycling. For their last photograph, the litter is organized to tell a story that transcends the cycle of production and obsolescence. As with the Australian performative works mentioned earlier, Muniz's photography is more than an allegory. It has a sense of largeness, of what theologians call world,[2] and which represents the fragility of our methods of generation. Both the energy and the somewhat morbid vision belong to the baroque. The sweeping perspectives, the triumphal and theatrical grasp of world, with its grand theatre of vigorous life, and its simultaneous depreciation are an element of baroque consciousness that prolifically produced the masterpieces of our museums. It entailed a remarkable spiritual evolution.

* * *

From the epoch of allegory we come to the epoch of theatre; from circumscribed charms encrypted with humanist scholarship during the Renaissance we arrive at the sensational stage-plays of the baroque. It is impossible to speak generically of baroque in the singular, for the variety of manifestations is baffling. Numerous different ambitions were cultivated during the period with impressive energies. In all the arts, there were contending aspirations and, in the visual arts, the genres were discovered, so to speak, and opened up opportunities to the concentrated talents of specialists. Hence, there were landscapes as well as history paintings, still-lives as well as allegories, interiors as well as religious icons; and even older genres like portraiture reveal an extraordinary range, as with the Dutch group portrait. Nearly all paintings in the baroque are remarkable for their fluency, the excellence in drawing; and many are *tours de force* in the co-ordination of multi-figured compositions.

Like the theatre, the baroque has a different mood for every act. There are settled yards and interiors in Dutch genre; there are erotic palpitations in abundance with naked figures cavorting and embracing on Italian ceilings; there are sombre and majestic countenances in portraits; there are melancholy heroes and heroines who take their own lives; there are frightening violent encounters and muscular brawls; there are exotic Biblical stories of incest, adultery and foiled rape; there are lyrical allegories about poetic inspiration; there are idle lads in streets; there are beggars, roosters, kings, traders and gods. There are turbaned people in tatty clothes with sleeves rolled up; there are beauties in contemporary dress, in historical robes or, as noted, no clothes at all; there are old men and women with furrowed brow, looking upward intensely to overcome their difficulties of sight; there are mythological characters who step with infallible elasticity over clouds or upon their enemies or into someone else's bed; there are children of all ages, some with the spry circumspection expected of a princess and some with the naughty conspiratorial air of potential thugs. Even the animals have the distinction of physiognomic difference, a wily nag, a haughty steed, a sagacious Labrador. The repertoire of types, actions, backgrounds, interior foregrounds, dress, historical trappings is daunting. But all of it was thoroughly visual. Painters mustered their artistic resources around their favourite periods and moods, choosing *dramatis personae* and scenes from an almost encyclopaedic range of options.

To call upon painters to observe the multifarious expressions and actions of all kinds of people in all sorts of spaces, new markets for art had developed.[3] The capital of landed aristocracy—with their obsessive etiquette and constant need for flattery—would no longer monopolize patronage. Lesser gentry would also want to buy paintings; and the whole class of merchants and other bourgeois would be served by the production of small-scale works, probably of suitably modest iconographic ambitions. Seascapes, for example, might have been particularly desired among mariners or shipping merchants. But even the greatest of traditional patrons called for variety in the address of pictures.

Since a number of Councils held in the later sixteenth century at Trent, the Church of Rome decided that images are useful in encouraging laity in their faith. They are most productive when accessible in content. In order to have widespread public appeal, painting would have to abandon some of its high-born intellectualism and cultivate certain sympathies with the class of people who habitually rolled their sleeves up to do their work. The humble figures in many otherwise illustrious themes were a part of this engagement. Today we would call it a marketing strategy. Of course, the almost comprehensive inclusiveness of low life only signals a general breaking down of the exclusivity of heroes, saints and patrons; it in no way implies a reassessment of the importance of these people. A change in status is not concomitant upon a change of subject matter. The baroque is not democratic in spirit, though it is properly catholic in its embrace of social background. The inclusion of lesser figures is often a means of seeing the whole world in order, with the great doing great things and the workers admiring them.

Artists undoubtedly underwent no humiliation in fulfilling the requirements of the Church in finding the means toward greater accessibility in their pictures. The new edicts would have prompted a wonderful new source of subject matter which assisted artists in their simultaneous interests in naturalism; for there is nothing more congruent with an illusionistic painting than a truthfully unideal protagonist candidly seized in unflattering dress or coarse action. Anyway, those artists who sought the exclusive domain of the courts and only wanted to paint in a classically elevated manner were free to find their niche among the privileged. The new propagandistic orientation of the Church only added to existing markets and did not diminish them or compromise developing markets.

The proliferation of types and scenes in baroque painting is matched by the sheer abundance of pictures. And big confident pictures, too! The century and a half from 1600 to 1750 is a most prolific period. The square metres in world galleries taken up by baroque works seem disproportionately high relative to earlier periods. Art during the baroque was in full vigour; and not till the development of film and television—whose theatricality, the baroque cultivated *avant la lettre*—did the visual have such a hold on the imagination. It is as if the whole energy of the period had a heightened visual expression; and no enthusiasm was left without its pictorial extrapolation.

Many seventeenth-century paintings are extraordinarily settled, like those of De Hooch and Vermeer; but the baroque distinguishes itself by also producing sculpture, architecture, furniture and pictures of memorable energy. There had never been buildings which take to swooning in voluptuous convulsions; there had never been tables which surge mightily with sculpted figures; there had never been ceilings which compositionally toss and roll around with the soaring and diving of figures; and so many baroque figures are realized in the strenuous climax of an action (even if a minor one) which picks up a muscular dynamic at its most climactic. All instincts of artists seem to have been honed to detect and translate the dramatic potential of gestures, sudden movements, the flickering of light and diagonal compositions, just as the instincts of designers were sharpened to invent the most powerful *contrapposto* of ornaments as they race and seethe in ebullience in the celebration of a supernatural cosmic energy.

In the previous chapter, the idea of High Renaissance magnificence was discussed, dwelling in particular on Michelangelo's Sistine Ceiling. The greatness of Michelangelo's conception and execution is not in question but his work seems simple and almost unambitious by baroque standards. Ceilings by baroque artists do not parade along stepwise with a series of independent tableaux, fragmented in their illusionistic space by frames and architectural borders. Such limits to the illusionistic empire of the ceiling were abandoned in works such as the *Allegory of Providence* by Pietro da Cortona in the Palazzo Barberini (sometimes known as the Apotheosis of the Barberini Family) or the *Glory of St Ignatius* by Padre Andrea Pozzo in Sant' Ignazio.[4] In both paintings, the major part of the ceiling is taken up with a single vista, proposing a single vanishing point which commands, so to speak, the logic of all architecture, humans and clouds which symbolize the heavenly universe. The action of each part is not contained but dynamically interacts with the whole.

The thrust of this energy is not manic but orchestrated. It is directed to demonstrating on a sensual level the authoritarian logic of glory. What makes for glory? Even if you think of the glorious as the naturally brilliant or sublime, it remains wholly unexplained. If you think of it as something from outside, as a kind of intervention, a visitation from an external world upon the tangible world, you have still avoided the question of what makes it glorious. Glory presupposes a structure, an almost political structure in the psyche. The glorious thing or person or event is superior and your experience is inferior. You even question the capacity of your experience to comprehend its own inferiority relative to the superiority of the glorious. Your apprehension of the glorious is always inadequate. The experience of glory is a reckoning, a coming to terms with your shortcomings.

The encounter with glory is awesome; for once having recognized glory you face a dilemma of potentially crushing consequences in either direction. You can stand firm and attempt to fathom the mysterious power that it has and, in the inevitable failure of your insights and the pathos of your exertions, you experience the depression of impotence. Or you can forget the exigencies of analysis and the identification of causes, resign yourself to the glorious and ecstatically absorb its superior force, experience the intensity of its elation and the worshipful thrill of being rapt by sublimity. But in the abandonment to these heady transports, you will be in no position to reckon self-reflexively, for you have foregone your responsibility to reason: you have relinquished those critical faculties by giving yourself over to a consuming spiritual narcotic which annihilates all critical consciousness. In a philosophical sense, you have become irresponsible.

In a cruder sense, things are considered glorious when there are people to admire them as stupendous. Not only does glory seem to be a guiding force in a great part of baroque production but the pictures themselves bear witness to the logic; for they are all structured around a relationship between a powerful core and a host of subsidiary motifs—often supplicating or stunned believers—who pay formal tribute to central commanding energies. Baroque paintings do not look horribly hieratic. They are spatially logical and there is an organic compositional flow which prevents them from having any iconic pomposity. But there is a deeper structural dynamic which is hieratic in a compelling way. In larger paintings at least, the lesser is always proffering support for the greater. There is often even a whole gallery of affirmative heads and forearms gesticulating in reverent amazement at the august constellation at the centre; there are angels for the Virgin as Queen of Heaven, vanquished giants for heroes, raucous urchins and labourers for saints, squirming sea-monsters for kings and queens, saints and prophets for Christ, frolicking sea nymphs for lovers, all minions and legions for God the father. One cannot simply paint a portrait of God but must represent his effect through all consciousness in heaven; and the same requirements flow to all glorious nobles and mythical personages. In this way, the wholehearted reception of glory is enacted within the painting itself. The deference and the giddy swoons are the enthused vernacular of glory, contributing iconographic zeal and compositional force which make for the internal collective bolstering of the picture. And, of course, the repeated structural reinforcements of such figures and the almost obsessive gestures of admiration are a cue, installed in the painting precisely to induce the same reaction of applause and support in the spectator.

There are allegories a-plenty in baroque painting (such as Simon Vouet's *Wealth* in the Louvre); but, either by their style or directly by their allegorical content, baroque allegories are all about one concept: authority.[5] Baroque allegories are unlike the semiotic inventions of the High Renaissance; they are seldom opaque and do not constitute mysteries in their own right. Their content is more consonant with their style, a single-minded determination to express the ineffable grandeur of authority, the majesty of providence which gives the world its authorities and the gracious benignity of the same authorities. Pietro da Cortona's *Allegory of Providence* mentioned before on account of its compelling compositional energies is the example *par excellence*. The almost sexual fluxing of energies in the rhythms of baroque compositions are already a commitment to that message; for they surge and pulse with a single focus around which all the energy conspires. Baroque aesthetics are the enchanting of authority.

For baroque artists raised for the vocation of representing glory, nothing could be more natural than faith. They are painters of faith, whether sacred or secular; for nobility beyond the cloth was granted a divine entitlement anyway and artists could demonstrate their skills by imputing glory to nobles and showing faith in their patrons. The same can be said for mythological subjects in which, of course, no one seriously believed. But to do an *Apollo and Daphne* or *Acis and Galatea* would be a great test of the artist's poetic and rhetorical prowess, just by virtue of the fact that belief in the theme was artificial and commitment to it a poetic contrivance. To 'produce' faith in a story in which nobody believed is in itself a miracle. The governing order of Christian faith would admit this extension, for it showed off what St Paul calls the fruits of faith, the faculty of vision which had already been exercised in that wonderfully wanton direction in the age before the Inquisition. However, the baroque exploitations of the Humanist convention add something. It is an emphasis on the glory of the mythological figures, their status as icons of immortality; for the prestige of the ancient names celebrated in Renaissance literature and now conflated with baroque glory would make an easy metaphor to express the natural authority of contemporary nobles.[6]

To stand in front of many large baroque masterpieces means developing a relationship with something glorious. You may not trust the authority who is credited with such glory but you cannot avoid recognizing the conviction with which the artist has projected the authority as glorious; and, owing to the excellence of technique and the integrity of the style and subject matter, you would probably not deny that the work is glorious in its own right. What works for us on a rarefied aesthetic plane would have worked on a spiritual plane with bewildering intensity among seventeenth-century spectators. The reasons touch on new relations between the aesthetic and the sacramental. The apprehension of glory is deeply sacramental. Not only does it in essence involve the presence of God—albeit once removed—but it deals with a humbling, a recognition of one's insignificance alongside an ineffable eminence. The rejoicing in this glory is your way of sharing it, as if God will dispense some part of it if you identify wholeheartedly with that majesty which you will never own.

This encounter with an unapproachable glory is also eminently ritualistic. The ritual is art. You cannot ascend to the contemplation of glory without the intermediary of an aesthetic representation, whether linguistic, musical or visual; and, once you enter a space whose aesthetic convincingly claims glory on behalf of divinity, you know that a kind of rendition of grace has been staged to afford the reciprocal awe in your reception of it. There is no difference in this sense between a painting—which is staged once and remains on the ceiling forever—and a musical performance which has to be rehearsed each time. The experience of hearing music is probably less repeatable than the experience of seeing pictures; but both are a symbolic miniature encounter with a superior spirit, a sublime crisis in which you subject yourself to the awareness of your inferiority and resign your critical independence in exchange for a joyful spiritual yoking to the almighty. The subservience of the intellect to an emotional paternal order is carried out in the performance. As you partake of the glorious representation, you develop a sense of devotion and happily sacrifice your spiritual autonomy; you submit yourself to be transported by the heady and passionate triumphal airs of glory. You lose the dignity of an independent subject, able to look at the world with objectivity, and become subsumed within the infinitely greater dignity of the glorious.

As a sacramental ritual, this process stands somewhere between the eucharist and ordination; for it is both about a sacrifice and a dedication. But clearly it is neither: it is art and has the great spiritual flexibility of the aesthetic. The sacramental absorption of glory has a wider metaphoric ambit than the traditional sacraments and readily allows its benedictions to be transferred from spiritual to temporal authority. What a marvellous commodity for the arrogant nobles of Europe! If ever there was a time to be deified by subtle implication, this was it: the baroque had a new sacrament powerfully rooted in the divine but available for secular distribution among exclusive authorities.

All the structures of mighty rulers and subservient fans would not have succeeded in expressing glory in the absence of an equally glorious technique. Critics and art historians of a connoisseurish variety have often bestowed upon the seventeenth century the distinction of being the high point of oil painting. The skills, ambition, confidence and poetic gifts of baroque masters excelled all before and have never been rivalled since. A technique as beautiful and luminous as Titian's was mastered by artists of the second order (though of course lacking Titian's peculiar vision) while artists of the first rank, such as the Carracci, Caravaggio, Guercino, Reni, Ribera and Velázquez, made enormous individual contributions to the history of technique and subject matter. Apparently all baroque painters mastered the art of drawing with consummate ease and were able to add to their perceptual clarity the habit of chromatic modelling which intensified and demonstrated their understanding of the drawn volumes. Some artists, such as Velázquez, Hals and Rembrandt achieved distinction with the summariness with which they could evoke a form in its exactness, seemingly dashing the paint down spontaneously and expressing the nature of paint as they did so.[7]

These qualities of stylistic perspicacity and perceptual power, as magic as they are, do not in themselves constitute a sacrament. But, as with the Venetians, they lend themselves to the expression of the carnal which has sacramental potential. To the habit of chromatic modelling and combinations of muscular scumbling and luminous glazing—both of which were developed in flesh painting of the sixteenth century—the baroque masters added the evocation of air surrounding the skin. It is an indefinable illusionistic charm, a final and exquisite stage of perceptual understanding of the way in which the surfaces of flesh, depending on their orientation relative to the viewer, reveal themselves with clarity or opacity according to their engagement with air.

It may be imprudent to hazard an empirical explanation of such a fugitive phenomenon and it is easy to imagine many painting teachers in the past articulating in vain the magic of atmospheric evocation in the old masters and being judged quite mad for attempting it. The magic cannot be given a merely technical piecemeal explanation; but insofar as it can, the ability to evoke the atmospheric engagement of skin has to do with edges. The outer contours of an arm, for example, are not always crisp. You cannot draw or paint the arm with a uniformly hard edge; for the trained eye in examining the contour will detect that parts of the arm vanish from sight with less suddenness than other parts. There is a pattern for the degree of crispness of edges. An edge is harder when the skin works its way around the volume in a rapid turn; the edge is softer if the skin works its way around the volume in a gradual curve, so that the tangent reaching your eye seems to touch on a larger expanse of flesh.

If you hold out your arm with bent elbow so that the forearm runs across your gaze, its outline will be crisp. But if you straighten your elbow, so that the forearm runs along your gaze, its outline will be fuzzier. When the arm is perpendicular to your gaze, the skin toward the edge very rapidly turns around the cylindrical shape and suddenly passes from view, hence the crisp outline. But if the arm is pointed away from your eyes and you therefore see it with a degree of foreshortening, a large expanse of skin is involved in conducting the arm from full sight to invisibility. The turning is thus very gradual. To use a mathematical term, the 'normal' to your sight-line is not a point but a whole expanse of skin open to the air. And because you are sighting along a whole lot of skin rather than just a brief passage, the engagement of so much skin makes the transition harder to judge. You are not quite sure which part of the arm really does the disappearing; there is a moment of indistinction where the definition of the edge is further dissipated by any unevenness in the skin, any hairs, for example, which interrupt the sight-line across the edge in a cumulative manner over the greater distance. Never mind the hairs. All skin is slightly irregular. It somehow has humid Lilliputian crevasses into which the air seeps or ridges around which the air is forced to spill. In this way the skin seems to entertain the air, taking it in and pushing it away. It follows that when a great deal of skin is seen intercepting the air across your sight-line, this organic interaction with the air will compound and deny the edge an exact definition. Photographs do not always register this 'fusion' of volume and atmosphere but the eye can sense it.

Seventeenth-century painters could control their edges with the greatest subtlety, making them crisp when the skin moves away rapidly and letting them linger when the skin lies flatter against the sight-line. Skilled seventeenth-century painters never give their outlines a general fuzziness but modulate the degree of interaction of volume and background to suggest the presence of the skin in its relationship both to the spectator's viewpoint and the almost imperceptible interpenetration of air and the fabric of the skin itself, multiplied by the obliqueness of the skin relative to the spectator's viewpoint. Baroque painters did not merely discover a geometric verity but a perceptual insight—admittedly logical in the highest degree—which enabled them to spell out certain sensual metaphors of the organic flesh. In their illusions, the body seems convincingly wrapped in air, not merely painted sharply or fuzzily on a canvas with perspectival accuracy. You seem intelligently to follow the skin around a form at its very edge, as if your eyes were the element of air, caressing the luminous and humid flesh and penetrating its texture at that point where its vapours, so to speak, are assumed into air.

Baroque poetry provides ample evidence of parallel interests. The sonneteering tradition already furnished baroque poets with a language of sighs (how many *sospiri* in Italian poetry, *oimé*!), breezes and erotic desire (or, as they say with shameless hyperbole, martyrdom). But baroque prosody relishes the sighing with an added sense of palpitation, the internal fluttering of an imminent grasp envisaged in arduous expectation, and would extend the breathiness to the sensation of one lover hungrily respiring over the other. The master of such heated breathing is Giovan Battista Marino, whose highly figured metaphoric sensuality engendered a brilliant following whom Italians call the Marinisti. The primacy of sexual feeling and the sometimes giddy convolution of metaphor cause the Marinisti to be opposed in literary history to 'the classicists'; but, in their heady fondness for the phenomenology of flesh and breath—indeed, for the organic carnality of experience and its extrapolation to higher levels of consciousness—the Marinisti form an essential libretto for the styles of baroque painting.[8] It is an irony, for while the classicists provided the subject matter in its learned subscription to antique authorities, the Marinisti provide us with a picture of the consciousness which underlies the genius of baroque technique.

Although prolifically enjoying sexual appetite in his verse, Marino is no pornographer and has an elevated interest in the phenomenology of atmosphere in all its manifestations. He is often evoking air, breath, the breeze and sighing, in conjunction with other sensory phenomena, especially light and colour, sparkle, radiance, glowing; his resources for such matters are immense. For Marino, the visual garnishes the tactile and the tactile is an ornament of the visual. His verse delights in the complication of going into a metaphor and coming out of it again in order to point up its artificiality and make jokesy *argutezze*; but this slightly wanton confounding of reality and metaphor allegorizes the great pregnancy of both his subject matter and his language. Marino has often been reproached, from De Sanctis onward, for being self-consciously ingenious rather than urgently moral (as Shakespeare seems to be) but the recrimination of artificiality ignores the wider allegorical potential of the poetic ruses. Of course there is a certain vanity and danger in oblique poetry; but to damn it for amorality denies a whole ritual zone of poetry. In particular, it imprudently forecloses on the fuller uses of metaphor, the wilful transposition of matter and spirit, that artful slipping between an object and its symbolic extensions which ultimately afford a sacramental function and signal an inspired and mystical access to divinity.

Poetic quicksilver throughout Europe replaced the stately humanist tradition. Throughout the baroque there is a clear enthusiasm for metamorphosis, for the interchange between one body and another. Ovid's *Metamorphoses*, for that reason, enjoyed spectacular interest among painters; and the idea of transformation also partly accounts for the love of dramatic moments in narrative painting, the spectacle of immediacy in the change of a person's countenance and gestures in suddenly coming into awareness of a tragic or painful circumstance. The same quicksilver is installed in the very fabric of the paint, its attention to the spatial and atmospheric 'volatility' of the outline of the skin, expressing its access of humours to the open air.

The consciousness of a seventeenth-century painter would have been steeped in poetic metaphors. Just as a mouth can hardly be painted but that it be capable of sighing; so each feature would want to fulfil its imaginative destiny of embodying a further kind of animation. The world was not to be looked on as an opaque and immovable given but as a transparent jewel which yields to suitably harmonious colours projected through it. The whole of nature was exoticized by metaphor. As a painter, you would have been more deeply moved by much of the poetic imagery than the poets were themselves. In baroque culture, all visibilia was held poetic hostage, to be forced potentially to dance with the narratives of desire; and the game of matching bizarre comparisons with a happy consonance would have enriched their vision with unimaginable interest.

When a baroque painter represented skin, it may not have been directly informed by any analogy which the latest published poems had hatched; but the habit of seeing all kinds of richness in the visible was probably the basis for the extraordinary faculties of perception in seventeenth-century painting. Painters looked into the flesh with heightened knowledge to find those parts which look more opaque, those which look more transparent, the parts where there is bone or gristle and the parts (as with the breasts) which are yielding. The drawing and the palette would be scrupulously modulated to register every sensual inflexion; for each nuance was not only beheld and recognized but matched with a whole thesaurus of metaphoric associations which enlarged their meaning and let them admit levels of poetic or spiritual charm. The painter saw all things in their symbolic sensual pregnancy, but especially the body and its details such as the face, the mouth and the eyes. Baroque poetry offers the cue to see in all features a peculiar adorable resonance.

Corporal, witty and adroit, the Marinisti are soul mates of baroque painters. However, it would be misleading to represent them as the only key to the styles of baroque painting, just as it would be misleading to construct their extravagant confluence of metaphor and reality as the only poetic transcendence of the age. There are other forms of spirituality which emerge from poetic style; and these proceed almost exclusively from the classicists, especially those in France.

Marino had some influence in France—indeed lived there—but the indigenous verse forms in French favoured something more directly argumentative, something more discursive and conducted in short sentences which fit neatly inside rapid rhyming couplets, each fairly discrete and preferably not beginning with the word 'and'. French literature in the seventeenth century aspired to the rigours of the ancient genres and was somehow more classical than antiquity. The height of French literary scrupulosity was reached in the rediscovery of tragedy, an art first revived by Italians like Trissino in the sixteenth century; but the zenith of the genre is achieved in the *grand siècle* in Paris.[9]

English literature may have the distinction of the greatest poet—Shakespeare—but the copyright for tragedy passed, as it were, directly from ancient Greece to the French and rather bypassed England. English literature, especially through Shakespeare, makes better drama, better poetic metaphor, finer sensuality, greater emotional range, better acknowledgement of social difference, better individual psychology, greater freedom with sources and rules, greater spontaneity and better vocabulary. By many criteria, French theatre is stuffy and hidebound, concerned with aristocratic virtue, ancestral honour and strenuous patriotism. But the purity of French tragedy—especially in the plays of Corneille and Racine—allows an almost archaeological recovery of the purpose and power of ancient tragedy. In plot and expression, they are sublime.

French tragedy only admits on stage protagonists of nobility and virtue. The contention in the drama is not usually between a good person and a bad person but two people of comparable virtue. They may, of course, have a fatal flaw; but they are not fundamentally evil (as is a King Claudius or a Lady Macbeth) and are often too virtuous for their own good. The genius of the plot is to contrive a catastrophic clash of two people holding different values—both good values in themselves—without a reconciliation being possible; for a compromise is inherently prevented according to their respective commitment to the values from which they cannot resile without dishonour. The protagonists also have to be intelligent, brave, sensitive and adroit. The sophistication of the Parisian court would have ridiculed any dramaturge for bringing on stage a person with a manifest psychological shortcoming, a sign of stupidity, excessive vanity, bloody-mindedness or pig-headedness. The axiom of nobility required that the calamitous tension must be forged within the mechanics of the plot rather than any defects in the nature of the heroes. Conflicting values had to be found.

Very demanding expectations attended the drama, unlike in England or Spain where a good *novella* from Bandello—with all its colourful tricksters, *accorti*, *sciocchi* and crooks—would provide instructive entertainment. France produced the most austere dramatic literature ever: the constraints concerning the morality of protagonists were matched by the forbearance in matters of stagecraft. The play was to be entirely free of set changes: following Aristotle's prescription of the three unities in tragedy (unity of time, place and action), the story could not exceed a day in the lives of the heroes, it all had to happen in one place and no extraneous stories could be told alongside it by way of leavening. The baroque in Italy, revelling in mutability of poetic conceits, slipperiness of metaphors, transformations of operatic sets, melodramas concerning metamorphoses of gods and humans into beasts and vegetation, was banished from the tragic stage in Paris. A play could be performed with nothing in the theatre but the walls of an august room and a single chair on stage.

The discipline of French drama extended to the language. Nothing but a chastened vocabulary was acceptable. Words needed to have a classical pedigree. A thought could not be conveyed with undue extravagance. Too many adjectives or adverbs would not be permitted. But perhaps the most extraordinary aspect of this poetic regime is its inspirational integrity. The poetry is exquisite, even though not terribly rich in texture; for the circumscribed possibilities of the language perfectly match the concentration on moral principle and the austere renunciation of dramatic variety.

Finally, the discipline of French drama was embedded in the verse form. The rhyming Alexandrines are no harder to write than many another form and a lot easier than *terza rima* or *ottava rima* which respectively required the poet to find two or three rhymes rather than just one. The pattern is very simple, aa, bb, cc, dd… and so on. The rapidity with which rhymes are encountered and then passed over creates a somewhat business-like pace. The form is suitable for parcelling thoughts in direct succession. It is not particularly geared to feint echoes of nuanced metaphors interweaving their way with one another but rather to clear communication. The numbers discourage ornament and figures. French tragic poetry is apt to seem rather dry on account of this. But its richness is strangely sacramental. It makes for a pious chanting, emphatic in its repetition and stately in a kind of stoic ceremonial discipline.

In the context of tragedy, these qualities take on a special value. In their favoured indigenous verse form, the French discovered the lyricism of downfall. The cadence of the verse—that is, the falling of the tones—has a powerful sense of delivering something final, ending, as it always does, on a note whose rhyme clinches the meaning of a preceding thought. In all cases where the poetry seeks to develop an argument, rhyming verse is the language of immanence: it sets up a phrase which is due to be met with a rhyming answer in the following line. When you get to it, you are reminded, somehow, that it was prefigured. The second line contains a rhyme which must have been foreseen in the laying down of the original line.

Technical matters like prosody seem 'merely technical' or merely formalist and for that reason are seldom taught or even discussed in today's academies. But this is the mistake of a non-sacramental age in unimaginatively judging a sacramental age. The verse form in essence is not merely formalist but is highly symbolic. It is an allegory of necessity, a kind of artifice which enshrines the inevitability of logical consequences, a reflection of divine guarantees that what must be will follow what must precede it; for the rhyme will be fulfilled in the exact number of syllables, as was prefigured in the line before. In its regularity and certainty, the verse form steps out the holy pace of providence, as if the lines have fortune built into them.

In the process of prefiguration by which the poets construct their rhymes, an almost inverted nemesis is automatically constructed. Nemesis as the force of downfall has its ideal counterpoint in the provident verse, because the necessary and correct succession of rhymes in advancing a linear argument relates the 'rightness of telling'; it figuratively acts out the confirmation of each thought and adds to each the sense of a fateful musical authority.

Perhaps because of this authority, the rhyming alexandrines are not only suited to tragedy—which concerns sacrifice—but are also suited to satire, which identifies vanities. Satire is not a pre-eminently sacramental genre; it is deeply skeptical and has a vein of humour which, while often employed benignly, takes its strength from a destructive potential. Satire is remote from rehearsing any kind of mythical killing, if not the victim of its own powers of demolition; but the best satire does not kill a person but a conceit, one presumably worthy of being debunked. The agent is human reason, not divinity, and the victim has no great sacrificial virtue. Nevertheless, some spirit of the times enabled French poets of the seventeenth century to engage the rhyming alexandrines in the ways that suit it best, for both satire and tragedy. The satires of Boileau in one sense read very similarly to the dramatic verse of Racine—eloquent, economical, fatefully accurate—because both reach for new levels of authority.[10] Both genres take up the powerful verse form to emphasize the ceremony of poetic thought. The one has strongly sacramental overtones and the other is purely secular. In the sophistication surrounding the French court, the two were transferable.

Of course verse is not necessarily holy. There have always been drinking songs and so on which are thoroughly debauched. Nor can you say that such-and-such a rhyme scheme has to signify holiness, because anyone can take a sacred form and make facetious nonsense out of it. But as a ritual structure, verse has a deeper integrity, undoubtedly arising from a grave ceremonial function, to tell of gods and the enchantment of the spiritual order to which they belong. The numbers in prosody are for a hallowed undertaking. The language of divinity is measured; the stresses do not fall randomly but have a cosmic order about them. They need to embody the ineluctable, to enact the stern determination of the world, to link the inner instructions of the world, as if by a knitting of Cartesian monads. Metred speech is a rhythmic symbol of destiny; and the poet is a kind of priest whose inspired vocation is to listen to the spiritual pregnancy of received stories and to find the measured language to express their rightness. Prosody is the sacramental stewardship of language.

Further magic is added when such ritual language is applied to tragedy. As with epic poetry, the verse supplies an incantational inevitability which supports the sense of mythical destinies; but in tragic poetry, it also supports the sacramental rhythm of events in that awesome steady progress of the story toward the killing. And in this sense it is a partner of Nemesis; it moves like a dirge and helps deliver the blow of the execution with the same sense of pace that guides the footsteps up to the altar. It may be that this ritual poignancy of verse belongs to remote antiquity when the myths entered poetic stagecraft in an active religious ceremony; but its echoes are felt powerfully in the rebirth of tragedy in the baroque. The rhythmic sonorous imperatives of tragedy are well recognized and strongly reinforce the sacred horror of the plot. It is probably the reason why comedy has long been considered best in prose. Comedy can be done in verse but prudence has suggested otherwise, following Aretino, Macchiavelli and many others in the Italian sixteenth century.

The naturalness of a tragic ethos to Catholic France should not be overstated. When the eminent dramatists stage their ritual undoings, the rehearsal of sacrifice is an artifice. It adds to the detachment of the genre that no one in the seventeenth century would have imputed to the play by Racine the sacramental qualities of the blessed eucharist or to consider the tragic sentiment efficacious beyond the purgative processes recognized by Aristotle. Parisian courtiers would have recognized that tragedy, when so well conceived, reaches new definitions of virtue (and nearly all secular virtues at that). Beyond this almost pedagogical agenda, our imaginary gentleman in the audience—rejoicing in suede, velvet, thin shoes, lace and stockings—would have taken delight in the grand machine, the 'engineering' of the script, the author's ability to throw around the stage the superb weight of greatness that comes with the fame of his characters, only coming unstuck through greater majesty and not really from any simple shortcoming or pusillanimity. And the quality that would have been admired most of all is the poetic manifestation of *gloire*, the legendary glory of each protagonist as they strive for every occasion to demonstrate it and savour it in their own speeches.[11]

Glory in France is not spread around a ceiling with gay extroversion but the stoic sense of containment and discipline of tragic heroes. Their verse is glorious but in an attenuated way, an argumentative, at times almost legalistic, exposition of state and personal justification. This is the context of sublimity that explains the grave spirit of Poussin, a painter of great poetic gifts whose sentimental range was also typically baroque, extending freely to the erotic (*Acis and*

Galatea), the comastic (*Triumph of Pan*), revelry in the dance (*Kingdom of Flora*), the lofty abstractions of Parnassus (*Inspiration of the Poet*), the passionately ethereal (*Diana and Endymion*), the love of a vespertine nature (*Landscape with the Ashes of Phocion*), the adoration of antiquity (*Et in Arcadia Ego*), the passionate lyricism (*Tancred and Erminia*), melancholy (*Echo and Narcissus*) and stoic piety (*Landscape with Funeral of Phocion*).[12] Poussin is a painter who obviously loved indulgence but loved academic discipline even more. His *Seven Sacraments* are evidence enough of the profundity of his feeling for worship.[13] And like most painters of his age, he found the occasions to induce upon his secular subject matter the glorious inflexions of his own style which derived from his ready access to the sacred.

It seems that even the quietest secular corner of the baroque is invested with a sacred demeanour and even, some have argued, content. So the still lives of Sanchez-Cotán have been interpreted as allegories of Christ's suffering, interpretations which are perhaps more reasonable in principle than in exact detail.[14] As in previous art, baroque painting is invested with an inimitable seriousness. Still lives are no different: they all work their way across your gaze with a concerted compositional gravity, opening up objects to the light as if offering up their living substance on a supernatural plane. Often they must also be credited with the sense of stagecraft that belongs to narrative pictures; their passive objects seem like players caught at their most vulnerable in the denouement.

Interiors, too, take on an exaggerated sense of the deliberateness of all things. The genre resolves itself with astonishing autonomy in artists like Vermeer, also a thoroughly baroque master in his technique and fondness for a sublimated theatricality which he shares with Rembrandt. In Vermeer's interiors there is always something going on. He repeatedly paints the same room or similar room, with the map, the tiles, the light, the beamed ceiling and the window which you can recognize in a number of his pictures; but he places characters in this interior to make each one available to a narrative interpretation. Here there is a woman looking out of a window; here is another reading a letter with the map behind her; here are a couple who have interrupted their music-making to converse by the virginal. You can weave any number of scenarios around these judiciously silent works; and Vermeer himself seems to justify the urge to offer allegorical interpretations, by painting allegories-in-progress, that is, the painting of the process of painting, as in the famous *Art of Painting* and the lesser known *Allegory of the Faith*, both of which show a staged woman posing in the conspicuously contemporary Dutch domestic studio for a further pompous allegorical depiction.[15] With these and other precedents, the urge to conjecture is justified. It is not wrong to interpret; but neither is it wrong to desist. His pictures are enigmatic not because the content is intentionally overloaded with cryptic symbols but because the very will to symbolize is uncertain: all the incentives for us, as interpreters, to insinuate a narrative upon the scene are ambiguous. In the context of such deliberate picture-making, the open-endedness of the cues is tantalizing.

In one work, *A Young Woman Standing at a Virginal*, there is a woman dressed in an impressive whitish and blue garment who looks up from toying with the keyboard.[16] She is caught fingering the surfaces of the clavichord without sitting down at the instrument to play it properly. She is disengaged. She stands without awkwardness looking to us. The light strikes her from a window behind, making her face slightly cool and retiring. It is impossible to look at her and not wish to penetrate her intentions. There is no clue, other than the fact that she stands beneath a large almost overbearing picture of Eros on the far wall, so much brighter and warmer than anything in the foreground. It makes naughty innuendo at the woman's sexual feelings. She stands in passive remoteness; but there is a sense of seething eroticism beneath the cool exterior.

Is this picture allegorical? Not really, for if it were, it would only allegorize this person in this situation and would not credibly pretend to the proverbial universality of allegory. But nor is it anecdotal. It does not relate the grope in the public house, the case of a misinterpreted pass or the offering of a token for sex. There is no incident, much less a garrulous contention. The painting takes the potential for an anecdote but holds it in abeyance for the greater self-sufficiency of the painting. The painting is about the visuality of the moment, not the moment itself. There is an emotional and moral context for the glance; the sense of narrative creates an undeniable suspense and invites speculation; but it does so with purposeful ambiguity, cutting off the narrative where it would be seized by flagrant desire. The painting is suspended from closure; the narrative declines to go forward and remains implicit but fugitive.

What kind of an art is this? It is as if the narrative interest is set up only to be disappointed and leave the spectator dissatisfied. But precisely at the point of default, the art steps forward and offers a sublimated consummation: the unresolved desire communicated in the image is diffused within the stylistic seduction of the formal and perceptual qualities in the painting. You initially look at the beautiful woman, notice her idleness, the absent-minded engagement of her hands, the potential for a playful and hot encounter behind the cool shades of her countenance; and, seeing the blessing of Cupid above, you know that something should happen in the silent room, broken by the incidental vibration of the keys. The erotic shiver goes nowhere; but as you look around for something to answer it, you find an extraordinary interest in the tiles, the warm and cool shadows spiling on the wall, the richness of the light on all surfaces, the resonance of the hollows, the fineness of edges, the infallible definition of the spaces. The painting is bristling with sensory information, so skilfully translated in aesthetically sanctioned mixtures of lyricism and objectivity. Nothing ever looks fiddly, nothing is overworked, nothing is too thin or too heavy, no part of the drawing is disconnected from the overall coherence of the space; in a word it is perfection, with a heady sensuality emerging from the evocation of all substances and the light that animates them.

In this transfer of sublimated erotic potential to the sensuality of the painting technique, a new kind of internalized allegory is invented. Vermeer's pictures allegorize the resignation of the sexual figure to a kind of artistic prestige, an aesthetically abducted libido, quiet and thrilling at the same time, which simultaneously trades off the woman's desire and transcends her identity. The subject matter is not irrelevant but its teleology is hijacked by the artistic fondness for all things which reflect and harbour light. Vermeer's women do not have a destiny to fulfil; they do not have a sacred or glorious vocation beyond the domestic walls and the street outside. They are accorded all tenderness but no future, for they are resolutely secular and have no symbolic aspirations, much less sacred aspirations. The aim of eternity which they lack as figures in art is transferred to the painting. The painting is an immortal celebration of its own resources, the perceptual understanding of space and light; and, above all, it is an immortal celebration of the symbolic potency of this formalist and perceptual sensuality, for it sublimates the ordinary erotic energies of the painted human object.

It is not far-fetched to claim sacramental status for Vermeer's paintings. It seems unlike any sacramental condition encountered before, as it does not appear to relate to divinity, not even by the most indirect metaphor. There is no insistent mythical background, very little portent, no apparent economy of propitiation and no piggy-backing on the aesthetic gravity of ancestral faith. Vermeer's paintings seem extraordinarily 'clean'. Historical references are to be found but they seem rather marginal alongside the dominant formalist and perceptual preoccupations. This purity gives the pictures the air of a secular sanctuary, hermetically quarantined from the spiritually tainted ritual languages of earlier and contemporaneous art. And in this very purity, Vermeer's pictures seems to prefigure modern art, similarly detached from the imposing spiritual order of the past, depreciating the symbolic terms of its subject matter and devoted to the purity of its own visuality.

But is this good logic? Just because Vermeer appears removed from the ancestral links with ancient altars, can we really say that the randy frolicking of naked gods on Italian ceilings are more sacred than the paintings of Vermeer?

Vermeer is certainly pivotal in the later renegotiation of art and the symbolic order. In fact much of the sacramental calibre ascribed to Italian baroque masters can be extended to Vermeer. For example, the intense carnality of his faces is breathtaking. Consider the three close-up portraits, the haunting *Girl with a pearl earring*, the *Girl with a flute* and the *Girl with the Red Hat.*[17] No one but Marino could have had an equal fascination with the flesh behind the teeth. The young women all have their lips parted and our gaze enters their mouths to discover a partially hidden sparkle, a damp redness of the gum with connotations of humid breath and the desire to kiss. They are tasteful works but ravishingly sensual in not merely acknowledging the outer form but almost obscenely promising to penetrate the inner body of palpitations and blood. Furthermore, Vermeer's technique of scumbling and glazing is as luminous and as theatrically carnal as that of any Italian coeval.[18]

But something about Vermeer's art also discourages us from over-emphasizing such arguments. The special sacramental status of his pictures lies in the very purity which seems to disqualify them from an ancestral sacramental connexion. In dramatizing the erotic visuality of his scintillating youthful models—not beautiful by classical stereotypes but very Dutch—but stripping them of a narrative continuum which would grant them an ongoing identity for posterity, Vermeer stages an abstracted sacrifice which will become one of the hallmarks of modernity: an aesthetic regime which puts people on an exalted altar of bourgeois taste which is characterized by haunting contradictions. The aesthetic brings to the sitter and his or her surroundings an impressive 'thereness', a quality of occupying space and absorbing or reflecting light, which gives the illusion a kind of palpable charm. At the same time, the figure is psychologically unapproachable; for he or she has few specific referents which define the mood or even explain the reason for being in a painting at all.

When humans first entered art without a narrative role or symbolic stature, they slipped in almost unnoticed through genre, especially the painting of domestic scenes. Initially, such figures also had a 'role' in that they represented the low life of a picturesque kind. With Vermeer, however, the figures are not exotic curiosities, with an inconsequential presence or jocular quaintness. They are demure, dignified, monumental and, without any dramatic exertions, they command the spectator's attention with the airs of enigma and serious contemplation. The spectator does not confront them so much as enters their world; and this entry occurs without the processes of recognition which were normal in the history of art. The pleasure of seeing is not one of fitting the character into a secular taxonomy; it is to muse on their inaccessibility and to become seduced by your own conjecture. Your interest in them is a mystery.

The painting is not pre-eminently about mystery, has no programmatic content or overt symbolic argument; yet the absence of a symbolic code paradoxically makes the work doubly indecipherable. In order to penetrate it, you work from the visual givens; but these ultimately yield only perceptual information and do not reveal a great deal about the psychological or moral condition of the depicted person nor any of the narrative contingencies which would make an interpretation possible. With Vermeer, art becomes its own mystery, a feat of conjuring presences which have never been envisaged before because they are too ordinary; but the feat is to have 'seen' that such presences are also intensely seductive, quietly bewitching when framed by an excellent perceptual technique. The spectator perceives sublimity where there was nothing before, no God, no myth, no altar. But through this solemnly abstracted theatre, the spectator also witnesses the vulnerable delicacy of an undistinguished moment.[19]

Everything in Vermeer is secular; but there is also a condition of piety, for the spectator's breath is held in sympathy with the frozen action; and the perfect resolution of the pictorial treatment encourages a deference before a greater order. Piety is a form of admiration balanced between melancholy and awe; you acknowledge someone's stature with deference but feel sympathy for his or her mortality. The sadness may not be expressed but it lurks as an unconscious backdrop behind your esteem for a human. Piety is not the same as reverence: it is not about the worship of one infinitely greater. Piety is a form of affection felt for a greater person but in the context of a perishable contact. It is a religious feeling but in a secular framework. With the works of Vermeer, the western mind discovers an exalted spirituality which lies beyond the institutional mystique of the sacred.

ENDNOTES

1 Vik Muniz, *Pictures of junk*, Sikkema Jenkins & Co, New York, September – October 2006. Some of the paragraphs below are grafted from my review of this exhibition, "Manhattan's trashy treasures" in *The Age* (Nelson 2006).

2 Leis and D'Amato (2005): "La humanidad vive en dos realidades: en una más permanente, la del planeta Tierra, y en otra más transitoria, la que resulta de la acción humana y que convencionalmente llamamos Mundo".

3 See the studies from the perspectives of economic and social history collected in North and Ormrod (1998), particularly the overview of historical trends in western Europe as given in the editors' "Introduction: Art and Its Markets," 1–6.

4 Pietro Berrettini da Cortona, *Allegory of Providence*, 1632–1639, fresco, Gran Salone, Palazzo Barberini, Rome; Andrea Pozzo, *Glory of St Ignatius*, 1688–1694, fresco, Sant'Ignazio di Loyola, Rome. For background on such projects, and a study of allegorical meanings in relation to patronage, see Beldon Scott (1991).

5 Simon Vouet, *Allegory of Wealth*, ca. 1640, oil on canvas, Louvre, Paris. Mérot (1995) richly contextualizes the work and influence of Vouet in the broader history of French baroque painting.

6 See Posner (1999), on sixteenth- and seventeenth-century discourse—and myths—of nobility aestheticized, and represented according to the *topos* of the theatre.

7 See, for instance, the account of Velázquez's technical skill and economy given in Brown and Garrido (1998).

8 See Pieri (1995), and the essay on the literary history and status of the Marinisti given in Pieri's "Introduzione," ix–xxvi.

9 See Ferroni (1980, 111–138), on Trissino and the 'restoration' of classical tragedy as a theatrical model in the Rome of Leo X.

10 See Pocock (1980) on neo-classical doctrine and the two authoritative functions ascribed to poetry; those of giving pleasure and instruction.

11 See Auchincloss (1996) on the ideal of *gloire* in its relationship to a heroic patriotism formed in the image of the Roman Empire.

12 Nicolas Poussin, *Acis and Galatea*, ca. 1630, oil on canvas, National Gallery of Ireland, Dublin; *Triumph of Pan*, ca. 1635, oil on canvas, National Gallery, London; *Kingdom of Flora,* 1631, oil on canvas, Staatliche Kunstsammlungen, Gemäldegalerie, Dresden; *Inspiration of the Poet*, ca. 1630, oil on canvas, Louvre, Paris; *Diana and Endymion*, ca. 1630, oil on canvas, Detroit Institute of Arts, Detroit; *Landscape with the Ashes of Phocion*, 1648, oil on canvas, Walker Art Gallery, Liverpool; *Et in Arcadia Ego*, ca. 1638, oil on canvas, Louvre, Paris; *Tancred and Erminia*, 1630s, oil on canvas, Hermitage, St Petersburg; *Echo and Narcissus*, ca. 1630, oil on canvas, Louvre, Paris; *Landscape with Funeral of Phocion*, 1648, oil on canvas, National Museum of Wales, Cardiff. See Olson (2002), who considers the discipline of Poussin's work as it was particularly addressed to a clientele from France's educated, political élite, the *noblesse de robe* under Bourbon rule.

13 Nicolas Poussin painted two series of paintings of the seven sacraments of the Roman Church. Usually dated 1636–1642, the first set was undertaken for Cassiano del Pozzo, and is now somewhat dispersed: *Marriage*; *Ordination*; *Extreme Unction*; *Eucharist*, and *Confirmation*, oil on canvas, Belvoir Castle, Leicestershire; *Baptism*, oil on canvas, National Gallery of Art, Washington. Also associated with this first series is *St John Baptizing in the River Jordan*, 1630s, oil on canvas, J. Paul Getty Museum, Los Angeles. The second set, dated 1642–1648, was painted for Paul de Chantelou, and remains intact: *Marriage*; *Ordination*; *Extreme Unction*; *Penitence*; *Eucharist*; *Confirmation*; *Baptism*, oil on canvas, National Gallery of Scotland, Edinburgh, on loan from the Duke of Sutherland. See Green (2000).

14 See Denny (1972), in which Christ's Passion is imputed as the theme of still lifes such as Sánchez Cotán's famous painting *Cardoon and Parsnips*, ca. 1604, oil on canvas, Museo de Bella Artes, Granada. See the catalogue entry on this work in Jordan (1985, 63).

15 Johannes Vermeer van Delft, *The Art of Painting (The Artist's Studio)* ca. 1665–1666, oil on canvas, Kunsthistorisches Museum, Vienna; *Allegory of the Faith*, ca. 1670, oil on canvas, Metropolitan Museum of Art, New York.

16 Johannes Vermeer van Delft, *A Young Woman Standing at a Virginal*, ca. 1670, oil on canvas, National Gallery, London.

17 Johannes Vermeer van Delft, *Girl with a Pearl Earring,* ca. 1665, oil on canvas, Mauritshuis, The Hague; *Girl with a Flute,* probably 1665–1670, oil on panel, National Gallery of Art, Washington; *Girl with the Red Hat,* ca. 1665–1666, oil on panel, National Gallery of Art, Washington.

18 See Wheelock, Jr. (1995) who details Vermeer's techniques and materials as an aspect of his artistic process.

19 See Boyd White (2001).

REFERENCES

Auchincloss, L. 1996. *La Gloire: The Roman Empire of Corneille and Racine*. Columbia, South Carolina: University of South Carolina Press.

Beldon Scott, J. 1991. *Images of Nepotism: The Painted Ceilings of Palazzo Barberini*. Princeton, New Jersey: Princeton University Press.

Boyd White, J. 2001. "The Depth of Meaning in Vermeer". In *The Edge of Meaning*. Chicago: University of Chicago Press. 257–288.

Brown, J.; Garrido, C. 1998. *Velázquez: The Technique of Genius*. New Haven: Yale University Press

Denny, D. 1972. "Sánchez Cotán, 'Still Life with Carrots and Cardoon'". *Pantheon* 30: 48–53.

Ferroni, G. 1980. "La 'Sofonisba': Un Classicismo senza Conflitto". In *Convegno di Studi su Giangorgio Trissino*, edited by Pozza, N. Vicenza: Accademia Olimpica. 111–138.

Green, T. 2000. *Nicolas Poussin Paints the Seven Sacraments Twice: An Interpretation of Figures, Symbols and Hieroglyphs, Together with a Running Commentary on the Paintings, the Drawings and the Artist's Letters*. Watchet: Paravail.

Jordan, W. B. 1985. *Spanish Still Life in the Golden Age 1600–1650*. (Fort Worth, Texas: Kyoto. [Exhibition catalogue.]

Leis, H.; D'Amato, J. L. 2005. "Para una teoría de las prácticas del ambientalismo". *Theomai*, First semester, no. 11.

Mérot, A. 1995. *French Painting in the Seventeenth Century*, translated by Beamish, C. New Haven: Yale University Press.

Nelson, R. 2006. "Manhattan's Trashy Treasures". *The Age*. 4 October, p. 24.

North, M.; Ormrod, D., eds. 1998. *Art Markets in Europe 1400–1800*. Aldershot: Ashgate Publishing Limited.

Olson, T. P. 2002. *Poussin and France: Painting, Humanism and the Politics of Style*. New Haven: Yale University Press.

Pieri, M., ed. 1995. *Il Barocco. Marino e la Poesia del Seicento*, Cento Libri per Mille Anni. Rome: Ist. Poligrafico e Zecca dello Stato-Archivi di Stato.

Pocock, G. 1980. *Boileau and the Nature of Neo-Classicism*, Major European Authors Series. Cambridge: Cambridge University.

Posner, D. M. 1999. *The Performance of Nobility in Early Modern European Literature*, Cambridge Studies in Renaissance Literature and Culture 33. Cambridge: Cambridge University Press.

Wheelock, A. K., Jr. 1995. *Vermeer and the Art of Painting*. New Haven: Yale University Press.

Cite this chapter as: Nelson, Robert. 'Substance and sublimity'. *The Spirit of Secular Art: A History of the Sacramental Roots of Contemporary Artistic Values*. Melbourne: Monash University ePress. pp. 5.1–5.18. DOI: 10.2104/ssa07005.

CHAPTER 6

THE INDUSTRIAL SPIRIT

Robert Nelson

One of Barbara Kruger's largest exhibitions was at the Australian Centre for Contemporary Art, where viewers encountered an overwhelming installation.[1] As spectator, you go into a room where gigantic text scrolls along the floor, like a conveyor at the airport. The floor becomes a projected page that spools in a loop toward the next room. The disorienting spectacle is a sliding blue carpet of verbal torment. Short grumpy refrains speak defensively, like 'Don't bother me' or 'Don't kill me'. Others are evasive like 'Don't praise me' and 'Don't trust me'; and some reveal cynical materialist philosophies like 'Feel is something you do with your hands'.

In the next room, the floor is pink, as if rehearsing some kind of *he says, she says* dramatic routine. The sentences fluctuate between delirium and malice: 'I can't resist you. I can't breathe. I can't take it any more. I dreamt about you last night. I think I love you. You scare me. You used to be nicer. You're not getting any younger...' and so on. Bland, hurtful, frightened, these skittish emotional utterances recycle themselves under your feet as an endless power game, as of soap opera. It is hard to know who's a victim and why. They're stock emotional exchanges on TV.

The third room contains a more obvious critique of commercialized girlish desire. It is a static list: 'Moisturizers, iPods, sneakers, drugs, computers, watches, cars, boats, gold, smaller noses, bigger lips, houses, diamonds, art, abs, breasts, shoes, blowjobs, sweaters.' Consumer goods are equated with surgically inflatable body parts and sexual favours. The large room that comes next is spatially dominated by a huge anti-consumption slogan running around the wall: 'Plenty ought to be enough.' The floor has nine tableaux, each filled with lettering, sardonically flattering men of means, as in 'You make history when you do business'. This is undercut by confessions of industrial guile: 'For the merchant even honesty is a financial speculation'.

None of this prepares you for the video installation in the largest gallery. All four walls are treated as large screens, with aggressive mug-shot conversations. From wall to wall, angry or embarrassed people exchange insults, niggle one another competitively, undermine, reproach, belittle, threaten and humiliate. This litany of toxic sentiments plays out the power games on an intimidating scale, with loud sound track and sarcastic slogans below. The contrast between this room and the rest is extreme. In the first two, spectators reckon with their vertigo, laugh and wonder at the spatial relativity induced by a floor that seems to move. Children in the gallery jump joyfully among the messages. The rooms with the still text are more severe, claustrophobic and brow-beating, symbolized by the typeface crowding out all available space; but the denouement in the large room with the belligerent videos turns spectators to passive silence.

What sense do you make of it? The display of agro in the video conversations extrapolates the dramas of TV. Maybe Kruger has created a critique of an insidious dynamic in commercial media. You can sell malice on TV in the soap opera and then sell goods for advancing sexual capital during the ad breaks. We then go out to shop for weapons to gain the advantage over one another. Beneath the vicious video banter, one of the running texts declares 'Not cool enough, not cruel enough.' Some people might really think that way: you lack street cred if you are a nice guy. Kruger lives both in NY and LA and would have first-hand experience of the cultures closest to the movies. Maybe no one takes you seriously there if you are not angry.

If that is the case—and people are increasingly rude and unsympathetic because of commercial TV—then capitalism has a lot to answer for. But is it true? The allegation is artistically poignant but only if it reflects reality rather than paranoia. It is doubtful that commercial media and marketing make people antagonistic and horrible. People watch violent bloodthirsty garbage on TV but with some sense of irony: they know it is trash because the language of TV is shamelessly attention-seeking. Most of it is festive; but one of the cheapest ruses for gaining attention is for bitter people to act appallingly in close-up.

Kruger takes advantage of the emotional rape. Thanks to commerce, we are deeply brutalized and compulsively locked in a competitive orgy of spite. Or are we? Kruger falls victim to the overstatement and sensationalism of her nasty over-capitalized subject matter. There's no love in Kruger that is not also a weapon to accuse the economy of abuse. The sentiment strikes me as pessimistic to the point of misanthropy and it makes me ask: whence this development of the artist as outsider, caught up in the bitter pith of social ills, seeking to denounce but forever the victim? After so many centuries of art as celebration, something happened with industrialization that created a new paradigm of art where the spiritual cadence is terse and stressful.

* * *

The Enlightenment distinguishes itself from all periods before or since by its absence of sacraments. The world without sacraments looks very neat; it has a good sense of order, knows how to classify things with a sense of tolerance, engenders delight in questioning authorities, has unrivalled satirical wit, values fairness and reason, is devoted to human improvement, enjoys machinery and politeness, champions political analysis and begins the industrial revolution. As a rule, it disapproves of the vanity of pompous structures without utilitarian value, dislikes symbolic orders based on arcane principles and, while having abundant sympathy for theism, develops contempt for arbitrary codes of worship. It detests religious zeal. Ideas of sacrifice are abhorrent and a ritual action by which little people try to make up to a big God for inherent sinfulness seems more than absurd: it offends the spirit of reason; for the rationality and benignity of such a God who is flattered and gratified by all the little people's genuflexions would be more than questionable. Insofar as the rites of propitiation—however abstracted—displace the discipline of analytical and critical thought, they are repugnant. The Enlightenment can be described as a polemic against the mystical.

One allows the existence of God; but it is God the theory, a provisional God without extensive holiness and with an obedience to reason. If God is not understood as reasonable, doubts arise that God has been correctly identified. If creation and all of nature's wonders can be put down to God, God qualifies for the title by virtue of superior reason. If some aspect of creation were unreasonable, it cannot be God's work. God is submitted to Reason; the jealous God of the *Bible* encounters a higher divinity—Reason—and, while everyone may acknowledge God as a necessary belief, the notion of divinity nevertheless slips into the fathomable and writers prefer to use euphemisms and personifications like Nature or the Sublime to describe the awesome and mysterious.

For many decades in the eighteenth century, no one seemed to have a heart for anything spiritual. A sign of this shyness of the ghostly is the way in which the sanguine lyricism of the late baroque gives way to the enchanted flutters of the Rococo. No one wants to see firm foundations for institutional persuasions; no one can bear the forceful sway of authority in a design and all sense of command and drive is deflected by daintiness and intimacy. Design loses its sense of gravity and energy; it only wants to tickle the airs of a late afternoon in rustic sweetness, whether the design of a plate, a dish, a chair, a candlestick or a table. Architecture turns its back on the severe structures of the classical tradition and leaves the force of urban traffic for gentler pockets of space. It craves the park, the designer grove, the hide-away, the overgrown theatre in the rural seat of some aristocratic patron, the humid pad of some invisible and indulgent lord who will allow one to perform spontaneous concerts and *fêtes*.

The charming and intimate paintings of Watteau are the best portrait of the great Rococo abdication. Everyone has an invitation to be an aristocrat but only for a while and only in fancy dress; no one need take up the burdens of office and everyone can play in the garden. All vegetation is figured as a kind of cushion; the world is a shady *parterre* and any classical architecture upon it is a condiment of the fluffy grove beyond rather than a powerful reflection of social purpose. Relieved of the incumbencies of administrative or political action, all people can investigate how to relate to one another with infinite gentility, etiquette, polish and intimacy. If there is a spirituality in the park it is of a personal and intimate kind, without the tincture of an institutional discipline.

The enlightenment may have reversed some of these directions; but the one feature of Rococo which remained for the modern world is the replacement of the institutional by the personal. With the Rococo, the artistic renunciation of authority begins; and any language of spiritual emphasis came to be seen as uncritical, backward and gauche. The Enlightenment may have deplored the frivolity of the Rococo but it did not have any ambitions to restore the compelling zeal of baroque architecture and pictorial programs. The Enlightenment, as it were, calls a practical diligent gardener into Watteau's park, cuts clean pathways through the shady groves, removes the ivy, chops the tall trees down, creates pastures with productive stock and gets all the make-believe aristocrats to do accurate measurements and useful calculations.[2] The world becomes more reasonable, more co-ordinated and orderly; nature is happily exploited and no one can reasonably complain without accepting the optimistic philosophy of ameliorating the world with reason and labour.

The reason why authority vanished from the compelling expressive agendas of art and design is not, of course, that the world experienced any less authority. It is just that the old forms of authority—highly visible, given to pomp and ancestral ceremony—were bit by bit being replaced by more powerful and universal forms of authority which, however, were intrinsically invisible. The new authority was capital. Money has no presence; it is by nature transferable, decentralized and free. No one has special allegiances to one pile of capital as opposed to another, for money is money and only trading labour or stock gives a person any tangible sense of proprietorship. There is nothing tribal about money, even when it buys real estate; there is no symbolic order surrounding it and its genius is the abstraction of all other social forces. Money determines almost everything that happens in a community but has zero intrinsic symbolic value.

As Adam Smith investigates the machinery by which money orders the economy, the western world prepares to commit investment in production on an exponential scale, creating the industrial revolution, beginning in the 1760s and continuing its course to the present time. We still live in the in the industrial revolution. There is no date at which it ceased. Nor is there a date (if you exclude the Communist hiatus) at which money ceased to exercise supreme authority. The power of capital is as dynamic as its influence is inexorable. Of course certain people had always had vast wealth but it was relatively static, an inherited fund associated with inherited lands and their revenues; but the discovery of the industrial revolution was that money could be mobilized. If you make textiles, for example, and generate a profit, you can invest the surplus in technological improvements to production, improvements in distribution, improvements in quality or position in the market and so on. The result will be further profit.

The entrepreneur of the free market looks for any opportunity to invest prudently. A better return may be indicated in the transport business associated with a local distribution network. It may not seem so sensible to invest greatly in new machinery when the gains appear more available in another area. An entrepreneur is not necessarily attached to a traditional activity but can transfer interests. Almost like a living personification, money looks for opportunities, plunges headlong into risky ventures with high stakes and wreaks spectacular changes. It rapidly builds factories, towns, whole industries, transport reticulation which, by the nineteenth century, included rail. Mining plunders the earth; farming is reorganized for greater efficiencies; more food is available to feed a growing population. The idea of progress is reborn on a daily basis.

Money, which is powerful everywhere, is visible nowhere. You can see its results; but the tangible presence of a grid of power-looms in a multi-storey factory looks like industry rather than money. In the days when money was static, it was naturally embodied in monuments. With the industrial revolution, the money becomes dynamic; its habit is expansion, not where it ends up, not what it supports by way of a big house for a successful capitalist, not its consumption. The essence of money is its agency, its immaterial energy in affording strategic opportunities, its funnelling into activities by way of investment. The symbolism of money is confined to investors and economists who study the allocation of resources and the functioning of money. Money has a symbolic order around it; but it is bizarrely hermetic and hypostasized; for the symbolism of money deals only with money, its power to generate more money, its bearing on money markets and money managers. In no time, this becomes a professional vocation: to watch money, to watch what money is doing, which pool of money is destined to increase and which is likely to shrink and so on.

The new status of money is symbolized by the idea of interest. Before the industrial revolution, money used to be conceived more or less as a medium of exchange. It never was so simple but suffice to say that under the title of usury, the reality of interest met persistent disapproval. During the industrial revolution, the idea that money must yield something—not what it buys but what it earns—takes hold of the imagination. You are no longer a person who has money; you own money and this ownership entitles you to an income one way or another. Money as a generator of wealth *per se* becomes somehow reified, not merely a medium of exchange but a thing in itself, an agent, in a sense almost a master.

With the rise of capitalism, the western world obviously organizes itself along materialist lines. For an economist, the reorganization is rational rather than ritual. The ancient spiritual order which once shared in the authority of the social order recedes from relevance. It is something to which people may retreat—it may retain a special value as a sign of a Jerusalem which, as in prophetic times, is rapidly vanishing from immediate sight—but it no longer assumes a position of leadership, for all ideas of progress are configured in materialist language toward material ends. In the spectacular matter of progress, there is no structural role for religious ritual. It is not just a case of being 'upstaged' by the inexorable spectacle of industrial change. The predication of that change is financially dynamic and supremely materialist; it is absolutely alien to the spiritual establishments of ancient tradition.

Bit by bit in this circumstance, the spiritual defaults to the personal. The spiritual is drained of its institutional authority and the very idea of religion (which one might define as institutionalized spirituality) is increasingly tenuous. In the industrial period, nearly all aspects of the relationship between the sacred and the secular would have to be renegotiated. The sacred privileges no longer seem as prestigious as they used to. It would be a terrible time, for example, in which to be an artist devoted to painting holy pictures or sculpting saints. The challenge to the traditional relationship between the sacred and the secular was never openly acknowledged. In previous centuries a challenge to orthodoxy was met by formidable councils of cardinals and theologians assembling and vigorously propounding resolutions and edicts in response to the heresies which were to be unequivocally anathematized. In the industrial period, such reactions were no longer possible. The heresy, so to speak, was not religious in nature. There was no language with which to argue against the onslaught of capitalist materialism and to promulgate its antidote. Capitalism was never a heresy. Its incursions on spiritual territory were passive. It could not be damned and in certain cases even had to be praised for creating wealth, missionary patronage and colonial expansion. But it inadvertently rearranged all institutional priorities in favour of material values. In the fervid preoccupations of money as a symbol of the transfer of authority, religion became little but an ancient ornament—almost exotic and quaint—in the great deritualizing of the economy.

The history of art bears witness to an intensely anti-institutional feeling which is often called Romanticism. Romanticism can be dated to the middle of the eighteenth century (immediately before the industrial revolution) in the etchings of Piranesi, in particular his series of *Gaols* or *Carceri*.[3] Although building on an old baroque tradition of bizarre visual fantasies (*invenzioni*) Piranesi's imaginative views of dungeons struck a note of sublime terror. They showed the prison as a deplorable place of torture, with disgusting cages, spiked wheels, dangling hooks and shackles and other horrific contrivances for the physical torment and psychological breaking of humans. The interior spaces of the prisons are giant extrapolations of Roman ruins but made somehow dysfunctional and irrational. They act as ciphers of the harrowed mind. The compositions crash this way and that with diagonal thrusts, registering in formal accents the violence suggested in the imagery. Although formulated primarily as exercises in the free use of imagination—and although remaining ambiguous and impossible to define in terms of intention—the iconographic result of the *Carceri* is radical. The individual is cast as outright victim. The institutional is represented as dire and depraved.

By the time Goya paints his gaols and madhouses around 1800, the industrial revolution was well advanced, especially in England and France though less conspicuously in Goya's Spain. One way or another, Goya's work adopts a kind of morbid rancour against the institutional. Like Piranesi, Goya does not define his intentions or allow the default of tradition to take care of his intentions. The work lies outside an established tradition in which the meaning was overwritten by institutional conventions. Goya does not paint the standard subjects of the previous centuries, such as *Erminia among the Shepherds* or the *Martyrdom of St Sebastian*, nor does he paint politically neutral genre subjects such as landscape or interiors. He hatches scenes of almost perverse originality. Often they are sinister, as in *Maja and Celestina on the Balcony*; sometimes they are morbid, as in the *Caprichos*; they can be violent as in *The Third of May 1808* or exaggerated reportage of detestable cruelty, as in the *Disasters of War*.[4] There are numerous scenes of witchcraft, from the *Caprichos* to the *Black Paintings*, in which Goya's position is almost impossible to determine.[5] He is fascinated by magic and wavers between relishing its alternative transports and satirizing its irrationality. Cruelty, too, is enacted as a hideous ritual of ambiguity. In numerous prints and drawings, Goya uses the convention of a wry title to comment on the subject matter; and through these lapidary lines, he often speaks through the chilling voice of the oppressor. Titles such as 'he deserved it' or 'he should not have written for idiots' somehow implicate the spectator in a disgusting agreement that the punishment of some poor victim is just and proper.

There is a pleasure in needling the conceits of the Enlightenment. The frontispiece for the *Caprichos* declares in simple Spanish that 'the sleep of reason engenders monsters'.[6] On the one hand, it could mean that it is necessary to remain vigilant against the sleep of reason, to avoid sleep, to command the mind with perpetual wakefulness lest the mind become abducted by irrational fantasies. On the other hand, it could mean that the sleep of the rational mind is inevitable and the zeal for constancy of reason is in itself irrational. I default to sleep; and, when I sleep, not only do I lose all watchfulness but I cannot control what I dream. This inner zone of the psyche is not subject to reason; and the tissue of quaint explanations of physical things which you call reason is only a thin overlay which conceals the real human beneath, wild with unexplained passions and instincts, fantasies and fears. Nothing in Goya's art ever lets us establish which of these positions he intended to express.

Goya is not alone in fostering an inscrutable motive for representing a given scene. The same fearsome closeness to a horrible scene can be witnessed in the paintings of George Stubbs, already mentioned in connexion with the performative photography of Monika Tichacek.His pictures of lions killing horses also share with Goya's the detached curiosity-value, an unwholesome distance between the immediacy of the image and the inaccessibility of the motive for representing it.[7] Stubbs could be representing the ghastly event in order to document scientifically the pathology of a screaming beast and the lust of a carnivore; he might want to show the moral truth about nature; he might be making an allegory of the predatory ruthlessly conquering the harmless. It is impossible to place Stubbs's sentiments. His pictures are poignant in their identification of natural forces; but they seem purposefully constructed neither to celebrate nor deplore their terrible subject matter. They represent a *tour de force* of painting as self-contained spectacle, without a scheme of references which explain it. The painting glories in its own extraordinary resources, a weird form of visual intensity detached from a direct communicative imperative. The autonomy of art draws nigh.

Ever since the enlightenment, artists became self-conscious in seeking subject matter. The commentaries in the *Salons* of Diderot bear witness to the interest in certain iconographic choices which artists were making, it seems, in a deliberately strategic way.[8] Artists can distinguish themselves by finding poignant themes. Poetic wits can then criticize the artistic endeavours on the basis of their accuracy or integrity relative to sources or the critic's own conception of human nature or any other form of nature. There is no longer an overarching confidence in iconographic convention or a compliance with governing authorities. The painter errs to novelty. It is unlikely that he or she reaches toward Ovid's *Metamorphoses* for inspiration. Before the dawn of the nineteenth century, artists had reversed their franchise with traditional spiritual authority.

All of this can be seen most clearly in Goya. His iconography is somehow instinctual and his often raw visuality supports the pre-eminence of an impulsive, inborn artistic sense. Vision with Goya becomes detached from the comforts of courtly certainties, a realm to which the painter apparently had ready access. For reasons internal to the painter, the delights of the exquisite buildings and the privileges of majesty are no longer convincing. He resiles from the polished and balanced look of luxurious portraits and turns to a world of irksome fantasies. It is possible that this apostasy relates to social conscience; perhaps, as every Goya-lover wants to believe, the painter heroically abjures a luxurious life in order to campaign on behalf of the dispossessed. But Goya never leaves enough information to tie down his personal convictions. He observes cruelty against the disadvantaged; he recognizes the darkness of the prevailing social order and the irrationality which it engenders in the poor and ignorant; but whom, ultimately, does Goya deplore? From just before 1800, everyone in Goya's art is in an unwholesome position; and even if some characters are innocent, their spiritually destitute situation overwhelmingly defines their identity. They are either victims, idiots, barbarians, bestialized by instinct or dehumanized by the machinery of authority, pompous inquisitors and deluded witches whose interest, perversely, is in wilfully transcending reason.

Once Goya ceases to represent the erotic economy of beautiful *majos* and *majas*, he defaults to misanthropy. The faith in a social order collapses and with it tumbles the artist's personal faith in human nature. Misanthropy undoubtedly becomes a kind of centrepiece of the Romantic imagination. But it would be naïve to construe this misanthropy as a purely social or political expression of the alienated industrial soul. It is an aesthetic position; it is artfully crafted to be profoundly grave but grand and resonant at the same time; it is ethically evasive, concerned with the unfathomable, the sublimity of pessimism, the disappointment of failed rationality, the horror of the bottom of human nature, the terror of the emptiness of the faithless soul.

Goya is far from an isolated instance. Other Romantic artists like the French Gericault and Delacroix have been equally famous for their disturbances of an inherited complacency, their interventions against the spirit of explanation; for they relish scenes of tremendous dread and alarm whose psychological impact is properly inexpressible. Pessimism, violence, misanthropy, but misanthropy as artistic celebration, writ grand, forceful, showy, theatrical and richly sadistic. Check this with the gratuitously sexual slayings of naked women in Delacroix's *Death of Sardanapalus*.[9] It is all mayhem and despair but for artistic gratification, not to say pornographic satisfaction.

But Delacroix's *Death of Sardanapalus* is hardly a unique case. In Delacroix, the celebration of despair is a commonplace, beginning with his early *Barque of Dante*. Works such as *Hamlet and Horatio in the Graveyard*, *Scenes from the Massacres at Chios*, the *Death of Ophelia*, the *Confession of the Giaour* and so on demonstrate the same passion for the gloom, the listless acceptance of horror, which forms the final virtue of the Byronic hero.[10] Any pretext for despair seems a suitable topic for a picture. Gericault's *Raft of the Medusa* can be interpreted as one of the first grand pictures which heroizes a topical event.[11] But the scene in which survivors cling hopelessly to a raft whose link with a life-boat has been selfishly severed is neither objective reportage nor a moral condemnation of an unconscionable deed against the survivors. The genre of outrage has not quite matured in the early nineteenth century. The rationale for the painting is artistic. The artist wants to paint despair and the raft lets him do it with nakedness, a great aesthetic condiment to vulnerabilty.

It is not totally theatrical and silly. A part of the cult of despair is necessary for the spiritual claims of art. The beauty of despair has a sacramental character; for in the spectatorship of disaster, despair demonstrates a heroism of awareness, a brave recognition of doom or certain death. Relative to heroic history pictures of the past, the view of spiritual virtue is mysteriously inverted. Greatness of soul is no longer registered as an abiding faith protested stoutly against ungodly adversity. Greatness of soul is defined as an absence of faith in the reckoning with mortality; it is the heroism which people have when they do not have God. Since the eighteenth century, no heroic moment would ever be shared with God. The encounter with death is staged entirely within the psyche of the individual; there is no appeal to the institutional, no hope of rescue by supernatural benignity; and indeed such fantasies are scorned as spiritual weakness. When the individual faces death with despair, a new sublimity of spiritual independence is found. It is not the quiet stoicism of the ancient Greek heroes but the anarchic dismissal of the artifice of institutional hope.

Romanticism comprises a new kind of rhetoric as well as subject matter. The rhetoric is also a scary polemic against the values of the enlightenment, especially against the positivistic philosophy of reason ultimately being capable of solving all problems. On a social level, Romanticism proposes a series of oppositions, many of which are artificial. For example, intuition is championed in opposition to tuition; the individual is opposed to the social. On an artistic level, the dichotomy must be framed in an opposition to classicism. Expressing passion is opposed to the static decorum of classicism; stylistically, energy is opposed to classical repose; vigour is opposed to classical organization; rough is opposed to smooth; complexity is opposed to classical simplicity; compositional tangle is opposed to classical clarity; effusion is opposed to restraint; abundance is opposed to sparseness; individual specificity is opposed to godly abstraction; stress is opposed to classical stability; imbalance is opposed to classical composure; and the spontaneous is opposed to the classically contrived. On a psychological or spiritual level, agony is opposed to sufficiency; emotion is opposed to classical impassivity; transport is opposed to intellect; impulsiveness is opposed to classical clear-headedness; mystery is opposed to reason; fantasy is opposed to intelligence; nature is opposed to culture.

Art as the detestation of complacency entails revolt. It means taking up the stance of rejection, of scorn for an imputedly self-satisfied *ancien régime* of the arts. You condemn any pictorial optimism as saccharine; you vigorously repudiate whatever spiritual values appear to have flattered political or intellectual conceits. Meanwhile, Romanticism means cultivating another form of grandeur, a sublime and even gruesome heroism which requires a renovated monumentality; and this is not without its conceits either. The greatest conceit of Romantic art is the heroism of the artist, able to resist the blandishments of aesthetic convention and instead entertain an agonized world of unpredictable imagination, violence, sublimity and instinct. It is self-flattering to a narcissistic degree; but the emotional force of Romantic rhetoric persuades the beholder that the spectacles do not arise from vanity but deep levels of insight and vision, an awesome inner clairvoyance which recognizes the tightest knots of the psyche.

In formal terms, Romantic paintings sometimes resemble baroque paintings, with their powerful diagonals, directional chiaroscuro, energetic shafts of form, circular compositions, the air of formal bravery as well as the iconographically sanguine. Of course they are entirely different in every other respect, technical as well as spiritual. One of the key differences relates to humour. Baroque painters in the Italian narrative tradition always acknowledge a kind of theatrical buoyancy in their fantasies; they know that the myths are ultimately only myths and leave a margin of disbelief in the very ornamental character of the work. And analogous observations can be made about their religious works—as pious as they are—for there is always a sense that the picture is but one reverent visual conjecture of an infinitely greater truth which is divinity. No matter how forceful and pompous, baroque painting leaves you in no doubt that the glory of heaven is greater. Romantic painting, on the other hand, lacks both the holy authorities which would induce such humility and the mythological enthusiasm which would encourage irony in pagan subject matter. Romantic painting is quite without humour. When it is grand, it is bombastic. And the pomposity is not leavened by a sense of supplication before the divine.

In fact there is nothing institutionally divine remaining in the artistic consciousness. The capitalist world of railways and industrial manufacture no longer structurally cultivates God, for the reasons suggested above. But the massive secularization of art which ensues—as in other epochs—does not entail a weakening in the spiritual claims of art. On the contrary, as with other epochs, art assumes greater spiritual status on account of its greater independence from a priestly order. In the Romantic period, the spiritual reputation of art swings from the institutional to the personal or to the individual's relationship with nature. The very idea of nature, of course, is antithetical to all institutions. When the word is used in the late eighteenth century or throughout the nineteenth century, it denotes a realm of innocence and autonomy from human organization. It is not quite the ancient Greek view of nature (*physis*), meaning growth, a form of biological development, the default process by which all things are formed if they are not actually made by art. Nor do writers around 1800 use nature quite in the sense of baroque theorists, as when they used to encourage artists to 'follow nature' or 'learn from nature', which meant to use unprejudiced objective observation in drawing rather than be informed by artificial rules or formulae when representing objects. For the Romantic period, nature is a moral force, a paradigm of action which is not spiritually killed by intellectual legislation. Nature is the place and the scheme in which cultural definitions and laws are ineffectual, leaving the poet or wanderer free to enjoy unpremeditated contact with the element.

At the very time at which the objects of nature were being colonized, so to speak, by the taxonomic genius of the enlightenment and empirical science, a construct of nature emerged which was metaphysical and poetic, fugitive and compelling, immediate and earthy but ideal and ethereal. Depending on your cultural bias, nature could act as a refuge from the disciplinary basis of culture; it would be a sanctuary for the imagination to avoid the regimentation of classificatory systems, for experience of nature would proceed directly and freshly from natural phenomena, unmediated by the hieratic order of the vitrine or scientific tables. Nature would give the poet asylum from the universal grid of the encyclopaedia, for the encounter with nature would directly evoke feelings, moods, atmospheric resonance, which would defy the structural regime of scientific positivism.

Nature represented an escape from both the political determinism of capital and the perceived emotional straight-jacket of scientific measurement of all phenomena. And because it offered such a refuge, it attracted reverence; in due course—at least among intellectuals and artists—nature overtook the spiritual prestige of God. Unlike the organized spirituality of a religion, the new cult of nature did not require a systematic structure; it needed no invidious hierarchy of cardinals authorized to cast grave anathemas on heretics. With the cult of nature, there was neither orthodoxy nor dissent (even though there may have been barbarians who do not appreciate it) but freedom to communicate with spontaneous force. The cult was attended by inspired mystics, enthralled observers, none of whom had superior gifts of prophecy but all of whom were pilgrims and intrinsic hierophants, artlessly given over to the rapturous contemplation of mountains, moss and trees.

Nature as a spiritual resource was an invention of the industrial revolution, which it has largely remained to the present age of eco-tourism in which rapt greenies take their holidays in planes and cars to visit wilderness. The machinery of both engineering and the social order inspired the recreational hallowing of nature. In previous centuries, nature was a realm of still-uncultivated land, rough, unpleasant, dangerous, unproductive, harbouring crooks and wolves. Mountains were an obstacle; travel across them was beastly. The industrial revolution redefined nature as sanctuary, not only because a spiritual antidote was needed against the psychological machinery of industrial life but because the same industry which forced people into the competitive struggles of capital also yielded leisure. The conspicuous consumption of leisure is registered in paintings toward the end of the nineteenth century, especially in those memorable impressionist pictures (such as *La Grenouillère*, painted by both Monet and Renoir) showing the bourgeois enjoying luncheon or boating outside Paris. The opportunities to move away from city life to absorb the restoring humours of the country must have been building up throughout the nineteenth century.

For the Romantics, however, the interest was not on a social milieu removed from Paris for the lyrical charms of a lazy weekend. The Romantic poets and artists—from Wordsworth to Wilson, from Eichendorff to Caspar David Friedrich—sought to be moved by the primacy of nature. They variously appreciated in nature the inclement transport, the imposingly grandiose vista, the raw impact of the endless complexity of nature upon the senses. Everything which could not be replicated by human construction, everything which defies the imagination, contributed to the cult. Nature emerged in Romantic consciousness as a pre-existing cathedral of infinite shrines, places where a person could go in prayerful silence and reflect on the wholeness of the world through contemplating a tiny fragment of the earth. Some Romantics may have imagined that the ultimate cathedral was that built by God; but the genius of the cult was to make the speculation on an institutionalized deity redundant. The cathedral, in this metaphoric sense, is *the godly*; for it is not an ornamental shell to be filled by sermons and liturgy but an animating spirit which organically creates and relates all living and inanimate matter. Nature in this autonomous spiritual guise received the dedications of the faithful, certain people (all relatively privileged on the social scale) who could let the sublime thought of nature into their soul, to be spiritually transfused by the encounter.

The artwork which promises to fulfil the terms of this encounter is sacramental. It replicates the physicality of the world on a spiritual plane; it rehearses a reverent predisposition toward the tangible presence of nature. The rich atmospheric dimensions of a vista are studied for their power of transfusing consciousness. It is what distinguishes the nineteenth-century landscapes of Constable, for example, from their seventeenth-century Dutch antecedents by painters such as Ruisdael and Hobbema. The masters of Dutch genre are powerfully atmospheric, evocative, and charming; but a part of their seductiveness is the way the picture is wrapped up, as it were, in a moody consistency, an aesthetic intonation, a resonance achieved by means of umbrous glazes. In Constable, the encounter with the givens of nature seems fresher, more palpably perceptual, capable of reckoning with organic anarchy, and lacks much of the aesthetic convention of the past. Constable's paintings are often iconographically unceremonious: you see the rear of things, a view from a ditch or the view of an illustrious structure (such as Salisbury Cathedral) which is substantially obscured by trees.[12] Meanwhile, the rich intonations of the layered transparent technique of the baroque masters is abandoned in favour of a more *alla prima* application of paint, sometimes extending to the placement of white on the canvas, untempered by ochres or any other earth glaze. The perception of the disorderly sparkle of wet surfaces no longer submits to the artificial unification of warm glazed tones; the hallowed technique of 'brown and green paintings' is rejected in favour of an 'importunate optic', a splashing and dashing, a flickering of lights which in nature are all varied and diverse. The illusion of a view gains a new primacy, for it separates itself from the coherent skin of the glazed picture plane. The new pictorial epidermis, so to speak, spontaneously acknowledges the multiplicity of visual information without the intermediary of a conventional dark and sonorous luminosity. Nature is all encountered through reflection of light; in Constable you do not have the sense of penetrating the shadows to see forms in their richness but rather the sense of forms impressing themselves upon the eye with immediacy. The painting technique seems uncontrived. The recognition of nature's richness invites the 'raw' handling of the medium of paint.

Painting becomes both more scientific and artistically spontaneous: it registers optical effects with a minimum of prejudice and it expresses a 'natural' engagement with the landscape and the medium. It is not exactly a mystical paradox (for it is logical and at times unemotional) but art emerges as an exalted clairvoyance into the untutored and irregular sights of nature. Not only does art involve a new seeing-power which realigns the subject matter but the optical recognition within the art expresses itself through the magic presence of the gestural brushstroke. Constable's application of paint is as unorthodox as his iconographic vision is unceremonious. But in dispensing with some of the inherited 'ceremonies' of painting, Constable more fully expresses what the century wanted from nature, ironically a kind of sacramental encounter which would abstract the genius of nature (and its infiltration of the eyes, lungs and consciousness of the beholder) and thereby act as an artistic substitute for the institutionalized sacraments of religion.

In many ways, Turner is not dissimilar. Although undoubtedly having greater affinity with past conventions and a greater readiness to assimilate them into the fabric of his pictures, Turner also represents the combination of a searching iconography which discovers hitherto unrecognized phenomena with a heightened expression of the medium.[13] The thrashing, surging and seething of Turner's seas, mountains and clouds are the qualities which most generally identify Turner as a Romantic, expressing the untrammelled emotional engagement with the moods of nature. His pictures have the air of narrowly avoided disaster. But the writhing sinews of his paint (often gorgeously intermingled with old-master glazing) are only one half of the pictorial renovation which Turner's pictures achieve. Like Constable, he can recognize an aspect of common reality which had never featured in painting, the new technologies of steam-power, the reality of wharves working through the night to load coal and save time—hence capital—or new transport systems, such as rail.

In a well-known picture memorably called *Rain, Steam and Speed—The Great Western Railway*, Turner shows a locomotive flying over a bridge beneath our gaze.[14] How radical this picture is cannot be summed up easily. In traditional terms the perspective is unseasonal. It proposes a viewpoint above the land. The train rushes toward us but beside us at the same time; there is a sense of its enormously dynamic presence but also its imminent vanishing, leaving the landscape to its wet silence and timeless stability. The approach of the train is a kind of visual crisis, emerging from a kind of inchoate suggestiveness amid the misty rain and enacting some overcharged epiphany which is chased by an almost simultaneous disappearance. Some of the radical pictorial content is conveyed by the title. There was never a picture in the past with the word 'speed' in it. The expression of distance divided by time is astonishingly abstract, especially in the context of old-fashioned nouns like rain and steam. Of course this variety of steam (steam produced by coal combustion) is unseasonal, like the speed and the perspective: it is industrial, an expression of modernity. But the painting equally expresses the way in which the infinite mantle of nature subsumes even the most violent interventions of modern machinery. The overpowering embrace of nature is a theme which Turner also visits in marine pictures showing a steamer struggling against high seas.

Turner's recognition of industrial objects is unusual. Most of the industrial revolution occurred without artists ever deigning to notice it. Why should they? Their business is sacramental. Considering the great bulk of nineteenth-century pictures, there are few factories, machines or distribution networks represented. To find a full-blooded enthusiasm for such subject matter, you have to wait till the futurists of the twentieth century and artists like Léger, by which time the interests in the reality of appearances is so severely challenged by internal pictorial interrogation that industrial plant and production are never really credited or dignified with the visual information proper to them. In a sense, the industrial revolution somehow escapes the sovereign spiritual notice of artists. And for a simple reason. The industrial revolution and all its machinery contained no sacramental cues. Turner is thus the exception that proves the rule. He paints modern powered machinery when it is upstaged by the sublimity of nature, when it demonstrates the infinite atmospheric lap of the earth in which dark and nasty little mechanical interventions contend with inelegant pumping exertions. Turner never shows machinery for its own sake and, if he had, we would not be looking at it today; for it would not be recognized as art.

The freshness of Turner's vision is not to be denied and is well celebrated by the vivacious and stressful technique; but the most modern element in his art is not the presence of machinery but—as with Constable—the absence of narrative. Neither artist wants monumentality to arise from an Aristotelian drama with a beginning, a middle and an end. The mythical personages in Turner's Claudian landscapes are pip-squeaks; even when he wants to recreate the baroque nostalgia for antiquity, the mythical substance of the themes is insignificant.[15] Turner just wants the sunset kissing the leaves and columns from the side, the expansiveness of the waters driving through the centre of the perspective; he wants the atmosphere of a distant kingdom but not in order to animate it with sanguine baroque immediacy but to drop it into a kind of historicist *sfumato*. His heroes no longer strut the heroic stage upon which they will commit sacramental actions; they slip to the props where they only enjoy their own decorativeness. Their role recedes from the potency of heroism to the insignificance of a pretext for painting a certain kind of picture.

From Constable to Corot, Courbet and the impressionists, the painted world reflects the anonymity of capital. The illustrious names of heroes are irrelevant to the artistic project. Ironically, there is a rich and seductive academic tradition of figure painting which keeps the Greek myths and Judeo-Christian narratives in currency; it is relatively well patronized and represents mainstream, orthodoxy, classicism, the establishment, everything, in short, against which Romanticism struggled. Academic painting continued to cultivate the names of ancient history and myth; but it added a large number of less familiar names which would have been esoteric for a baroque audience. With relative prosperity and the airs of pomp and authority, academic painting strains hard to achieve excellence in learning and moral probity; it seeks to be both grand and useful, bristling with antique names, lessons and rhetoric. Academic painting throughout the nineteenth century shows no signs of collapsing or losing its technical finesse. Sometimes, the historical themes seem artificial and the gestures of protagonists are hammed or stilted; and, compared to baroque painting, academic painting is unnatural, stressfully ambitious and psychologically remote.

Of course painting as edification in academic painting has almost nothing to do with capital or industrial progress. But like Romanticism, it works by opposition to the mainstream of organized production. Art is understood as something about itself. It does not reflect the social conditions of the day but the greatness of soul of former times. Neo-classicism is nostalgic and Romanticism is challenging and forward-looking; but both are structurally united in their preoccupations internal to art itself. Art is about being art. It is not about the changes to the fabric of cities or the development of technologies. It is about the resources of a medium, pre-eminently painting—from the optical to the literary—which would help lift the spectator to a higher plane of contemplation. Absorbing this material attention to the agonized gaze would be prestigious and spiritually transformative. Art is about secular sacraments.

Within this somewhat introverted economy of self-challenging picture-making, an artistic ethos emerges which, at least ostensibly, pays direct attention to the appearance of the age, Realism. Realism rejects the rhapsodic spirituality of Romanticism but has no time for the oratorios of neo-classicism. The movement is not unrelated to its immediate predecessors. Realist artists such as Corot clearly owe much to Constable, as does the whole Barbizon School.[16] But when it comes to painting the figure, the distinctiveness of realist motivation emerges more clearly. The key personality (and such a personality!) is Courbet, an energetic self-publicist and rebel, endowed with the confidence to establish his own exhibition—at a time when solo shows were rather unknown—when his works were rejected by the academy because of their radical content and treatment.

Courbet professed to seek no manner of artifice in his works. His celebrated challenge "show me an angel and I'll paint one" well characterizes the determination of the materialist spirit. No Ossianic fantasies, no revelry of woodland nymphs or esoteric assignations of lads and lasses of Boccaccio's Florence. Courbet ambitiously sought heroic content in the boring days and menial work of ordinary people, especially those in the countryside, some distance from the sophistication and prestige of Paris. From there he painted his best known works, the *Stonebreakers* and the *Burial at Ornans*, paintings of new and surprising pathos.[17] In the *Burial at Ornans*, the unceremonious obsequies for a recently deceased member of the village community shamble their way across the canvas: the composition takes its cue from the randomness of the bleak landscape, and the scenography of poses and gestures reveals a disjointed combination of poignant grief and the indifference of the funerary routine. The presence of the dog at the burial seems indelicate, scandalous, indecorous; the hole dug for the coffin yawns horribly and the pious blessings induced by the cross seem ineffectual.

In the *Stonebreakers*, Courbet shows a very young man assisting a lean older middle-aged man in breaking rocks. Presumably their toil is for screenings, perhaps for a railway or road—who knows?—but their labours are not related to an end-use. They are required by the destiny of capital to bend their backs to the work, to slave away at the most unrewarding task (proverbially making little rocks out of big rocks) in order to feed themselves and their families. There is a suggestion, too, of mortality: the boy will grow into the figure of the older middle-aged man, with no opportunities for corporal grace or dignity. This is what it is like, you sense Courbet saying, if you are underprivileged. Your life is bespoken by poverty. There are no ways out. You just have to bend your body to whatever unglamorous work is available and be rewarded by such a tiny pittance that no escape form the oppressiveness of a miserable life will be dispensed by fortune.

Courbet is only cheerful if the picture is about himself or his erotic investments. *Bonjour Monsieur Courbet* is an example of the painter's conceited buoyancy; in numerous other self-portraits, his narcissism is apparent.[18] None of his pictures is without a rhetorical temper. They tend to be large and have an air of monumentality in their drawing. Courbet professed to seek no kind of inflexion on the accurate visual recording of the things which he saw in front of him. But if that were the case, his pictures would be expressionless. And that they are not. If anything, they tend to the operatic, as in *The Bathers* of 1853.[19] And the two works of thorough realist conviction (the *Stonebreakers* and the *Funeral at Ornans*) are intended to convey the most poignant expression, namely the social desolation of the rural proletariat. They are painted in the most objective manner possible but they can hardly avoid the rhetorical temper of projecting pathos, the sense of the histrionic, the stage-managed rehearsal of poverty by a sophisticated and ambitious painter. Try as he may to persuade us that he only paints what he sees, Courbet asks people to pose in his studio: a whole ritual is undertaken by people who definitely are not so oppressed that they have no time to act for him as studio models. The artificial nature of working on 'low life' can be seen in the picture with the most tellingly paradoxical title, *The Artist's Studio (A Real Allegory)*, in which numerous down-and-outs have been clustered in one part of the composition to represent not themselves for themselves but the radical subject matter of art for the radical painter.[20] They are answered by the figures on the other side of the composition, poets and intellectuals who similarly synthesize the facts of the great unwashed to produce the insights of genius.

Courbet's socialism is crucial in all this. As a socialist, Courbet believes that everything *that is* and everything *that ever was* has a material cause. There is no mystery, neither in the patterns of historical change nor in the motives for contemporary religious beliefs; at the heart of organized spirituality there is a habit of manipulating people into submission, perhaps at best based only on superstition to which no self-respecting intellectual would ever succumb. There are no sacraments but any number of greedy spiritual groups ready to prey upon the gullibility of the oppressed and uneducated masses and recommend submission as supreme virtue. This critique may all be fair enough; and as Courbet really believed it, he must be recognized as the first artist ever to have consciously and actively defied the spiritual basis of art.

For the most part, Courbet's paintings bear out the philosophy. At least in the late 1840s and early '50s, they are relentlessly ordinary, showing a staunch rejection of spiritualized subject matter and stylistic conventions. But there is a philosophical contradiction in Courbet's materialism, a paradox out of which the artist creates a new kind of art, an agonized art of implied manifestos and theoretical difficulty. As a socialist, Courbet would seek revolutionary overthrow; he would want his work to contribute to class struggle and convey a point about social justice. He would not go so far as to create propaganda for the revolution but neither would he want to create ideologically neutral art; for that would mean acceding to the capitalist complacency of bourgeois consumption. Alas, the same ideology also asks him to stick to the facts, to paint only what he sees (as he says himself) and to exaggerate nothing. In following such Realist principles, Courbet denies himself a whole level of expression. He cannot easily engage allegory, narrative or symbolism, much less expressive exaggeration or theatricality, rhetoric in gestures or emphasis; for these tropes fly in the face of the Realist credo to paint only what one sees, proceeding from materialist principles of objectivity and faithfulness to unromanced perception. The social campaign which would follow from the same principles is disappointed by the artistic requirements.[21] Courbet cannot easily be both socialist and Realist. And of course he errs to the artistic side of the dichotomy.

Courbet's later work is seductively erotic (as in the Lesbian *Sleep*); it appeals to cheeky bourgeois taste and could easily be read as an ideological sell-out.[22] But rather than interpret the later work as a sign of failure for Courbet's philosophy, it makes more sense to read it as a proof of the stresses which make Courbet's earlier work so compellingly modern. The agony is inherent in all Courbet's work: first, to paint something which is candid and untampered, so to speak, by artistic ruses and, second, to champion the cause of social reform or revolution. That leaves very few things to paint. Courbet probably exhausted many of them with the few pictures of the rural proletariat from early in his career; thereafter, his art becomes more and more an imaginative demonstration of the self-conscious agonies themselves, as in *The Artist's Studio*, mentioned before.

With Courbet, art gains an avant garde; it gains a sense of being progressive in strong alignment with a political avant garde. After Courbet, it would become more and more difficult for an artist to be understood as progressive without being implicated in a whole network of contradictory and almost impossible demands. It would no longer be possible simply to paint an expressive picture along the heroic lines of the Romantics; for pictures with a simple expressive power do not display efforts to grapple with the material ideological status of the work; in fact, they elude such an effort beneath a subterfuge of expressive bombast. Painting at its most progressive cannot glory in the rhetoric of tall tales, high mountains and high seas, when that very rhetoric insulates art from a tough engagement with its own material ideological underpinnings.

In all this, however, art remains art. It still has a pre-eminently aesthetic or perceptual charter and cultivates the magic of seeing-power to a high degree, discovering exciting artistic potential in topics hitherto considered unworthy of art and undoubtedly cued by photography. As noted, Courbet's paintings of low life are on a monumental scale, the same scale as assumed by ambitious Romantic painters. And despite all theory to the contrary, Courbet's images are usually immensely rhetorical, engaging every strategy for artistic self-importance which Romantic painting ever projected. The difference with respect to the Romantic tradition is the substitution of its spirituality, the rejection of the numinous assumptions behind the reverence for nature, the rejection of nature, in fact, as a spiritual force or even an interesting motif in art. This turning away from the spiritual assumptions of the previous traditions is similar to all the stages of secularization considered so far; for the challenge to the anterior metaphysic occurs while the awesome properties of the tradition—Romantic painting as a statement of rebellious magnanimity—are still conferred upon its successor. The stirring thrill of the Romantic revolution animates the zeal of the Realist; and the whole Realist urgency and pregnancy owes everything to the rebellious agonies of Romanticism, the very art whose spirituality Realism rejects.

Courbet, in this sense, is a shameless appropriator; he glories in his status as genius rebel with implied greatness of soul and monumental vision and he paints his miserable rural proletariat with a kind of majestic authority. He would undoubtedly like to think that his expressive remoteness from the poor was due to his uncompromising objectivity and dispassionate distance; but it could equally be ascribed to a natural coldness and lack of sympathy, the same kind of objectivity that allowed Stubbs to paint horses being mauled by lions and let Delacroix paint the vicious mayhem of a lion hunt. The thrill of transgression is offset by the hallowed celebration of greatness of soul, the artist's power of witnessing the sacrificial, the confession of the artist's sturdiness of spirit in relaying the truth of the victim.

The sacramental character of Romanticism is carried forward in Courbet by the further heroism of ideological conviction: the expressive prestige of his art is sacrificed to a higher social good, on account of whose strenuous requirements the artwork is agonized, denied its age-old privileges of fantasy and inventive licence, its imaginative seduction, its poetic liberties. The artwork is submitted to paradoxes and the artist is a kind of priest who proffers impossible reconcilement between aesthetic privileges and moral obligations. Art, in this sense, becomes a jealous God, subjecting its artistic mediators to agonized devotions. With Courbet, the archetype of the modern artist is born: to make the ideal of progress sacramental. From the empiricist view of the Enlightenment—to effect progress by undoing the religious tradition—the movement of socialism into art paradoxically reintroduces a mysterious element of poetic judgement in an otherwise rational domain. The severity of a materialist philosophy at some stage bends and becomes art. It is the classical moment of reinvestment of spirit, the adoption of privileges of a previously spiritualized art to serve a more skeptical and critical aesthetic order. The outward spiritual rationale is denied but the sacramental privileges are retained for the greater prestige of the new art.

ENDNOTES

1 Barbara Kruger, Australian Centre for Contemporary Art, 111 Sturt St, Southbank, 2005–2006. The following introductory text is grafted from a synchronous article in *The Age* (Nelson 2006).

2 Partly because it privileged the 'inaction' of reverie (as opposed to the 'action' of historical narrative; labour; the pursuit of knowledge), Watteau's subject-matter of idyllic love and landscapes was not accorded high status by his peers. See Cafritz (1989, 149–181); also, Plax (2000) provides an account of Watteau's artistic achievement that highlights his complicated relationship with the culture of the Royal Academy of Painting and Sculpture.

3 Giovanni Battista Piranesi, *Invenzioni Capric di Carceri all Acqua Forte* was the title of the first series of etchings featuring imaginary interiors, issued ca. 1745. The second series was a re-working of the first; titled *Carceri d'Invenzione*, it appeared in 1760, and then in its finished form in 1761. For a sustained comparison of the two series or states, see Gavuzzo-Stewart (1999), who also permits systematic comparisons of the images.

4 Francisco José de Goya y Lucientes, *Maja and Celestina on the Balcony*, 1808–1810, oil on canvas, collection of Batholomé March, Madrid; *Los Caprichos,* a set of eighty-four etchings with aquatint first published in 1799 by Goya himself; *The Third of May, 1808 (The Executions on Príncipe Pío Hill)*, 1814, oil on canvas, Museo del Prado, Madrid; *The Disasters of War*, 1810–1820 but unpublished during the artist's lifetime—the first printed edition of these eighty plates appeared in 1863, almost forty years after Goya's death.

5 Francisco José de Goya y Lucientes, *Black Paintings*, 1820–1824, oil transferred to canvas from mural, Museo del Prado, Madrid. Executed in oil on the plaster walls of the cottage known as la Quinta del Sordo, these fourteen paintings were given to the Prado Museum in 1881. See the very readable portrait of Goya and his work by Hughes (2003). See also Junquera (2003) on the matter of archival evidence for the attribution of these works.

6 Francisco José de Goya y Lucientes, *El sueño de la razón produce monstruos*, plate 43 of *Los Caprichos* (intended as the title plate), 1796–1797.

7 See Morrison (1997, 108–116).

8 See Diderot (1995).

9 Eugène Delacroix, *The Death of Sardanapalus,* 1827–1828, oil on canvas, Louvre, Paris. On the scandalized reactions and reflections that this painting provoked on being exhibited at the Paris *Salon* see Jobert (1998, 78–88), who quotes at length from contemporary documents.

10 Eugène Delacroix, *The Barque of Dante,* 1822, oil on canvas, Louvre, Paris; *Hamlet and Horatio in the Graveyard,* 1835, oil on canvas, Städelsches Kunstinstitut, Frankfurt; *Scenes from the Massacres of Chios*, 1824, oil on canvas, Louvre, Paris; *The Death of Ophelia,* 1853, oil on canvas, Louvre, Paris; *The Confession of the Giaour,* 1825–1840, oil on canvas, National Gallery of Victoria, Melbourne.

11 Théodore Géricault, *The Raft of the Medusa*, 1819, oil on canvas, Louvre, Paris. See Grimaldo Grigsby (2002, 165–235), who reads this painting in terms of the cultural politics, violences, and ambiguities of colonial contact: "And certainly Géricault's picture also redeems the raft survivors as martyrs—as victims not victimizers. What has been sublimated is the narrative of brutal sacrifice: of women, of blacks, of foreigners, of the poor ... Géricault's painting redeems the raft's survivors but it does so in terms at once more radical and more difficult than the [popular, contemporary] narrative offered by [Jean-Baptiste-Henri] Savigny and [Alexandre] Corréard" (232).

12 John Constable, *Salisbury Cathedral from the Bishop's Grounds*, ca. 1825, oil on canvas, Metropolitan Museum of Art, New York; *Salisbury Cathedral from the Bishop's Garden*, 1826, oil on canvas, Frick Collection, New York. The former is a full-scale oil study for the latter; both are amongst the numerous views of the Cathedral made by Constable during the years 1811–1829, as a result of a commission from Bishop John Fisher.

13 See Venning (2003). In its analysis of the historical context of Turner's works, Venning's monograph foregrounds the complexity and variety of the artist's *oeuvre*, in particular as a function of Turner's own conception of history.

14 Joseph Mallord William Turner, *Rain, Steam and Speed—The Great Western Railway*, before 1844, oil on canvas, National Gallery, London. See Rodner (1997).

15 See Nicholson (1990): in her study of Turner's use of mythical subjects and traditions of idealized landscape painting, Nicholson prefers the idea of "interpretive play" between narrative and other elements. "The stories [Turner] told about heroes like Regulus, about the gods and nymphs of the *Metamorphoses*, or about ancient civilizations, exalted nature's critical role in the narrative of antiquity ... The straightforward account promised by the paintings' ostensible subjects (and the titles Turner himself crafted) is inevitably complicated and enriched by the development of the imagery" (291).

16 See Adams (1997, 48–52); as well as John Constable, the author singles out painter Richard Parkes Bonington for his influence on early nineteenth-century French landscape art.

17 Gustave Courbet, *The Stonebreakers*, 1849, oil on canvas, formerly Gemäldegalerie, Dresden (destroyed 1945); *Burial at Ornans*, 1849–1850, oil on canvas, Musée d'Orsay, Paris.

18 Gustave Courbet, *Bonjour Monsieur Courbet (The Meeting)*, 1854, oil on canvas, Musée Fabre, Montpellier.

19 Gustave Courbet, *The Bathers*, 1853, oil on canvas, Musée Fabre, Montpellier.

20 Gustave Courbet, *The Artist's Studio (A Real Allegory)*, 1855, oil on canvas, Musée d'Orsay, Paris.

21 The contradictions characteristic of Courbet's approach were strongly reflected in interpretive discourse on his painting in American art criticism of the second half of the nineteenth century: see Meixner (1995, 142–193).

22 Gustave Courbet, *The Sleepers (Sleep)*, 1862, oil on canvas, Musée du Petit Palais, Paris. See Kosinski (1988, 187–199).

REFERENCES

Adams, S. 1997. "British Art and Restoration France". In *The Barbizon School and the Origins of Impressionism*. London: Phaidon. 48–52.

Cafritz, R. 1989. "Rococo Restoration of the Venetian Landscapes and Watteau's Creation of the Fête Galante". In *Places of Delight. The Pastoral Landscape*, edited by Cafritz, R.; Gowing, L.; Rosand, D. Washington: Weidenfeld and Nicolson. 149–181.

Diderot, D. 1995. *Diderot on Art,* edited and translated by Goodman, T. 2 vols. New Haven: Yale University Press.

Gavuzzo-Stewart, S. 1999. *Nelle Carceri di G. B. Piranesi*, Italian Perspectives 2. Leeds: Northern Universities Press.

Grimaldo Grigsby, D. 2002. *Extremities: Painting Empire in Post-Revolutionary France*. New Haven: Yale University Press. 165–235.

Hughes, R. 2003. *Goya*. London: Harvill.

Jobert, B. 1998. *Delacroix*, translated by Grabar, T.; Bonfante-Warren, A. Princeton, New Jersey: Princeton University Press. 78–88.

Junquera, J. 2003. *The Black Paintings of Goya*, translated by Evans, G. London: Scala Publishers Ltd.

Kosinski, D. M. 1988. "Gustave Courbet's The Sleepers: The Lesbian Image in Nineteenth-Century French Art and Literature". *Artibus et Historiae* 18: 187–199.

Meixner, L. L. 1995. "Courbet, Corot, and Democratic Poetics". In *French Realist Painting and the Critique of American Society, 1865–1900*. Cambridge: Cambridge University Press. 142–193.

Morrison, V. 1997. "The lion and the horse series". In *The Art of George Stubbs*. Sydney: Sandstone Books. 108–116.

Nelson, R. 2006. "Belligerence that silences the viewer". *The Age*. 25 January, p. 18.

Nicholson, K. 1990. *Turner's Classical Landscapes: Myth and Meaning*. Princeton, New Jersey: Princeton University Press.

Plax, J. A. 2000. *Watteau and the Cultural Politics of Eighteenth-Century France*. Cambridge: Cambridge University Press.

Rodner, W. S. 1997. *J. M. W. Turner, Romantic Painter of the Industrial Revolution*. Berkeley: University of California Press.

Smith, A. 1977. *An inquiry into the nature and causes of the wealth of nations.* Chicago. University Of Chicago Press (first published London: W. Strahan and T. Cadell, 1776).

Venning, B. 2003. *Turner*. London: Phaidon.

Cite this chapter as: Nelson, Robert. 'The industrial spirit'. *The Spirit of Secular Art: A History of the Sacramental Roots of Contemporary Artistic Values.* Melbourne: Monash University ePress. pp. 6.1–6.19. DOI: 10.2104/ssa07006.

CHAPTER 7

MECHANICAL REPRODUCTION

Robert Nelson

A film by the Luxembourg artist Antoine Prum, *Mondo veneziano*,[1] features the beautiful Italian town, captured with cameras roving majestically over the echoing courts, which are grand and intimate at the same time. This is the backdrop for two artists, a theorist and a curator to debate the fortunes of art. They meet in loggias, argue across bridges, harangue from a cherry picker, and compare notes over coffee. Each speaks from a script, full of the ingenious jargon of the high-arts press.

Venice, la Serenissima, is unsettled by the inevitable tensions of the Biennale—which seems to be imminent, as if in the air, like the damp—as the national camps assemble their agendas and try to represent them as morally or aesthetically supreme. So Prum's protagonists are identified as German, Russian and American, all countries with historical antagonisms, archaic grounds for hatred, now played out in the refined language of art debate.

Their clashing perspectives erupt, it seems, in a gory world of fantasy, where—inspired by chilly stillness and silence—they take to one another with pick, rifle, surgery and crucifixion. These acts are separated throughout the film as premeditated rituals. After the executions, the victims return as before, apparently allegorizing the cyclical and liturgical nature of sacrifices in art. The host (or slain lamb) is also the butcher and priest. Somehow you can't dismiss this film as sensational or capriciously indulgent. The production values are high, with the filming (in 35 mm) managed with exquisite light, movement of perspective, economical sound and action. The conversations are grand, urgent, impatient, smug, sardonic; and the oscillating moods of their interchange are captured with Shakespearean mixtures of humour and gravity.

In Prum's film, the world has descended on Venice with poisoned competitiveness and ruthless ambition. The global contestants extract one another's innards and eat the sacred meat of the slaughtered expressionist, the critical theorist or the situationist, to sustain the next life of art. The contribution of the one to the other is seen in sacrificial terms; and some of the dialogue invokes ritual as an integral element in art. For some of the interlocutors, the agenda is thoroughly Marxist and materialist; but it makes no difference in the end because, once in the sacred citadel of art, their behaviour is structurally identical to that of the Romantic egotist, lustful for for a redemptive killing of the order that they seek to displace. It is a great insight on Prum's part.

The artist or theorist kills the immediate source of inspiration, alienating a font of sustenance that he or she might once have absorbed. The lamb is the artist or theorist that you might have been, killed by your own hand in the hope of transcending the barriers of style, positionality and content. This reflects on a pattern that becomes increasingly common, as the artist hacks off the artificfially disowned, a part of the tradition forsworn through a pitiless impatience with limitations. The destiny of Courbet's materialism prefigured this; and the motif of ideological probity twisting itself into pious execution continues in contemporary Venice every two years, with spiritual blood-lettings on every day in the intervals.

* * *

Courbet's determination to achieve objectivity in his pictures drew him to the great new visual technology of the industrial period, photography. Many of his paintings from the middle of the nineteenth century have a photographic appearance. Some have tell-tale signs of a photographic source, such as the light in *Young Women From the Village* of 1852.[2] It is one of the earliest paintings to document the sharpness of shadows in sunlight, an effect which painters in the western tradition for the most part have studiously avoided, for the sharpness of shadows inhibits the rendering of volumes by means of tonal and chromatic gradation, for centuries the prowess of all good painters. But the camera is not informed of such niceties. It registers the shadows as sharp if the sun is out and a form is split midway over any kind of edge or even sharper curvature. Such are the characteristics in Courbet's painting: the rocks have a sedimentary stratification with many sharp edges; all the shadows fall with crisp mineral accents and the rounded fulsomeness of previous landscape is abandoned.

The same is true of the women in the picture carrying parasols. The women deliberately screen themselves from the bright sky with umbrellas; the shade which the umbrellas cast is crisp and sudden. Meanwhile, the illumination of the shaded faces is gently effected by backlighting, that is, by the flush of reflected light bouncing off the broadly lit clothes and ground. A person who is not screened from the direct glare of the sky is subject to a light-source which is unusual—even unknown—in the history of art: vertical light. If painters ever looked at forms in broad daylight they would have rejected them as unsuitable for painting. Broad daylight (which includes an overcast sky) does not flatter the beauty of the vertical human form, for it deposits shadows underneath the forms rather than to the side. There is an unceremonious dollop of shadow under the nose, a gash or an elongated hole for a mouth, and black caverns for the eye-socket, plunging the expressive magic of the eye into the gloom. The chin hugs the face from below with a beard-like wadding of shade, reaching down the neck to the clavicle; and, in the nude, the region from the bottom of the belly to the genitals is obscured by an inky mat of shadows.

Artists from the baroque to the academic tradition of the first half of the nineteenth century possessed techniques for showing light in any circumstances. They could easily have represented anything under the open sky; but they chose not to. The reason is that the human body is presented in an unflattering way when the light falls from above. When photography first began showing forms in natural light, the results would undoubtedly have seemed somewhat inartistic. It would take some time for photography to develop lighting systems (or sensitive photographic plates capable of capturing an indoor sitter in front of a window, as in baroque portraiture) to use the more oblique lighting of the tradition of painting. With the consciousness of a photograph as a careful manipulation of light and chemical treatments which purposefully represents a person or object, photography became an art. It has been honoured with that status, more or less begrudgingly, from the middle of the nineteenth century to today.[3]

At face value, photography seems a perfect expression of the materialist values of nineteenth-century progress. Photography is mechanized and saves labour. In its potentially undiscriminating attention to all visibilia, photography also reflects the free movement of money to address all goods and services regardless of their symbolic character: photography registers the shape and shade of things in a transferable way, because a camera can be pointed at a prince, a mendicant, a rat, a temple or a slum: it can show illustrious achievements, abject squalor, the erotic body and the mutilated body. It also seems more democratic than traditional media. Proficiency in photography and figurative painting requires uncommon skill and decades of training; but the prerequisites for photography (not necessarily good artistic photography) are simpler. Through a technical series of procedures, a photograph can be taken by anyone with a modicum of visual intelligence; whereas the art of figurative painting—whether academic or romantic—requires many years of diligent training. A convincing illusionistic painting takes many months to produce whereas a photograph (even counting the time setting up, shooting, developing and printing) may be produced in a lot less. A person wanting a portrait no longer had to sit for weeks in front of a painter—risking, in the result, the inaccurate or unflattering personal inflexions of the artist's inspiration, malice or ineptitude—but could now sit for an hour in the assurance that an accurate and credible result would ensue.

With its greater convenience and speed, photography seemed ready to make painting obsolete, in the same way that rail freight had made the system of barges and canals redundant. In some areas, a kind of artistic redundancy did occur; but they are fairly marginal. The most notable is miniature portrait painting. This specialization is painstakingly difficult and results in a form of art which does not enjoy enormous status, perhaps a reputation unfairly related to the size of the object, as the miniature was placed inside a pendant or locket and worn as jewellery. Furthermore, many of the qualities of painting which are most esteemed are discouraged by the tiny scale and, if nevertheless executed with vivacity and gestural strokes, the stylistic virtues are likely to remain concealed to all but experts. Meanwhile, what painting did with great inconvenience, photography did with special distinction. From the times when the resolution of photographs was not high, a miniature could be depended upon to concentrate the information to a point of great sharpness. Making things small is a task that photography can perform with particular ease. It is not surprising, therefore, that the once-flourishing art of the miniature portrait dwindled drastically in the second half of the nineteenth century, almost to the point of extinction that we know today.

For the rest, photography posed no threat to painting. Any celebratory image to hang on the wall of a public interior had to be painted. In domestic interiors, which photographs rapidly penetrated, similar points can be made in regard to placement and scale. The photograph took some time to ascend from small frames propped up on little stands upon sideboards to the greater axial address and authority of large image on wall. It is not just a question of status and snobbery. It may be related to ancestral prejudices against the 'cheapness' of the industrial image; but there are other issues of taste and sensitivity to materials which deserve sympathetic attention. First, there is a technical fact: photography did not produce pictures in colour. They were confined to black-and-white. They could be hand-coloured but the results are somewhat quaint; and the whole air of magic sophistication of the photograph is somehow undermined by an unhappy labour of colouring-in. In many instances, the results are clumsy. For example, skin tones are impossible to 'get right' unless the artist is prepared to balance warm earth colours with cool ones. It is a painter's vocation, not a photographer's. If the work of hand-colouring has such sophistication that it can comprehend the subtleties of flesh timbres, it is effectively a form of painting which negates the process and materials—the very genius—of photography. But what it takes to assemble the colours to act out the quality of the volumes leads to more fundamental aspects of the difference between photography and painting.

Second, painting confesses by gestural brushmarks the consecutive nature of its construction; and this habit of building up the surface and the illusion is congruent with all other aspects of the built environment in which the painting is situated. A house is assembled brick by brick; the floor is hammered together from separate planks resting upon joists and so on; even the apparently uniform plaster work, though smoothly evened out, is applied by consecutive actions and is subsequently worked over by careful muscular actions; and in any case, the plaster of the wall is just one articulated component between the skirtings and cornices which frame it below and above. Everything in the house is crafted by actions which follow one another. The painting on the wall belongs in its innermost conception to this order of labour and construction. Each feature is separately pored over and analysed in a perceptual link between a motif and the manipulation of the paint; everything is articulated by the brush, spelt out in a series of gestures which distinguish themselves by chromatic inflexion in order to show a certain aspect of a volume. In today's avant garde, the process of perceptual painting—as opposed to photography—is sometimes pejoratively described as fetishistic crafted mark-making; but this stigma undervalues the ceremony of perceptual recognition which a painting enacts when it enumerates the separate aspects of the spaces and volumes of its motif in a stepwise series of brushstrokes. Ideally, the brushstrokes are not exaggeratedly present for their own sake (and hence perhaps correctly charged for being reified and fetishistic) but as a trace of the stepwise figuring of the intellect as it finds its way around all the forms in a series of coherent spatial relationships. Photography, meanwhile, creates all motifs simultaneously. They are all apprehended in the same instant; and in the development and printing process, all aspects of a scene are treated with the same commitment on the surface. There is no basis for any textural variation and, if the surface were puckered by different rhythms here or there, the photograph would be considered to have been adulterated.

Third, the gestation of a painting—like its execution—is not a simultaneous affair but is rooted in a drawing process. The painter does not commence with a field (as through a viewfinder) but begins with a blank sheet of paper. A core of form develops as a notion of a motif is pursued and, especially when the motif is partly imaginary, the nascent drawing supplies the artist with the cues to grope further for the ideal form and clinch the desired purpose. There is no obvious counterpart for this organic method of developing a composition in photography. The technique in photography is essentially lens-based rather than drawing-based. Even when the photographer is assembling a constructed image (that is, a display of objects and people prearranged to form a narrative or allegory or *tableau vivant*) the square or rectangle of the camera acts as a pictorial quantum which has to be filled with motifs. Of course there are many ways partially to overcome the limits of the viewfinder. The photographer Oscar Rejlander already created a large allegory of *The Two Ways of Life* composed of several negatives.[4] But in essence, the process of photography avoids the dynamic gestation of lines in the drawing process to create a composition.

Photography as a process can be described as 'a roving rectangle in search of a motif'.[5] The camera is predisposed to see so much and no more, depending on its distance from a motif. The photographer walks around the world looking for things to put inside the rectangle, changing position to accommodate the best viewpoint, to eliminate the useless information and contain the entropic randomness of the gaze; for once you hold a camera to your eye, you notice the way that any given view defaults to visual chaos in the superabundance of available detail. The nomadic and scavenging character of photography makes for an art of great complexity; but it is essentially different from the constructed technologies of the past and, in spite of the two media sharing certain axioms of perspective, it is hardly surprising that they look very different from one another. Photography is immediately recognizable for what it is. There is very little confusion between photography and painting. A split-second glance at either will normally let you form an accurate judgement about which it is. When there is confusion about whether the art work is a painting or a photograph, it is usually the case of a painting looking like a photograph (as in the photorealist painting of the 1970s) rather than a photograph looking like a painting (with the exception of pictorialists like Edward Steichen in the early twentieth century).

It makes sense, therefore, that photography never posed a threat to painting but it did pose a threat to the media which historically anticipate it *as* mechanical reproduction, especially engraving, etching and the relatively recent art of lithography. The rationale of printmaking was mechanical reproduction, contemporary with the birth of the printed book in the Renaissance; lithography followed, appropriately, to serve the greater demand and print-runs for mass media. But even with printmaking, photography only made incursions on the drawn image *qua* journalism. Images intended for reportage would eventually be exclusively photographic; and the drawn picture, with its lesser reputation for objectivity, would—with the exception of cartoons—rapidly recede from journals and newspapers. Any images involving rhetorical exaggeration were left to the hand-drawn media, just as the case remains today in the witty genre of political cartoons. And for obvious reasons: it is not possible to manipulate photographs to the extent of cartoons, much less engage fantasy of personifications tumbling out of the sky or transforming themselves into other objects. As the rest of the tradition of hand-drawn images withdrew from the capitalist press, printmaking would paradoxically gain in prestige as an art form. The art of printmaking (not a term in use before the twentieth century) ascended to the status of high art, full of relish in fantasy and poetic imagination. Printmaking would particularly suit the literary flair of the Symbolist movement, a form of late Romanticism characterized by a self-conscious feeling of spiritual decadence in the face of mainstream materialism. The often morbid but lyrical preoccupations of the Symbolists seemed exquisitely refined and precious when impressed upon paper, the medium of poetry, which lacks assertive monumentality and classical spatial authority. But of the Symbolists more later.

Photography began its trajectory toward visual dominance when it interacted with print-media. The photograph as object upon the wall grew enormously but not to the extent of displacing painting or printmaking. The photographic portrait had great popularity but, again, not to the extent of diminishing the appeal of the painted portrait. In sheer quantity, though, the pre-eminence of photography was apparent from early times, prefiguring the situation today in which most images are generated through lenses, even if the recording of the visual information is electronic rather than chemical. Only a tiny proportion is produced manually. Painting has retained its prestige partly due to natural uniqueness, its rarity and the assumed difficulty of its production. Photographs, on the other hand, are reproducible and easy to generate. Of course certain photographs may be harder to produce than certain paintings; but let that pass.

The dichotomy of painting and photography was topical (and is still topical) not just because of the natural competitive instincts of practitioners. Artists of a certain medium have always vied with those of another medium, the most famous case being the duel between sculptors and painters during the Renaissance, a competition to which the Italians attached the name *paragone*. The contrast of photography and painting is structurally different because it is based on the historical priority of one medium, painting, whose visuality initially determined many of the aesthetic ambitions of photographic artists. The dichotomy would have been topical had there been no antagonism or chauvinism among swaggering artists. The quest for photographers was either to find an autonomous aesthetic which was in some sense unrelated to the mainstream tradition of painting or to graft a useful and artistic dimension onto a pre-existing tradition of painting, to adapt rather than to forswear. In this sense, though a photographer could be naive and know little of the painting collections in the museums, the relation between photography and painting is inherent in the profession of the new art.

Some intrepid photographers sought unusual subject matter or bizarre viewpoints which appeared (a) to create a new visuality and (b) attain the uniqueness of painting, hence perhaps artistic prestige. An example is the aerial photography of Nadar using a hot air balloon to take the photographer above ground and to bring the horizon down in the conspectus of the lens. No one had ever seen Paris represented from the air before. The old representational technologies of oil painting would not have allowed the view to be seized on a brief trip above the rooftops. The excitement of the new medium was fabulous. But for all that, the example is telling. We still admire what Nadar did and cannot deny that he helped create a new visuality.[6] But the extraordinary novelty of the vision does not automatically confer upon the image the prestige of even an ordinary landscape painting. The aerial topography of Paris is more likely to stir the soul on account of historical or archaeological information concerning architecture and town-planning than anything deeply aesthetic.

The best shots, so to speak, of photographers risked confirming what any pictorial chauvinist might have imagined about photography: that it is mechanical, a means of recording mere visual fact, a soulless exercise in lugubrious black-and-white for the visual mortification of living and lived-with objects. In spite of the excitement which attends every new and imaginative photographic image, there is a sense that *au fond* photography lacks something which the other arts have at their innermost core, namely a sacramental status, an artistic interaction with a motif by which the artist demonstrates a kind of reverent devotion, a gestural worship with carefully layered sacrificial connotations. A beautiful photograph can be taken by a total cynic; there seems nothing about that mechanical process which requires a deep inquiry into the sensory and emotional or spiritual relationship with a motif. The photographer has limited resources with which to demonstrate pious fondness for a motif; there is no caressing, no touching nor contact of any kind, no tactile homage nor caring veneration. The language of painting, with its copious repetition of patting actions, is a physical demonstration of wilful choices by which the paint submits to an active intellectual recognition of how the object looks and behaves; in its ritual dimensions, painting is powerfully celebratory. There is no corresponding physical and sacramental level in the language of photography.

Not surprisingly, many photographers took advantage of those aspects of the conventions of painting which lend themselves equally to photography. Photographic portraiture, for example, would be conceived to resemble painted portraiture. In the case of the English photographer Julia Margaret Cameron, certain sitters—such as the poet Lord Alfred Tennyson—would agree to pose in robes in order to resemble types from the tradition of painting, in Tennyson's case, a Renaissance monk.[7] In other works, she would contrive a beautiful woman and small boy to sit in Renaissance clothing in order to rehearse the archetype of Madonna and child in Renaissance painting. The beauty and seduction of such works are difficult to describe. They are sentimental but in a powerful way. From the first glimpse of Cameron's *Blessing and Blessed* (a composition of mother and son based on the Virgin and Child archetype), you are in no doubt that you are looking at a photograph and not a painting.[8] The art is not in the deception. It is another form of homage, a new act of reverence which confesses its materialism, its absence of metaphysical pretensions, its unabashed position of contemporary ordinariness and bourgeois domesticity. The photograph does not begin with a Platonic idea or sketch of a heavenly intuition but with a person and her child. You are in no doubt that you are looking at a woman of the nineteenth century and her child. The boy has a frame which had never been recognized by painters: the shoulders are relatively broad and, perhaps on account of the posture, the space between them is slightly concave across the thorax. The lozenge-like shape of the boy's head and his look of bewilderment would never have been comprehended in the art of painting. The specificity of photography is inherently unidealized. It is the opposite of the 'artificial' constructive language of painting which somehow celebrates a form even when it does not conform to stereotypical canons of beauty, as in Dutch art of the seventeenth century. Photography observes the oddness of everyone and everything. The only way to make it ideal is to enforce a rigidly exclusive determination to photograph only the world's most stereotypically beautiful models, as in the fashion photography of contemporary popular magazines. And even then, the sense of accident and incidence is impossible to expunge from the glossy page. In fact the desirable accident is zealously sought by the photographer who will spend scores of expensive medium-format film strips in order to chase a more inspired moment. But with all that, even the most successful fashion shots are not immortal images beheld in the imagination as perfect and unadulterated ideas and then translated, as if by magic, through the artist's powers of synthesis. They may be pre-conceived and staged in advance; but they are only found on the day when it appears that the model ought to whisk the head this way or that while beckoning seductively to an industrial accessory. But let us leave the unedifying visuality of the twentieth century to its proper place.

The fascination in Cameron's work is that it does not strain to produce heavenly archetypes. Through the imagination of an art-lover well versed in the construction of pictures, the heavenly archetypes are all readily available and predisposed toward a photographic outcome. Cameron has only to suggest these archetypes to her sitters and their lending of themselves to the shared idea represents something touchingly quaint and naively ritualistic. The result is something never seen in the history of art. What you witness is not the advent of a vision of the Virgin and Child—say—but the performance of two people who are trying to stage the presence of the Virgin and Child. It is the record of a cultural happening quite distinct from anything produced by a paintbrush and it is not without a sacramental dimension.

Cameron is noteworthy for several artistic qualities. In spite of the theatricality of her images, her portraits can only be described as sensitive; her sitters seem delicate and sensitive, too; and her representations of children are exquisite, perhaps because of the natural delicacy of children. The recognition of the physique and behaviour of children is a nineteenth-century achievement owing everything to photography. Children's bodies are both bonier and pudgier than adult bodies. The peculiar distribution of weight for each age group, the corresponding proportions and behaviour, are accurately registered by a patient photographer (though the photography of children is not easy!). It would be impossible to correlate the appropriate shape, look and action unless the artist performed a recording process very similar to photography. It would be an impossible research project for a painter to undertake. Besides, painters have their own ideas; they tend not to be so scrupulous about the facts but seek the expression of what they want to see. There are few incentives but major obstacles to overcome for a painter depicting children.

But Cameron's photography of children is not remarkable purely on technical grounds. It is not merely that, like other photographers such as Lewis Carroll, she has given us an accurate record of the appearance of children.[9] Her images show the special intimacy of photography, what you could call the conversational sacraments of the art. In photographing children, you have to maintain a conversation; you have to propose everything very sweetly and encourage the child to act appropriately but 'naturally' as well, not to be stiff or so self-conscious and withdrawn that the result inhibits expression. Or if the child is shy and you want to recorded it, the expression must still seem spontaneous and not a result of anxiety from the photographic session itself. The special grace of the event of formal photographic portraiture is a kind of baptism or confirmation in light and conversation.

The conversational background to photographic portraiture and allegories is arguably seen at its most sacramental in the least pious of all genres, namely erotic photography and even pornography. The ethical calibre of the art form is problematic, for there is a powerful feminist case against the exploitation of women as sex-objects in any art form; and pornography more frequently shows naked women than naked men and therefore more often serves the sexual gratification of men than women. But these scruples concerning equality should not prejudice the evaluation of a whole genre which is capable of addressing itself to sexual difference and not merely to the mainstream exploitation of women by men. For example, there are scores of explicit photographs of women spanking one another's bare bottoms with all manner of whips (*Jeux des dames cruelles*) which seem to be addressed to female fantasy rather than male fantasy. The expression of diverse sexual preferences and perversity tends to be personally titillating and socially embarrassing; but for all our concern about the correctness and taste of such imagery, it must be taken seriously as yet another dimension of the photographic proliferation of difference, resulting in the new visual expression of hitherto unacknowledged psychological conditions.

But let us not get caught up in the rightness or otherwise of pornographic extremes. Erotic photography occurs because (a) there is demand for it and (b) a photographer obtains the agreement of a model to stage his or her nakedness in front of the lens. In this ritual, the status of the model changes from the 'formal prop'—which models were in the academies, that is, beautiful or interesting specimens of flesh and bone for classical drawing—to people who have agreed to allow the lens to visit their intimacy and record the reality of their body.[10] Photography records the person not as the *idea* of a person but as the identity of the individual. Even when the face is hidden, you are conscious that the model really was there, was not an embellished figment of an artist's imagination but really did have those forms and disposed them in such a way. Erotic photography is not necessarily explicit sexually but it is always explicit about a person acting in front of a lens. A photographer can idealize with lighting and so on; but the image remains the permanent record of the light at a certain time in a studio which reflected from a specific person's body.

Photographic erotica presents itself with greater immediacy than painted or drawn erotica. You are always looking at the moment in a ritualistic sequence during which the model stripped and struck the pose. Erotic imagery often has a pretext of narrative—even something so trivial as 'taking a bath'—to make the display of flesh seem less gratuitous; but in the case of photography, the narrative does not default to the ostensible scene (whatever it is supposed to be) but is hijacked by the palpitations of the model on being exposed to the lens for all the world to see. This ritualistic performance which really did happen—unlike the bath, say—is full of erotic tension of its own and probably offers a superior erotic fantasy to any titillating confection invented by the photographer. Because the person is a specific individual, a prolonged study of the image induces you to think that you know him or her. You are implicated in the intimacy of the moment. In disrobing, the model loses all modesty and, like virginity once lost, this sacrificed modesty can never be recovered. Once the naked body is submitted to the lens, it is exposed to all gazes for posterity and can never enjoy its former chastity again. The erotic photograph is the sacrificial image of the nineteenth century.

If nineteenth-century pornographic photography seems in better taste than its twentieth-century counterparts, it is because the personal presence of the individual is somewhat dulled and abstracted by the certain knowledge that the person has been dead for a century. The individual is present in the picture but rather like a ghost, a sign of a being who once was a specific person but so long ago now that the immediacy of his or her presence is no longer felt. Now that the nakedness of the model is archaeological, the erotic thrills of staging it in front of the predatory lens acquire a secondary aesthetic dimension which paradoxically relates them to mortality and makes the sacrifice of modesty seem almost tragic. The abstraction of the model's personal presence through time is analogous to the abstraction of the model's physical presence in the process of painting.

The major effect of the new medium upon the old medium is positive rather than negative. Instead of displacing the art of painting, the new medium sought new outlets and found new subject matter or new views of old subject matter. This flowed to painting. Photography has an extraordinary poignancy in discovering sights, realities hitherto unseen by painters or anyone else. The new visuality of the photograph relates to its relative lack of interference. Viewers were confronted with the great variety of appearances in humans, interiors and outdoor scenes. The almost accidental convergence of motifs was first registered in photography, where the representation of a human would simultaneously record a bill-board, a street-light and a wagon, objects that a painter would never have included, perhaps because of their compositional complexity, perhaps because they entailed extra work in rendering them, perhaps because they were unfamiliar, perhaps just because of their contemporaneity which seemed out of place in a painting. Before long, painting of a 'conservative' kind filled up with detail.

Even painters of a staunchly classical disposition reveal the influence of the new visuality. An example is the enviably successful academician William Bouguereau, a painter of antique domestic subjects, heroic scenes, bacchanals, religious pictures and other histories.[11] Bouguereau was also inclined to a fashionable kind of allegorized portraiture, something long cultivated in painting but also seen in the photography of Julia Margaret Cameron and others. Bouguereau's figures have an unusual individuality; many of them are far from the classical ideal which the artist studied and knew well how to replicate in any circumstance. In Bouguereau there are people with big chins, large lips, darkly shaded eyes; his children have the slightly larger knees in proportion to the flesh of the thigh and shank; they have a variety of flirtatious gestures—all very correctly observed—revealing an extraordinary sympathy for the sensuality of childhood, even to the point of risking a paedophilic air. There is frequently a light source from above, which causes deep shadows in the eyes and requires backlighting to reveal the forms. Bouguereau never lets the overhead light diminish the definition of forms; his control is legendary and, perhaps as a final sign of virtuosity, he allows the flat lighting of an overcast day to inform his pictures, requiring the most masterful variations of tone and colour to spell out the volumes in the absence of a more powerfully directional light source. Strong shade is reserved for the volumes close to their edge. It is a cue directly provided by photographs, but assimilated by a painter in full command of his own medium through decades of drawing.

Bouguereau is by no means alone in adapting the photographic information and lighting. Other masters like Gerôme and Leighton, Alma-Tadema and numerous others show the influence of photography in a late classical tradition, an influence which is scarcely ever narrated in standard texts.[12] The reason for the neglect of this influence upon classical painting is that the Academy is framed by modernist art historians as fundamentally conservative, the archetype of the reactionary, the necessary antagonist of the avant garde, deeply entrenched in the habits of the past, resisting technical and iconographic progress, disavowing modernity and clutching to the discipline of drawing as the imitative basis of art. It is a grotesque distortion of the truth; for although the academic classicists remained attached to the discipline of drawing as the imitative basis of art—and very legitimately—they were by no means recreating Poussin's vision or Le Brun's vision from over a century earlier but were richly informed by the visuality of the industrial period. Their work is as much a faithful record of the values of the period as any avant-garde work.

Meanwhile, the famous cases of the influence of photography upon painting are the impressionists. The historical emphasis on the impressionists is understandable. Not only did artists like Degas, Manet, Monet, Morrisot, Pissarro and Renoir, absorb further elements of the new photographic visuality but their subject matter is accordingly contemporary. No Greeks or Romans walk their boulevards or haunt their gazebos; they are all Parisian citizens enjoying the leisure which their relatively privileged bourgeois occupations afford. For social historians, impressionist painting almost functions like photography, for it reveals what people did, how they dressed, how they related, how they paraded their children, how they interacted or adopted a certain abstracted day-dreaminess in a busy city location. The mood of a public bar or a back-stage chat among junior ballerinas is discovered and celebrated in a vivacious way that even exceeds the immediacy of photography.

The means by which the artists composed and applied their paint also owe much to photography. The famous habit of cropping a scene is perhaps the most striking. In Manet's *Boating* of 1874, for example, the sail and gunwale of the little yacht are cut off by the edge of the painting; and all attention is drawn to the insouciant couple as they are lulled by the gentle movement in a kind of trance.[13] You have a strong sense of the roving rectangle of the camera, looking from a fixed vantage point at a certain distance and seeking to fill up the available area with the optimum information. The integrity of the boat as either a form or a vessel is nigh irrelevant. The scene and the moment are 'suspended' in the arbitrary cutting of the frame, just as in a photograph. The same habit of composition can be seen in countless images by Degas and Monet and others, in which the form of a person or object is arbitrarily chopped off by the frame as either the person moves out of the frame or the object just happens to be sitting on the divide, in the manner of photography.

And just as photography records movement in a peculiar way—either catching movement 'on the hop' if the exposure is very rapid or blurring the object if the exposure is a little slower—so the paintings of the impressionists insinuate dash and scatter in the rendering of fleeting objects and people. The definition of things begins to fail. Objects and people are no longer circumscribed by a drawn delineation; they are registered as patches of colour which suggest the dynamism or elasticity of an object in movement rather than its exact volume. And even without movement, the painting allows its motifs to become indistinct on the basis that the eye does not really see a great deal of detail when it rapidly scans a scene from a distance. Testimony is found in the camera which has a limited depth of field and can only focus on objects within a certain range; and in any case, objects in the distance are weakened in their definition because of the foggy atmosphere. Painters often deliberately sought the disruption of architectonic definition by atmospheric muffling, as in Monet's studies of the *Gare St Lazare*, in which the steam of the trains clouds the clarity of the calculated forms of industrial engineering.[14]

True to the new optical cues of photography, the impressionist painters were not interested in space as such. If there is space in the viewfinder (as in a street scene), it will be registered by the general laws of perspective; but no special expression of the spatial relationship between objects is possible. The field of the camera is objective in that sense; for the film simply registers the light, not the form. It has no understanding of volume but records the intensity of light in a wholly unprejudiced and undemonstrative way. The impressionists similarly conceived their paintings in a kind of grid of unaccented brushstrokes, each registering the intensity and colour of light at a certain point in the field. They do not demonstrate, as in the baroque tradition, how the form wraps around its outline or how the shadow feels its way across a table. Everything is seen in patches, unrelated, unbiased and mobile. Painters would actively renounce their previous appreciation of 'building' the volumes in the old tradition of drawing; the drawing-knowledge would only inhibit the equality of the pitter-patter in the chromatic registration of light. Of course, by the nature of figurative painting, various items are delineated by a drawing process; but the habit of assembling form does not comply with wilful sympathy for the form but places appropriate tones and colours with 'optical disinterest', that is, professing no special interest for the spatial character of the form *per se*. The impressionists by and large disliked mixing their colours on the canvas. They did not enjoy carving one colour into another. Each stroke was independent and consecutive, not negotiable and not informed by a notion of space.

And so impressionist painting takes on a certain stylistic autonomy from the spatial order of the world. The palette was no longer arranged to provide the stable tertiary mixtures suitable for tonal modelling but was renovated in what painters call a divided palette, that is, organized as separated, relatively unmixed contrasting constellations. The picture would reflect this in its rapidity of contrasts, frequently bouncing between complementary colours and acquiring a new and impressive radiance. The architecture of things is lost but a new rhapsodic lyricism is gained. Painters often went out of their way to find spaceless motifs in order to be able to hang their paint upon it without the interference of a powerful illusion. It is the case with Monet's famous series of *Rouen Cathedral* or the *Poplars*.[15] The bulk of things is dismissed in favour of an overall tremor of chromatic patches.

But while the gestural and compositional basis of impressionism owes its 'optical disinterest' to the new visuality of photography, the resulting two-dimensional skin of contrast and complementary sparkle is a purely painterly discovery quite unrelated to the uniform film of black-and-white photography. The expression of the medium itself had never been more acute. The slapping of dabs of paint on the canvas is demonstrative; the effects of contrasting colours are emphatic and the genius of the painting as a two-dimensional surface begins to assert its autonomy. All impressionist paintings are figurative—none is abstract—yet the window has frosted: the vista is vague and heady; the enthusiasm for defining things has fallen out of the retinal project and the vivacity of atmospheric and evocative paint overtakes the expectations of spatial definition in the long tradition of western picture-making. With impressionism, painting as an autonomous rhapsodic mark-making lullaby, in hedonistic search of a neutral but lyrical pretext, has arrived. The qualities of the picture plane (the surface that you could slap with the hand) have precedence over the perceptual calibre of the illusion. And it follows that the formal qualities of the picture plane also have precedence over any symbolic or narrative characteristics. Indeed, they are inconspicuous, receding to atmospheric evocations of a loose and general kind.

Whereas Symbolist artists were at that very time constructing elaborate ciphers of psychological conditions with profound spiritual ambitions, impressionist painters were content with the ambient dab, spreading general optical happiness over the leisure haunts of the middle classes. Between the high-minded social agenda of Realism and the awesome psychological inwardness of Symbolism, the art of the impressionists seems to many viewers rather light-weight, barely serious in its seduction by sweet paint and sweet subject matter. But this criticism ignores the sacramental disposition of the movement, its devotion to an optical consciousness which functions like a hallowed screen, filtering the chaotic visual information of the industrial world into an abstracted atmospheric charm. impressionist painting may well be hedonistic and can be denounced for lacking a critical ideological basis; but its contribution to the history of ideas is to translate the potentially destructive logic of photographic visuality (the roving rectangle with fuzzing and cropping and weak spatial expression) into a discipline of chromatic arguments proper to the autonomous painted surface itself. It finds a new ideal, the ideal of painting: through the practice of registering the independent quanta of light emanating from a motif, the prestigious independence of the painting itself is asserted. A merely mechanical impulse is translated into a high aesthetic, a zone of lyrical and contemplative absorption. Never was the transformation of the mechanical to the spiritual so seamless.

On a perceptual level, impressionism lacks 'guts' but its formal flatness is congruent with a major direction of modernism in design. Especially in the last decade of the nineteenth century, graphic design emerges with an extraordinary self-confidence and commitment to its own resources. The design of advertisements and posters for most of the nineteenth century had been based on bordered windows framing illusionistic images in a context of copy (the word designers use for printed text). In the stylishness of the *fin de siècle*, the architectonic separation of these elements seemed pompous, bookish, busy and unimaginative. Popular artists and designers like Toulouse Lautrec created a whole new visuality again, running copy over images, with extensive flat local colour in all motifs, so that the images read as signs, matching the flat elements of letterforms which were crafted loosely by hand for greater agreement with the flamboyancy of the drawing. There was no architectonic sense of articulation of copy versus illustration by means of borders and so on but an organic marriage of all elements in a surface lyricism. Typically, in the case of Toulouse Lautrec, the rhapsodically freakish rhythms of the spontaneous design would support the concept being advertised, an entertainment event, a leg-show, a comic performance, extroverted, bizarre, hedonistic.[16]

The common source for the flatness of impressionism, graphic design and Symbolist painting and printmaking has sometimes been identified as Japanese prints, whose conventions did not contain the perspectival systems of western illustration. In the case of graphic design, the added factor of suitability for printing must be considered. In the case of impressionism, photography is also a factor. But in all cases, and particularly with Symbolism, the breach with the conventions of western illusionism was integral to a new claim for artistic freedom. Artists repudiated the systematic nature of illusionistic drawing; they disliked its submission to empirical reason and spatial order. They sought other pictorial effects: rhapsody in the case of impressionism, strikingness and *eclat* in the case of graphic design and inner clairvoyance in the case of Symbolism.

Symbolists are not united by a style. Some, like Gustave Moreau, had a pale academic manner; others, like Odilon Redon, seem to have deliberately weakened their drawing with incoherent combinations of bleeds, spidery lines and foul-biting; others again, like Paul Gauguin, engaged a radical language of flat local colour within cloisonnist outlines; and emotive distortion was engaged by artists like Edvard Munch. What they share is a spiritual quest to find icons of superior consciousness either in the supernatural or inner feeling and fantasy; they share a rejection of materialism and identify the impressionists with scientific positivism. The anti-empirical dimension of the movement was strongly advocated by theorists, such as Albert Aurier, who attacked the physical sciences as 'bastards' and sought art as a haven for the promotion of abstract ideas to the spiritual.[17] And on the other hand, theorists who enjoyed Realism and impressionism considered Symbolism decadent, 'a retrograde movement', in the words of Emile Zola, the eloquent champion of Manet who could not relate to the Symbolist love of riddles and enigmas.[18]

But the Symbolists were anything but retrograde. They had little interest in physical realities such as sunshine or weekend resorts or boulevards; but more than the impressionists, they redefined the role of art toward the direction of modernism: they favoured a disembodied representation of rather spaceless presences, avoiding an assertive expression of the physicality of things and invoking instead a higher order of spiritual logic by means of mystical archetypes. And with the Symbolists, the archetype of the artist becomes self-consciously spiritual but in opposition to the institutional. The artist, like his or her subject matter, was alienated, able to identify neither with the power of capital nor its materialist Marxist critique. The artist became an ideologically neutral outsider, structurally committed to the celebration of unsettling fantasy, seductive evil, the bitter power of erotic compulsion, a whole arsenal of mortal anxieties, sadism and deadly women. The movement has been seen as misogynistic but it is more than that; it is misanthropic, able to entertain only those instincts which end in the ritual undoing of people.

In dealing with mortality, the Symbolists are interested in a death by neither noble causes (such as heroes suffer in tragedy) nor accidental causes. The undoing of the human has to conspire around a principle of exotic evil; the morbidness must be insidiously engraved in the psyche in order to have the appropriately aesthetic intonation. There have never been so many sphinxes (Moreau, Knopff), Salomes (Moreau, Lévy-Dhurmer, Beardsley, von Stuck), Sirens (Klimt), Medusas (Knopff) and personifications of Death (Redon, Munch, Böcklin, Gauguin, Rops), sinister love-making (Klinger, Munch) and Sin and Perversity (von Stuck, Delville). But perhaps the major *Leitmotiv* of the culture is inner transport, the dream which shuts out external awareness and proposes the fulfilment of inner meditation, the closed eyes of reverie or the trance-like stare of the hypnotized (Moreau, Delville, Redon, Gauguin and the early Mondrian). The abstracted eyes are the simplest common sign of transcendence; but it is a transport to the spiritual which renounces conventional religion as much as it denounces the materialism of the capitalist world. The vehicle for spiritual transport is the fantasy which brings up unconscious chimeras, perhaps archaic cultural archetypes from mythology, perhaps personal figments, in all events the part of the psyche least contained by reason and least explained by science or theology or any traditional academic discipline. The *via regia* to the unconscious for Symbolist artists is obsession. It is the culture from which Freud emerged in Vienna at the end of the nineteenth century, already publishing *The Interpretation of Dreams* (*Die Traumdeutung*) in 1900.

But the genius of Freud was to place such expressions of the unconscious in the framework of the dominant empirical materialism of science, to see psychological processes in a material economy of dynamic forces and energies.[19] That is a whole further story. The symbolists did not go so far and would never have exchanged their artistic birthright—that priestly claim to spiritual clairvoyance—for a tough materialism which ultimately discredits the spiritual pretensions of art and religion. Apart from reservations by skeptics like Zola, Symbolist artists were positioned exactly where they wanted to be: the inheritors of the privilege of spiritual transcendence, proprietors of intimate and immediate contact with mythical archetypes, irresponsible songsters of obsession, prophets of terminal introversion, indulging in pessimism and the spectacle of evil with aesthetic relish.

More than any of the artistic movements of the nineteenth century, the Symbolists mark the critical stage in the subservience of the spiritual to the aesthetic which forms the egocentric basis of modernism. Symbolism is a movement which submits all institutional aspects of the spiritual—developed prehistorically in myth and encoded through liturgy and sacrifice—to personal fancy larded with an artistic rhetoric of inner depth. The aspirations for art to transcend this nasty material world and reach a plane of higher consciousness were undoubtedly genuine; and the vocation of art as an other worldliness and spiritual seduction was not normally professed in bad faith. But in the process of cultivating the higher symbolic levels, a conflation of spiritual powers was uncritically induced upon art; and the art whose aesthetic was not informed by a host of spiritual conceits seemed merely decorative or mechanical.

Ironically, the other-worldly aspirations of symbolism licenced a range of styles which were highly decorative, because suggesting the ether, the vaporous *au delà*, the vague depths; drawing was pursued for its rhythmic character rather than analysis; spaces dissolve and the discipline of constructing volumes flagged amid rhapsodic transports. Many visual clichés arose and were obviously regarded as very stylish. The other-worldly aspirations of symbolism also explain how colour came to be applied in arbitrary zones, achieving an almost autonomous presence as a single entity rather than an integral component of the perceptual description of a volume. Arbitrary colour—referred to later as the liberation of colour—was assigned to parts of an image because of the intrinsic symbolic value imputed to the colour; for the feeling among artists like Gauguin was that colour, by its own associations, could suggest concepts around a motif, hence adding both to the supposed symbolic argument and to the strange other-worldly appearance of the work.[20]

When the spiritual passes so inextricably into the aesthetic it gains a new inscrutability. Any claims can be made for the spiritual intentions and calibre of a work and they can never be referred to the authority of tradition; for symbols are used intuitively and there is no external authority for their correctness. Any reasoning is self-referential and contained in the work; but the work is contrived so as not to yield an obvious interpretation (for it is not structured upon a coherent vision shared by anyone beyond the artist) but to constitute a mystery. The intention, in fact, is to create mystery. Symbolism is not an art by which painters use symbols to denote qualities—as in the Renaissance—but to relish the enigmatic resonance of the symbols and archetypes which the semiotic patrimony leaves at their disposal.

The artist does not have a good idea of the meaning of the work; the spectator does not know what the work adds up to; but, as their common hope is to be seduced by mystery, the hermetic insularity of the project is very functional. It is better that the work is wholly ambiguous, for then it can be a receptacle for abstracted spirituality, that is, a spirituality without shared belief. The aesthetic of enigmas was the great commodity of the unauthorized spirituality of the end of the nineteenth century. In the severe face of materialism, poets and intellectuals wanted to believe in a spiritual dimension of existence; but the spiritual authorities of the past had lost persuasiveness and could not supply the necessary faith. The peregrine spirituality of the age had to be aestheticized and free; it could support nothing dogmatic but anything mysterious in its open-endedness. The picture which aims to seduce by invoking spiritual ghosts, not to bring them back to life but to subsume their archaic potency within a rhapsodic aesthetic, is the last sacrament of art in the nineteenth century. It sets up the structural paradigm of art in the age of modernism.

ENDNOTES

1 Exhibited in the Venice Biennale, 2005, of 30 minutes duration. The introductory paragraphs are grafted from my article "Brilliant Fantasy Worlds Capture Travesties in Motion" (Nelson 2007).

2 Gustave Courbet, *Young Women From the Village*, 1852, oil on canvas, Metropolitan Museum of Art, New York.

3 See the catalogue entry by Childs (1999, 25–33), a lucid survey of the begrudging and other attitudes to photography amongst painters and artists from the year 1839 (when the new medium of photography was made accessible to the public), and through the nineteenth century.

4 Oscar Rejlander, *The Two Ways of Life*, 1857, albumen print, George Eastman House, Rochester, NY. For an excellent technical account of Rejlander's combination print, and the allegorical content of the resultant *tableau*, see Crawford (1979, 53–56).

5 Personal communication from my friend and colleague at Monash University, Geoffrey Dupree.

6 See the account of Nadar's achievement that links his documentary photographs of Paris with the modernity's cults of the city and of death, in Rice (1988, 156–171).

7 Julia Margaret Cameron, *Alfred Tennyson*, 1865, albumen print, Overstone Album, J. Paul Getty Museum, Los Angeles. For the range and variety of Cameron's portrait studies of Tennyson, see Cox and Ford (2003, 354–358). Amongst the artist's male subjects, the portrait painter George Frederic Watts and the poet laureate "are in many ways Cameron's most important sitters" (291).

8 Julia Margaret Cameron, *Blessing and Blessed*, 1865, albumen print, Overstone Album, J. Paul Getty Museum, Los Angeles.

9 On the concept and cult of childhood as rendered in the photographs of Lewis Carroll (Charles Dodgson), see Nickel (2002, 55–72). Produced to a high quality, this exhibition catalogue includes individual commentaries for each of the plates reproduced.

10 Certainly this distinction regarding the status of the model is also a matter of the frame and context bestowed on the image. From an art-historical perspective, see, for example, Garb (1998, 54–79), whose study was well attuned to ways in which the photographs in the early twentieth-century French monthly *La Culture Physique*, and other magazines, could simultaneously serve those formal, aesthetic purposes associated with academic art, and a wider audience for erotic nude photography. See also McCauley (1994, 105–194).

11 For an overview of Bouguereau's career, see the catalogue of the important Bouguereau exhibition of 1984–1985 organized by the Montreal Museum of Fine Art (d'Argencourt et al. 1984).

12 On Alma-Tadema's extensive photographic archive, see Pohlmann (1996, 111–124). As well demonstrated by this catalogue, more recently, art museums themselves have helped to motivate a serious re-appraisal of nineteenth-century classical painters and their vast bodies of work.

13 Édouard Manet, *Boating*, 1874, oil on canvas, Metropolitan Museum of Art, New York.

14 See J. Wilson-Bareau, *Manet, Monet, and the Gare Saint-Lazare* (Washington and New Haven, 1998).

15 Claude Monet painted over thirty canvases of the façade of Rouen Cathedral during the 1890s. The following examples all pertain to the collection of the Musée d'Orsay, Paris: *The Portal (Grey Weather)*, 1894, oil on canvas; *Rouen Cathedral (The Portal and the Tour d'Albane, Morning Effect)*, 1894, oil on canvas; *Rouen Cathedral (The Portal, Harmony in Blue)*, 1894, oil on canvas; *Rouen Cathedral (The Portal and the Tour d'Albane in the Sunlight)*, 1894, oil on canvas.

16 Bunbury (2004, 35–39) gives a compact discussion of the Parisian cafés-concerts 'scene' as stimulus to Toulouse-Lautrec's style, in the exhibition catalogue *From Paris With Love: The Graphic Arts in France 1880s–1950s*.

17 A nuanced characterization of attitudes and trends in late nineteenth-century symbolist art criticism can be found in Marlais (1992).

18 Emile Zola's essay "Une nouvelle manière en peinture: Edouard Manet," was first published in the *Revue du dix-neuvième siècle* on January 1, 1867. For an analysis of this text, and of its role in shaping subsequent art historical treatments of Manet's modernism, see Armstrong (2002, 31–47).

19 See Gamwell (2000, 13–25). This exhibition and book project on the realm of dreams as a source for twentieth-century science and art was undertaken to commemorate the centennial of the publication of Freud's now classic work.

20 The French painter, designer, and writer Maurice Denis theorized the Symbolist movement in its own day; in 1890 he published an article that became a manifesto for Symbolism. It opened with the following resonant claim: "Remember that a painting—before being a charger, a nude woman, or one anecdote or another—is essentially a flat surface covered with colours assembled in a certain order." See Clement (1996, 443–444, 471).

REFERENCES

d'Argencourt, L., in collaboration with Walker, M. S. 1984. *William Bouguereau, 1825–1905*. Montreal: Montreal Museum Of Fine Arts. [Exhibition catalogue.]

Armstrong, C. 2002. "A New Manner in Painting: Emile Zola on Manet". In *Manet Manette*. New Haven: Yale University Press. 31–47.

Bunbury, A. 2004. *From Paris With Love: The Graphic Arts in France 1880s–1950s*. Melbourne: National Gallery of Victoria. [Exhibition catalogue.]

Childs, E. C. 1999. "The Photographic Muse". In *The Artist and the Camera- Degas to Picasso*, edited by Kosinski, D. New Haven: Yale University Press. 25–33. [Exhibition catalogue.]

Clement, R. T. 1996. *Four French Symbolists: A Sourcebook on Pierre Puvis de Chavannes, Gustave Moreau, Odilon Redon, and Maurice Denis*. Art Reference Collection 20. Westport, Connecticut: Greenwood Press.

Cox J.; Ford, C. 2003. *Julia Margaret Cameron: The Complete Photographs*. Los Angeles: Getty Trust Publications, J. Paul Getty Museum.

Crawford, W. 1979. *The Keepers of Light; A History and Working Guide to Early Photographic Processes*. Dobbs Ferry, New York: Morgan and Morgan.

Gamwell, L., ed. 2000. *Dreams 1900–2000: Science, Art, and the Unconscious Mind*. Cornell Studies in the History of Psychiatry. Binghamton: Cornell University Press.

Garb, T. 1998. "Modelling the Male Body: Physical Culture, Photography and the Classical Ideal". In *Bodies of Modernity: Figure and Flesh in Fin-de-Siècle France*. London: Thames & Hudson Ltd. 54–79.

McCauley, E. A. 1994. "Braquehais and the Photographic Nude". In *Industrial Madness: Commercial Photography in Paris, 1848–1871*. New Haven: Yale University Press. 105–194.

Marlais, M. A. 1992. *Conservative Echoes in Fin-de-Siècle Parisian Art Criticism*. University Park, Pennsylvania: Pennsylvania State University Press.

Nelson, R. 2007. "Brilliant Fantasy Worlds Capture Travesties in Motion". *The Age*. 30 May, p. 17.

Nickel, D. R. 2002. "Ducks That Lie in Tempests". In *Dreaming in Pictures: The Photography of Lewis Carroll*. New Haven: Yale University Press. 55–72.

Pohlmann, U. 1996. "Alma-Tadema and Photography". In *Sir Lawrence Alma-Tadema 1836–1912*, edited by Becker E., et al. New York: Rizzoli. 111–124.

Rice, S. 1988. "Souvenirs". *Art in America* 76: 156–171.

Zola, E. 1867. "Une nouvelle manière en peinture: Edouard Manet". *Revue du dix-neuvième siècle*, 1 January.

Cite this chapter as: Nelson, Robert. 'Mechanical reproduction'. *The Spirit of Secular Art: A History of the Sacramental Roots of Contemporary Artistic Values.* Melbourne: Monash University ePress. pp. 7.1–7.17. DOI: 10.2104/ssa07007.

CHAPTER 8

THE NEW AND THE TRUE

Robert Nelson

Modernism arose out of impatience and grew into orthodoxy with bewildering speed. It is most easily understood as an outgrowth of Romanticism, the ongoing and forever-incomplete critique of the Englightenment. For according to all poetic views of economic and technological progress at the end of the nineteenth century, civilization was more than ever in need of a great intellectual cleansing and artistic insurgency to overthrow the dominance of the prevailing mechanistic paradigms of reason. Part of the basis for our affection for modernism is its inspired virulence, its often self-declared revolutionary spirit, seeking unabashedly to destroy and replace, to abolish and efface, to create a new world free of the rules of the old world. If you think of the authoritarian norms of the epoch, the modernist zeal is beguiling and infectious. It freshly valorizes, for example, the art of children, the idea that an energetic and pleasurable expressive process is more important than a polished result with learned literary connotations; it championed the motif of spontaneity and the creative spirit in a given person which reflects his or her unique subjectivity. The denunciation of canonical aesthetics worked decisively in favour of the individual and what grows organically within his or her consciousness as opposed to an institutional aesthetics.

Consequently, everyone was a modernist for his or her own reasons. Some modernists sought new rules for themselves; others wanted to find freedom from all systems, all systematic thought and prescribed ways of looking or methods of constructing the world. It is impossible to sum up the diversity of approaches and it will have to suffice to offer a number of instances. But from our point of view, the grounds for modernism among its revolutionary and inspired instigators are less important than the way modernism was subsequently understood, or even understood from its first apologists. For in that larger framework of interpretation, the project of modernism is to make stylistic innovation a symbol of spiritual improvement. The basis for this is not naïve, even though style is not a primary motive, say, in the art of Cézanne, to whom special attention should be directed. But the primacy of style as the historical hallmark of modernism is central to most texts and is most eloquently and authoritatively summed up by the eminent Australian art historian, Bernard Smith, who characterizes modernism as a late nineteenth-century period style—which he calls the formalesque—that flourished throughout the first half of the twentieth century.[1]

The peculiar kind of reaction that was modernism has a stylistic expression, even though it sometimes proceeded from enlightened spiritual motives and occasionally social motives, as with the Bauhaus or Constructivism. Modernism is not a reaction against the triumph of the industrial. Modernists were keen to address themselves to the terms of modern life in its newness: they sought the refreshment of novelty in exaggerated colour and proportions in their representations; they often enjoyed the intrusiveness of the rapid pace of industrial life, the disrupted views and disjointed rhythms; they often relished the bizarre and unseasonal growth of capital cities, the fabulousness of huge design projects in steel (such as bridges and the Eiffel Tower) and they sought, above all, to internalize such novelties into the stylistic manipulation of the media of art.

It was not possible to be a modernist simply by representing accurately the new and exciting physical structures around you. It was necessary to reflect something of their impact, especially through artistic process. A realistic rendering of a bridge would not have conveyed sufficiently the power of the structure as a symbol of progress. Such a representation may show off the engineering better than a modernist representation, with all its distortion and exaggeration; but, as a symbol of progress, the power of the structure would have to be celebrated as transcending its material construction. The modernist treatment of the bridge (or whatever) would have to rehearse, in the technique and drama of the painting process, the disruptiveness and unseasonal energy of the motif.

This is already true of work by Seurat and Signac toward the end of the nineteenth century. The scientific appreciation of a given tertiary colour is 'analysed' on the canvas in small dots of pure primary and secondary colour, mingling on the retina to produce a bristling synthetic version of the colour found on the motif. Any sense of newness conveyed in their subject matter—such as factories, entertainment venues or gasometers—is dramatized by the 'systematic strangeness' of the painting technique. For that reason, modernist pictures are often indeed systematically strange: they indirectly reflect in the internal celebration of their technique the oxymoronic organized chaos of the modern world relative to the stable and eternal perspectives of the premodern world. The spectacle of modern life is both regular and bizarre, with its airs of ritual and stiff performative routine, interrupted by the crazy assembly of outrageous gestures, high jumps from the trapeze and high kicks, dramatized in the pointillist application, which is controlled yet manic, illusionistic yet artificial, scientific yet synthetic. These paradoxes poetically match the balance of authority and impulse in the free bourgeois economy or regattas, leg-shows, circuses and parks. The little modern tradition running from the neo-impressionists to the cubists and on to various kinds of geometric abstraction reflects the will of artists to embrace the newness of their world in a superpictorial dimension.[2]

In the middle of the nineteenth century, the poet Baudelaire exhorted artists to paint from modern life, a famous cliché which prophetically signalled the forthcoming fascination of artists by modernity. But the enthusiasm for modern life is not the whole reason for modernism. In fact, when it comes to iconography, the bulk of modernist painting and sculpture is not about modern life at all, nor is the work of most of their immediate radical predecessors. Impressionism is certainly about modern life and the post-impressionists Seurat and Signac share the enthusiasm; but other post-impressionists have only a co-incidental involvement with the iconic novelties of public and private ritual. When Van Gogh paints a mental asylum, he does not mean to comment on contemporary medical institutions or the pathology of certain social disorders of the industrial age. Insofar as he means the motif to convey a message beyond the demonstrative muscular process of painting, it is rather to express his internal anxieties, appropriately sited in the place where he is being treated.

When Gauguin represents the peasants in Brittany or the Indigenous inhabitants of Tahiti he inadvertently confesses a peculiarly colonial malaise, much heightened by the capitalist prowess of the industrial period, namely the exoticizing of the inferior Other, the ethnicity or group which is the marginal opposite to the dominant order of cosmopolitan western society. As with Romanticism, the consciousness of modern life is registered only by reaction. Factories and newspapers and hoardings which increasingly define the visuality of the modern world do not feature. Fantasies of a more primitive spirituality fill Gauguin's pictures. He travels to places supposedly uninformed by western sophistication—a cultural asylum which is in itself a sophisticated western myth—and produces pictures which deflect the pictorial expectations of the western tradition of illusionism. Like Van Gogh and Munch, Gauguin is a symbolist. He is not interested in the physical appearances of things but the realm of ideas and spirit, not properly capable of being comprehended by objects but for which objects, extrapolated by chromatic lyricism, could provide cues.

The more avant-garde the symbolist, the less the expression takes place in the subject matter and the more the subject matter is subsumed by the style. Rodin, for example, commits very few radical innovations in subject matter but he alters the formal character of sculpture and consequently the way the three-dimensional art functions as a monument. Rodin does not create statues but sculptures: a new purity and spatial autonomy enters as he gives his works an organic pulsing give-and-take in their texture which celebrates the process of execution but resists the statuesque authority of an architectonic plinth of many horizontal bevels and chamfers. For two thousand years, sculpture had enjoyed a haughty partnership with architecture but, with Rodin, sculpture and design part company. Sculpture moves from its status of landmark to self-sufficient artwork: it is no longer intended to act as a focus of a designed environment but rather occupies an art-space, projecting the work as an autonomous artistic conception.

Tellingly, the contribution which Rodin does make to the history of iconography can also be interpreted as a stylistic innovation. He casts bronzes in a fragmentary representation of the body, creating works such as his *Walking Man* which deliberately has neither head nor arms.[3] The figure lacks corporal completeness not in order to symbolize humanity without brain or manual skills—nor even to show the 'essence' of the figure without incidental encumbrances such as the upper limbs—but in order to express more urgently the presence of the medium and the heroism of the artist's command of it. By subtracting from the anatomical wholeness of the standing figure (that is a person with a face and gestural faculties) the bronze itself emerges as the subject matter. This promotion of the medium is not a simple case of formalism displacing iconographic meaning. The figure is still a necessary force to confer iconic might upon the artist's conception. The sculpture stages the submission of the heroic figure to the mark-making gestures of the artist. The iconography of the figure is essential in this ritual and is by no means marginal. The formidable elements of the figure, the virile looking legs and torso, lend themselves to the heroization of the interventionist plasticity, the conspicuous manipulation of the medium and the artist's stylistic boldness.[4]

The radical does not need new iconography but less iconography. It wants the old subject matter but with less iconographic independence; for the objects depicted must submit their simple and inalienable presence to a celebratory stylistic conquest. The basic symbolic virtues of subject matter are thus arrogated by style; you have the forceful presence of a motif but stripped of its independent function. The radical wants to reduce the information in subject matter to certain archetypical signs, a demotion in favour of the stylistic presence, a gestural or compulsive intervention which (a) overcomes the subject matter with formal rhetoric and (b) draws from the archaic potency of the subject matter to express the heroism of the stylistic innovation. The new stylistic mysteries have no need of new subject matter. The idea that Rodin might draw inspiration from the radically new metal shapes appearing throughout the factories of the western world would have been naïve: art is concerned with its own mysteries, not the marvels of a material reality to which it would have to defer and submissively offer illustrative celebrations.

Nor does the industrial iconography of the modern world infiltrate the radical pictures of Cézanne from the last decades of the nineteenth century. His subject matter—and to some extent even his technique—would set the parameters of the full-blown modernist movement, cubism: still life, portraiture and landscape, all of a somewhat neutral and inexpressive character. When Cézanne paints landscape, he avoids atmospheric effects, disliking either bright sunshine or storms and rain. The view he selects will normally have no sudden precipice or magically picturesque character but seems a relatively dull vista to be viewed from a withdrawn, inconspicuous platform. For Cézanne, the emotive associations with which landscapes are generally loaded are non-pictorial elements particularly to be shunned. When Cézanne paints people, they are seated impassively and have no impressive gaze or posture and no discernible nature. When he paints still life, the results have no suggestion of wealth, ritual or family life.

To the uncommunicative isolation of his subject matter Cézanne adds the systematic plasticity of his pictorial process. Cézanne avoids all the bright colours which had been fashionable in impressionist painters and were elevated to lyrical heights among fellow post-impressionists. He resists the gesture of a florid brushstroke for inflecting a characteristic feature of a motif and instead evenly chips away at his surface so that a tree, a cloud, a mountain or a patch of water all have a congruent gestural accent: leaf, trunk, land-mass, vapour, sky, liquid are all accorded an analogous emphasis. If Cézanne paints a peach, its texture will be negligibly different from that of a jug. It is only by association that you infer the furriness of the peach relative to the ceramic glaze of the jug.

These symbolically sombre traits are neither due to laziness nor inadvertence. In the best sense of the word, Cézanne's pictures are laboured and, in spite of the sometimes undifferentiated angular brushstrokes, the pictures are by no means dashed off. If anything, they seem almost overworked with a kind of oxymoronic 'violent deliberation', as you imagine the canvas submitting to days of warfare, with countless revisions in every quarter. The communicative limitations have to be construed as intentional. They can all be referred to one further characteristic of the pictures which might also seem a fault but which appears similarly purposeful and doggedly prosecuted. In spite of all the volume given to each object, Cézanne denies perspectival space. The purposefulness of this contradiction can be seen when he inclines the lip of a jug or bowl so that it no longer aligns with the horizontal plane of the table-top.

The most common explanation is that Cézanne aims to register the forms in front of him without sacrificing the integrity of the picture plane. At the close of the nineteenth century, academic drawing had prescriptively codified the artist's way of looking. The draughtsperson looked at a central motif through an implicit perspectival grid that defined the diminution of all things according to their distance from the eye. Since Alberti, this idea had proved expedient and was never challenged, for its self-evident systematic logic and consistency. But for Cézanne, this geometric paradigm apparently denied the key elements of both perception and painting. Using perspective to bore a hole in the picture plane adversely affects the compositional rigour of the work. The preoccupation to describe or mimic spatial recession neglects the fundamental organization of the picture plane.

But for Cézanne, the sin against perception is undoubtedly the greater. Perception intrinsically does not arrive at once, with all rays striking the retina—and hence arriving in consciousness—simultaneously, as of the sixtieth of a second in photography. Rather, perception is an experience, an organic process by which the eye directs itself to fathom the space according to its intelligence.

The eye looks, adjusts its lens and shutter but above all its field in countless movements for every glance. Perception is thus essentially motile, a logical scrambling for the links in light and space; and to the spatial organization of the world, you must therefore add time, for it takes the duration of cerebral activity, ocular scanning, focus and triangulation. For a painter, this is greatly heightened, for it is necessary not just to glimpse nature (or whatever motif) but to understand its spaces, its incidental accommodation of light and shadow and its fundamental forms.

Cézanne builds his images without any implicit perspectival grid, much less photography or any other mechanistic system. His works express the experience—the subjective activity which yields consciousness—of seeing a motif. Cézanne follows multiple pathways over, across, in and around the spaces, allowing equal weight to object and background (or space itself). And because he does this with unswerving concentration and energy, the works express the subjective immediacy of perception. In its vigour and spatial logic, Cézanne's work celebrates visual perception as something dynamic, binocular, somatic, elastic and intelligent, not automatic or mechanical as you might assume from photographic processes or even perspectival systems. A whole arsenal of perspectival contrivances had been available for generations; but, as clever as they may be, they falsify the analogue experience of seeing and they offend the subjectivity which lies at the basis of consciousness, visual and otherwise. When it comes to registering the somatic impulses of seeing and responding, the perceptual painter rejects such systems.

Cézanne's vision favours a fragmented space in which objects cohere with the picture plane rather than with pictorial illusion. The objects have a relationship with one another; but it is a compositional relationship, not a perspectival relationship. There is not much space in a Cézanne painting. Meanwhile, there is a sense of colossal volume in the objects occupying the picture. The angular brushstrokes demonstratively celebrate the roundness of things. An apple has a volumetric rigour, a carved solidity, which dramatizes the perception of its shape and gives it an almost geological presence. The presence of objects in Cézanne is unprecedented in the way the brush dynamically articulates volumetric change and, with appropriate tones and colour, forcefully acts out the arrangement of planes. But with all that 'staggering' volume, there is no space, no vista with fixed viewpoint, no predictable platform, no perspectival clarity. Cézanne's relationship with objects is a form of groping rather than a form of optics.

Cézanne effectively confounds space. Apart from the obvious unity of treatment of all parts, Cézanne also engages compositional liaisons to flatten out the pictorial space. In landscapes, he sometimes negates perspectival space by running a tree across foreground, middle distance and background, so that they are all in some sense equated. In still life, he unites all the planes by lifting the point of view to such a gradient that most of the painting fills up with the folds of a tablecloth or the clutter of the surface, so that the architecture of the motif is not traceable. Part of the difficulty which he undoubtedly experienced in painting his pictures—what with their chiselled brushstrokes leaving demonstrative tracks of all internal negotiations—would have been the decision to show volume but no illusionistic space. His mission is to paint a contradiction.

This ambition is consistent with the desire to follow perception in its inscrutable organic closeness with time and experience; but the resolution must nevertheless have struck any traditional artist as perverse. A portrait or a still-life would be much easier to produce with all the volumes sitting in a coherent perspectival space, optically correct and well-drawn; because, given practice and talent in the exercise (which artists at the time possessed in abundance), the artist knows exactly where to put things according to perspective. In abandoning the secure and orderly link between volume and perspectival space, Cézanne determines to make his pictures subjectively agonized, a process of sorting out chaotic impulses in beholding—and subsequently forming—the objects before him. His style (to return to Bernard Smith's critical term) allegorizes the process of seeing and painting when one has no communicative reason to paint beyond one's subjective perceptual experience, which is part of the act of painting itself.[5] The will to paint is to constitute a discipline unto itself, a discipline of solving pictorial contradictions that reflect consciousness, spatial incongruities that arise through seeing in time, which can only be handled when no other expressive issue arises in the picture, such as narrative, symbolism or even atmosphere. Even the time of day in Cézanne is suppressed, so that light can come from the east as much as the west. And that is why Cézanne's style is paradoxically resolute. It is a discipline of being wilfully disturbed, a routine of grappling with irreconcilable formal demands and reaching the purity of the means of painting by focusing on nothing but a kind of pictorial impossibility.

No one else at the time painted as Cézanne did; but his unusual and perversely compulsive ambition is not merely a historical and anal eccentricity. It matches the extension of other movements and anticipates a number of directions which extend from Cézanne, such as cubism. Painting as paradox, as aesthetic tension between a motif and a style which refuses to dignify the motif with perspectival continuity but instead fragments motifs in order to chase the motile character of perception or, as in cubism (which largely abandons Cézanne's perceptual concerns), to enjoy a bizarre formal franchise with the picture plane: this is the introverted strategy of early modernism (fauvism, cubism and German expressionism) prior to the abstraction of figures like Mondrian and Malevich. Here, there is nothing to paint for a communicative purpose. The radical innovations in the styles of representation involve no iconographic developments but a kind of communicative mortification of the old subject matter which had been passed down by tradition. You take a bay with yachts, a hill with houses, a window, a static person, a jug or violin—things of almost arbitrary familiarity—and challenge their visual presence with chromatic or spatial hyperbole, outlandish effects with which you then have to wrestle in order to retain a suitably inexplicable relationship with the motif. The new aesthetic depends on the inscrutability of purposes in attaching either exaggerated colour or dislocating planes to the motif. After Cézanne, there is no longer a consciously perceptual basis for the stylistic extravagance of the avant garde; for then the whole project would default to a communicative phenomenological celebration of the nature and feel of things, and there would be no self-referential agony, no tension in the picture between fierce pictorial means and detached subject matter. The painting must be consumed by its own intransigence.

It is not just classical space which is abandoned in the course of early modernism but the classical link between style and iconography. In the past, artists frequently sought a stylistic emphasis which added a meaningful formal inflexion on the subject matter and added an evocative dimension. It is the case throughout Romanticism and can be seen at its most stressful in Van Gogh. The hefty commitment and occasional brutality of Van Gogh's brushstroke are a consistent cipher of the psychological and communicative interest which the artist found in the motifs. The tree or Church or star-lit sky with writhing cypresses become more expressive on account of the obsessive exaggerations in the application of the medium. The paintings seem to cry out with a stylistic menace which matches the awesome imbalance of the subject matter. And even when the subject matter is neutral in associations—which is infrequent in the work of the

Dutch symbolist—the style induces a mood upon it which charges the work with communicative zeal.

Since it was identified as a phenomenon by art historians, modernism has had a linear genealogy assigned to it. It is a common understanding that various kinds of modernism simply extended the exaggerations of post-impressionist artists like Munch and Van Gogh. Instead of the little vermiculated bricks of colour put down by Van Gogh, the expressionists relished a still broader application of large slabs and slashes. It is as if Van Gogh's brushstrokes 'grew into' or matured into the unrestrained patches and scruffy dashes of the expressionists. This paradigm of an organic development between post-impressionism and modernism insinuates a historical necessity on the modernist project; for it is seen as a fulfilment of the campaign against the traditional academy: colour is liberated and the brushstroke is freed of all conventional restraints. This interpretation is misleading; for it accords the expressive purposes of certain post-impressionists upon the modernists who succeeded them. Of course there is some dependence of each generation upon the previous generation but modernists do not inherit the expressive agendas of Van Gogh or Munch. Modernism frequently avoids direct communication and expresses a process rather than a feeling: the cold aesthetic shadow-boxing of formalism in innovatively skew relationships with a motif. Emotional expression has little place in it.

The signal case of this is German expressionism. Paintings by the artists of *Die Brücke*, Kirchner, Heckel, Nolde and Schmidt-Rottluff, have a rawness and intensity of formal clashes which distinguish them from the already daring boldness of French expressionism or fauvism. But whereas it could be argued that the fauves from 1905–07 (Matisse, Derain, Vlaminck) sought to express the lyrical pleasure of the Midi, it is impossible to identify an expressive counterpart among the Germans. The technique of these artists seems very expressive and earned them the title of expressionists; but the reason they are modernists is that they have nothing in particular to express. A face showing an open mouth by a German expressionist cannot be judged an expression of anguish any more than an expression of joy. The fierceness of the colour and the summariness of the execution seem expressive *per se*; but you can never declare simply by looking at the picture which emotion they express. The same is true of street and outdoor scenes (such as Schmidt-Rottluff's *Red Tower in the Park*.[6] The houses and land, roadway and sky are assembled in the roughest possible manner, with no care taken to have patches of colour meet at an edge without the naked canvas showing through. The colours are dissonant and the composition equally raucous. It all seems very turbulent and ferocious; but there is no single emotion to which the turbulence and ferocity commit themselves: it could be a wild emotional condition associated with claustrophobia or schizophrenia or the positive celebration of freedom. And finally, the nude: almost any example by Kirchner will reveal distortions of anatomy which, when combined with the same reckless technique, suggest an emotional torment.[7] But again, it is impossible to identify the emotion as crippling anxiety or sexual bliss. And if these opposites cannot be distinguished, the emotional impact is somehow not the point. There is an exaggerated emotive emphasis in the treatment of the scene but a wholly ambiguous communicative result. You have the emotional means but not the emotional outcome. The expression is there as rhetoric but not as impact. By forcing the emotional expectations and yet supplying so little satisfaction, the project amounts to a paradoxical negation of expression.

The only way to save the emotional expression of German expressionism is to posit the existence of a new modern emotion, an emotion proper to art and to no other realm of existence. Emotions are never general; but the *art emotion* is different from other emotions in that it is not specific. All other emotions are specific, even if they are not exclusive: the reason you know the feeling of joy is that it distinguishes itself from fear or pain or dread or hate or what have you. That is not to say that joy cannot be mixed with other emotions—such as the analogous emotions of love and hope and so on—and even to be somewhat confused with contrary emotions; but ultimately the emotion experienced is a single condition of feeling which has an integrity proper to the moment of feeling it, even if the words are diverse in its definition. Hence the great privilege of painting and the other visual arts is especially precious because they do not need words to clinch that peculiar constellation of feelings. But that is the point: each emotional state, regardless of its composition or causes, is peculiar. German expressionism gives you an emotion that is not peculiar but is an indiscriminate amalgam of indecipherable opposites. The essence of the new art emotion is its lack of uniqueness and consequently a defiance on the natural integrity of an emotional state. It is an abstracted symbol of the power of emotion, but quite without any emotional power of its own.

With the German expressionists, art is not primarily about an emotional exigency but a priestly sacramental ambition to effect emotional abstraction in the picture and confer emotional transcendence on artist and viewer. The project is not formalist, as it is in the tradition of Cézanne, but it ends at a similar point: the abstraction from time and place, from the contingencies of circumstance and narrative continuity. The contribution of the German expressionists is to have pursued the abstraction of emotion rather than the abstraction of form. In a sense, it is the emotional extortion of art; for the viewer is pressed into responding to an emotion and giving sympathy *carte blanche*, not knowing anything of the emotion but accepting the mystery of emotion. The art achieves this by (a) wringing the picture of all objectivity so that it congeals and reifies a turmoil of subjectivity and (b) eliciting an emotional response in the absence of an emotional argument. The picture provides no emotional justification for the welter of subjective mark-making and distortion. Art, for the German expressionists, is the process of transforming the arbitrary and gratuitous emotional response into a pretension of universal emotion; and for the viewer it is a challenge to proffer uncritical sympathy, to suspend the faculties of analysis and indulge the work with the emotional generosity which one would never extend to a beggar.

The German expressionists fulfil the paradigm of the artistic movement from a relatively spiritual condition to a relatively secular and universalizing abstraction while nevertheless arrogating the spiritual claims of the anterior art. The expressionists step into an emotive and mystical tradition, engaging the exaggeration and subjective composition and colour of artists like Munch and Van Gogh; but they remove the hallucinogenic effects from a narrative or symbolic source and so divorce them from an emotional engagement. The liturgical element of Munch and Van Gogh—let us say the cathartic artistic enactment of an emotional crisis—is dropped; but the claim to spiritual status is implied all the more strongly on account of abandoning the temporal and spatial associations of the earlier art; for the new abstractions upon emotive techniques ascend to the status of universal archetype of the emotional.

The fauves are not so different, even though their works are more cheerful and reveal a bias toward the friendliness of sunshine and leisure, which among Europeans is almost considered indigenous to the south. For the most part their paintings do not provide any emotional justification for the strongly reductive technique, the arbitrary colours and the degradation of space and volume. In Matisse's famous *The Green Stripe*, for instance, the stately and prepossessed carriage of Mme Matisse's head does not indicate any of the heightened colours which conspire around the form with planar dynamism and effect an unusual chromatic counterpoint.[8] The colours in the face, neck and tunic do faintly echo the stronger colours in the background: the unity of the work is formidable and, in a sense, helps convey a certain imperiousness in Mme Matisse's aspect. But the colours and composition are not arranged as a psychological analog to the sitter.[9] They transfuse the sitter with an aesthetic tension, for they are neither proper to the colours of the skin, the tunic nor a normal light source; but one is interested to see how the pale tertiary colours of Caucasian skin can have powerful colour induced upon them—almost against their nature—while still remaining the sign of a sensual carnal person.

Many fauve works seem gladdening and outgoing (as do some brilliant works of Kirchner), for the brightness of the colour and buoyancy of application match the hedonism of the subject matter. But the work is not allowed to be merely decoratively charming: there is always stressful argument between impulsive force and equivocal flimsiness; parts of the canvas are left bare and the paint, even in local zones (that is, when the hue does not change) waxes and wanes and often seems thin in an ugly way. Indeed, were it not for preserving a classical aloofness—as in *The Green Stripe*—the work of the fauves seems wilfully incompetent. The classical aloofness, though, means the same reluctance to embrace an emotion as in the German expressionists. The stylistic claim of their pictures insists on a certain emotional calibre: they have the extremity of means which would be suitable as rhetoric for conveying powerful emotion; but they retentively hold back on any message but the most general. The pictures have little to say but deck themselves out with chromatic and compositional formidability; they project the clout of emotional engagement but withdraw both from the communication of emotion and the psychological or moral consequences of invoking an emotional message.

The work of the fauves can be compared to that of the cubists. In the so-called analytical phase of cubism of Braque and Picasso circa 1910, the motif accepts any number of interventions, not of bright colour but planar fragmentation. The integrity of the form fights against the disruption; the disruption is not there for the expressive sake of the motif but rather *vice versa*: the motif is a pretext, a passive and inexpressive vessel for slotting planes into with a geometric inflexion which equates all objects and spaces and further reduces any latent expressiveness which the objects may have had in their familiar symbolic life on the tabletop. The term analytical cubism is understandable insofar as it conveys the somewhat systematic and unemotional nature of the project, but it is misleading in suggesting a process of analysis; for analysis is an intellectual strategy for appreciating the composition of an object. You engage analysis in order to separate the ingredients of a single entity; and breaking down the single entity into its distinctive components enables you to understand the operation of the entity, to appreciate the cause of its behaviour or its likeness to or difference from other entities. This scientific process has little to do with cubist pictures which, if anything, conceal the nature of objects rather than reveal any aspect of their constitution or bearing in space.[10] On the level that so flattered abstract expressionism, analytical cubism is a method of making all objects (preferably neutral objects, somewhat pleasant and with lyrical associations) entertain the same spatial disruption and so share a similar conformity with the picture plane; though some credence has to be given to the fragmentary figuration as an extension of Cézanne's project to express the motile, time-based character of perception. Against the idea of rationally analysing the discrete parts of an object—or even the possible viewpoints of an object—analytical cubism is a way of synthetically agonizing the presence of an object, confounding its spatial logic with disparate viewpoints so that, by a stylistic litany of jerks and jolts, it is extracted from its integrity, pulled out of its contours, overcoming its circumscription; and with these elastic and percussive strokes, it is drubbed into an artificial agreement with the picture plane.

Like the fauves, the cubists have a general expressiveness, the expression of modernity. Their work conveys the enthusiasm for a renovation of vision, proposing the redundancy of spatial figuration and privileging the reality of the picture plane over an illusion. But the purpose of this renovation is structurally fugitive. It is neither to be beautiful nor expressive. One does not have that kind of unequivocal purpose; in art, one seeks the abstraction of purposes, a general spirit of progress which is not revealed by a single intention. Through the abstraction of purposes, analytical cubism absconds from prestigious traditions with the symbolic clout of progress firmly in hand but none of the expressive incumbencies. In shedding the communicative responsibilities of earlier art, it also acquires a new prophetic status in the modern desert—the unwatered iconographic terrain of formerly prolific narrative and symbol—in which progress is necessarily expressionless because necessarily abstract. Art is about progress; it hypostasizes progress with self-referential circularity and wants to be the symbol of nothing but the sacraments of progress.

Modernism as an artistic term describes the project of making modernity sacramental. It is not an extension of the Romantic movement, avoiding industrial circumstances with anti-institutional disdain and cultivating the spiritual Other. It is a cult of the new whose zeal for progress and scorn for tradition paradoxically parallel the aggressive energies of capitalism. Modernists may have sympathized with the political avant garde—with notable exceptions, as in Italian futurism—but, in spite of socialist ideology, their reformist passion harmonizes with the alienating upheavals of industrial progress. It is no accident: there is a structural link between the visual renovations of modern art and the dislocating aggression of capitalism. Both have idealistic motives but both are structurally phallic: they look upon the cultural ambience in a predatory spirit, happily dismissing the franchise of tradition and redefining the terms of production beyond common grasp.

To some extent, modernism does carry forward the conceits of Romanticism, especially the celebration of the artist as individual genius, full of instinctual innovative passion and contempt for traditional authority. But the Romantic spiritual affinity for nature does not belong to the modernist enthusiasm for innovation. Modernists are by and large too egocentric to submit their understanding of spirit to a superintending order such as nature, inducing a feeling of admiration or even worship for a sublimity infinitely beyond the artist's powers of comprehension (albeit for the sake of egotistical identification). Spirituality had already defaulted to the personal in the avant garde of the previous century. The gifts of innovative creation give modernists a personal proprietorship of the spiritual, for the spiritual now resides in the realm of the personal and available through individualized abstractions. Modernism involves a faith that spiritual states can be contacted through the very act of innovation, thus making redundant a referent, such as nature, God or tradition.

When modernists approach more spiritually pregnant cultures and appropriate their artistic forms, tinctures of Romanticism also appear; but the interest in the narratives and liturgies of another culture's mythological cosmos—however naïve—is absent from the modernist motivation. The persistent undercurrent of primitivism in many modernist groups is unlike Gauguin's sojourns in Tahiti to bring back the imaginary paradise of innocence and untroubled cohabitation with haunting spirits in decorative symbols. The influence of African carving and masks on Picasso from 1906-08 and the noble-savage imagery of the German expressionists circa 1910 does not extend more than a cold handshake to the beliefs and customs of other ethnicities. They want the masks in order to project a new brutality, to licence their new visual rudeness and, above all, to induce an archaic urgency on their stylistic excursions. If for example, the expressionists of *Die Brücke* wish to represent naked figures in the forest, as did Kirchner and Schmidt-Rottluff, this must not appear a rehearsal of the pastoral genre or the Rococo frolic in park but must communicate the intrepid cultural freedom of woodland warriors against western convention. One paints with the air of the savage and this appropriation has a chauvinistic glamour. The primitivist associations confer cultural profundity upon the formal recklessness of the work. In Kirchner's *Four Bathers*, the women are depicted with gashes of paint, with little care taken to represent the body.[11] The people depicted are not primitive; they are sophisticated German artists and models who want to shed the inhibitions of western culture. The expressionists in this sense do express freedom; but it is a freedom all bound up with the making of art, introverted in its abstraction from any circumstance in which freedom counts in concrete terms. Freedom only enters if you consider the subject matter of the picture to be the style of the picture. This collapse of the pictorial dichotomy between subject matter and technique—a dichotomy which underlies the whole western dialectic of looking at pictures—is abstraction.

Abstraction is the underlying paradigm of modernism. There are many historical routes to abstraction but nearly all of them have a mystical character. Even when the motive toward abstraction could just as easily be empirical and rationalist, it tends to be the opposite. An example is Kandinsky. There are times when his apologia for abstraction could almost proceed from the emancipatory rationalism of the Enlightenment. Why should visual art always mimic a pre-existing optical reality and so confine itself to picture-making, with whatever degrees of distortion? Why can it not free itself of the yoke of the imitative image, thus transcending the limitation in the visuality of the chaotic world around us? Why not synthesize the visual? Music, after all, has achieved this more or less for millennia. Programmatic music may have a representational element; but the genius of music is melody, an abstract rhythmic concatenation of notes which does not in essence represent anything but its own relationships. Why is this privilege confined to music? Why can the visual arts not shed their dependence on representation? For if they could, a whole realm of the aesthetic would become available to the artist, unthinkable beauties of pure form, unencumbered by the submission to, or negotiation with, the known visual environment. The artist would have to compose in a non-spatial framework, as if colours might equate with musical pitch and distance upon the two-dimensional plane might equate with time in music. From there it would only be necessary to think of the visual melodies.

But Kandinsky's voice is different and the new offices which his abstraction promises are spiritual. He wants to touch the soul with the new non-representational art; the ensembles of abstract form would offer direct access to the soul because, in their purity from contingencies and the limitations of circumstance, the uncompromised visual music would be superior to all before it, demonstrating a purity with harmonies infallibly sympathetic to the pure chords of the soul.[12]

The spirituality with which Kandinsky's art is larded was also necessary. Major claims would have to be made, not so much to distinguish the new abstract art from new figurative art (cubism and expressionism) but to distinguish it from abstract motifs in the tradition of ornament. In the key period of Kandinsky's development, the first two decades of the century, the tradition of ornament in western design was still unbroken and enjoyed the authority of two and a half millennia of cumulative richness and an aura of immortality. Its lively apologists in England (Pugin, Ruskin, Jones and Morris) were relatively recent; and concerted scholarly work through continental figures like Gottfried Semper and Alois Riegl related the field to systematic method.[13] As prestigious as this tradition may have been in architectural circles, it was definitely not the paradigm to invoke; for the 'merely' decorative had already been seen as intellectually and poetically inferior, and a work of fine art which seemed to ape the applied arts would be stigmatized with connotations of routine, pattern, fill-in, the mechanical and so on. A strong expression of this contempt was the anti-decorative polemic of the early modernist architect Adolf Loos, *Ornament and Crime*.[14]

The abstract enterprise also encouraged spiritual overstatement in order to outweigh the inadequacies of the visual outcome, and indeed the inherent inclemencies of a practical execution. The theory suggesting that the visual arts can be like music has obvious appeal; but the beauty and usefulness of it are apparently confined to theory. When the artist gets to the canvas, he or she discovers that colours in no way equate with pitch; likewise, distance on the two-dimensional plane presents no analogies to the idea of interval in music. Colour has elements (hue, saturation and tone) which are unlike those of sounds. And even if you could pretend that your palette were so many octaves, where do you put the chromatic notes in order to make visual melody? Up, down and across are extraordinarily complicated indices in painting, suggesting relationships of depth, very different to the unidirectional linear progression of time in music. And this is before you start thinking about chords or modes. The whole project is an embarrassment. Paintings do undoubtedly have a musical dimension; but it is no more certainly achieved by abstraction than by figuration. A Giorgione or a Poussin, for example, is much more sonorous and melodious than a Kandinsky. This is the basis for Bernard Smith coining the term formalesque, because 'formalist' does not belong to modernism alone but equally to Tiepolo or Watteau.

The evidence of Kandinsky's abstract paintings just before the first world war is not encouraging. To equate with music means seeing them as somehow sonorously sumptuous; but it makes no more sense to call them beautiful than ugly: the forms are amorphous and ill-defined; they seem to have little lyricism to make their puffiness convincingly connected. The liaison between the forms seems somewhat messy and almost every brushstroke announces a fresh search for a rationale. In painting which is declared to be an 'art of inner necessity' all aspects seem conspicuously unnecessary. The paint has little to do except collide with itself, merge, smudge, stand apart, form balls or clouds or constellations of equivocal relationships. Especially if you consider the tradition of western music as being argumentative, a pattern that makes a case for a certain mood, the analogy with Kandinsky's paintings seems strained. As the visual seeks, in his hands, to realize an imputedly true nature, unhampered by representation, it forsakes its previous evocative strength, which is arguably its point of closest contact with music. The attempt is forlorn because it co-opts the paint to act as something that it is not. The paint as music is less true to the essence of the medium—if such an essence can be imagined—than the paint as illusion.

Abstraction is easily dismissed by conservative critics: there is nothing to paint; therefore there is nothing to say. And as the mystical component is not evident in the painted result, it can be happily ignored. But Kandinsky's approach to abstraction is less mystical than Mondrian's. As a Theosophist, Mondrian is almost automatically inclined to the abstraction of spirituality; for the theosophical spiritual movement called for a kind of syncretism among the several major religions, an abstraction, in effect, by which each religion would tend to forego its peculiarities while the shared religious motifs would be emphasized. The areas of commonality among the belief systems would have extraordinary prestige in their power of suggesting convergence toward universal spirit.[15]

The movement can be compared to the philosophy underlying the immediate predecessors of De Stijl. The spirituality of the symbolists as articulated by theorists like Albert Aurier has a classical inflexion, not so far removed from Plato's view that mere objects carry very little virtue on account of being embodied in material; but the idea (or form) which informed these objects already has a claim to a kind of universality, not limited to the single incarnation in a given material but capable of being rediscovered any number of times or exchanging energies with other ideas. Behind each object lies the idea of the object; and these ideas (or forms) can be perceived in a certain order by the clairvoyant, running from the specific idea of a functional object to the general idea of a category or abstraction which comprehends a great number of meaningful signs. One proposes a rather hieratic regime of ideas, in which the more general are higher than the more particular. At the apex of the triangle lies pure spirit or God. The spiritual mission of philosopher and artist is therefore to identify the most universal ideas—those capable of suggesting a great depth of meaning—and celebrate them with the expression of spirit which is proper to them.

Taken to its logical conclusion, this philosophy means abjuring the celebration of individual objects and the particular circumstances in which they are encountered. In a celebrated series of paintings from 1908–1912, Mondrian paints a tree, progressively losing the tactility of the bark, the pendulousness of the outer twigs, the elasticity of the branches, the diagonal thrust of boughs connecting them to the trunk, even the distinction between the tree and its background. It is as if he asks the question: sure, that is a given tree but what is the essence of the tree which would also be the essence of all trees? It is to grow up and then out. It proceeds from a shaft in a vertical direction and then spreads horizontally. And so Mondrian moves from a red, somewhat expressionistic tree on a blue symbolist background to a gridded abstraction (which would involve the essence of things other than trees): as the sequence is completed, he achieves a pictorial composition which has very little of the botanical specimen but an arrangement of horizontal and vertical lines and planes in warm grey.[16] The tendency is also true of his *Pier and Ocean* series of slightly later date, effectively concluding in the pure abstract *Composition* of 1916, a patch-work of muted reds, blues and yellows, 'hosted' by a discontinuous grid of thin and short black lines.[17]

Parallel to the geometric abstractions of the Russian suprematists, Mondrian's works after the first world war eliminate further traces of incident and accident in the application of paint. The gestural patches in the early abstractions of Mondrian are replaced by the artist with hard edges; and the sense of pitter-patter in their multiplicity is exchanged for larger areas of local colour. The thin and scattered discontinuous lines which interspersed the earlier work are geometricized and strengthened to act as pictorial girders. The colours are now the pure primaries, blue, red and yellow, as well as black and white. In this austere reduction of the multifarious appearances of painting, Mondrian confines his work to the elements, that is, the essential components out of which all possible pictorial manifestations are constituted, in the same way that all shapes can be described in mathematics by a relationship between the x, y and z axes, the essential dimensions of space. In Mondrian, the elements are vertical and horizontal, red, blue and yellow, line and plane, black and white.

The artistic excellence of Mondrian's work from the twenties, usually bearing the general title *Composition*, depends on three generous givens: the first is that an intellectual or spiritual ascension to the universal (not a humble mission) is a credible aesthetic experience. The second is that the collapsing of pictorial variety to the chosen ingredients is a credible symbol of the same ascension to the universal, the higher state of being or consciousness by virtue of shedding the incumbencies of matter and the chaotic circumstantial messages which attend it. The third is that the formal result of echoing the intellectual or spiritual ascension to universality is sublimely beautiful, resolved and self-contained, suggesting not only some ultimate tranquillity but ultimate aesthetic intelligence. All three propositions are dubious, not the least because the very effort to shed particular information in order to achieve the universal ultimately strips the artwork of a communicative faculty. The planes and lines *as such* do not have great meaning, even as they gesture toward the absolute. The very universality which they institutionalize visually denies them a specific meaning; for meaning, like emotion, is always specific, even when its address is general.

The spiritual autonomy of the abstraction is inherently self-disappointing. It is impossible to know the high spiritual intention of the artwork without being told about it. The work on its own is fairly blank, perhaps subtly balanced, perhaps peaceful, perhaps daring in its contrasts, perhaps interesting in the way that the lines do not meet the border of the canvas and perhaps remotely engaging in the novel fact that it uniquely uses primaries, black and white. But the spiritual claims made on behalf of the whole aesthetic exercise are not inherent in the work. The great purity of the spiritualized abstraction is a paradox: one wishes to have nothing in the painting which has a non-pictorial rhetoric—like representation or narrative—but the effectiveness of the work in achieving any pertinence to the spiritual is dependent on an external exegesis. Abstraction as the great self-sufficiency of the visual is a failure. Of course, anyone who claims to be spiritually moved solely by beholding Mondrian's *Compositions* has an incontrovertible privilege to assert it, as with the enthusiasm of those who believe that they have seen God.[18]

But the art which abstracts has no obligations to deliver. The purity is aesthetic, not therapeutic; it is aloof and, in the manner of a statue of Apollo, it basks in its own self-sufficiency, serenely free of any demands made upon it for the graces which it possesses but never promises to dispense. Like Mondrian, the Russian suprematists set the high tone of abstraction as the genre of pure spirit. Like Mondrian, Malevich increases the austerity of his paintings, even exceeding the Dutch artist's economical planes and lines. In 1915, Malevich was creating hard-edge abstractions featuring geometric shapes jostling with one another, with an implied magnetism acting between them upon a light ground.[19] In the same year, he would abandon the dynamism of parallel elements, and produce his famous *Black Square*, in which there is no trace of even that abstracted narrative of his other suprematist compositions.[20] The blank canvas purposefully represents the degree zero of visual information and expression of experience. But it is not intended to be nihilistic; on the contrary, it is conceived as taking the next step, indeed the final step, in the necessary progress of art from totemism through illusionism to abstraction. The *Black Square* is thus the 'ultimate painting', a genre which has been cultivated by numerous artists such as Frank Stella ever since. Each artist attempts to do the ultimate painting, a painting beyond which nothing can be more radically basic.[21]

Once art is tied up in such claustrophobically absolutist agendas it is difficult for it to disentangle itself from an apocalyptic heroism which is also folly. Since Romanticism, the genius of art had been defined as progressive, anti-conservative, anti-traditional. There was no possibility of going back. The avant garde progressively paints itself into a corner, with an ever-more radical position being demanded of each artist as if by destiny, as if by the deterministic trajectory of art history. It is not long before artists feel that the arts of painting and sculpture are exhausted. Those who do not feel pessimistic either owe their complacency to a sweet compromise between the radical and the traditional or they owe it to the incorrigible conceit which the image of rebellious cultural hero had vested in artists since Romanticism. Both options encourage mannerism, the uncritical cultivation of stylistic tropes to garnish obsessive imagery or obsessive absence of imagery. In popular parlance, all artists have to have 'a thing', that is, a gimmick, such as an exorbitant elongation or scrawliness. Many gimmicks relate to medium-consciousness, that is, a self-reflexive address to the medium itself.

Modern art aspires to universal forms; it wants to make all visual contact submit to geometricized schemata or an emphatic expression of the medium, even when figurative. The incidental quality of the visual world (as seen in realism and photography) has no place and must be either totally expunged (as in abstraction) or suitably abstracted (as in modern figurative art) in order to enjoy the higher pertinence of universal forms. But the zeal for making all forms 'universal' causes in figurative artists peculiarly systematic distortions—as in the biomorphic sculptures of Henry Moore—which induce upon a work-a-day form a transcendental pertinence to a higher idea. All mannerisms have to be spiritually portentous, even though they have no symbolic referent beyond the internal argument of the medium and the style. Modern art must not communicate directly, as in the former representational traditions, for that would mean relinquishing the newly acquired essentialism which seems to grace any mannerism with a spiritual resonance, the sacramental element of making a form belong to a universal abstraction, borne infallibly to spiritual pertinence. The inadequacy to communicate is not seen as a failure but a success: the internalization of the process-oriented relationship between style and medium, the new limitations of the new art, become the symbol of spiritual pregnancy.[22]

The history of the diverse modernist movements cannot be related here but those signal examples which involve abstraction structurally conform to the paradigms already noted. Just as in previous centuries, the progress of art during modernism commenced upon a spiritual footing linked to archaic symbolic regimes; but its charter was to abstract the spirituality inherited from the immediate past, dispense with the haunted narratives, the overt symbolism, the imagery of a cathartic or liturgical function (as in the emotional stresses of Symbolism or the aesthetic *askesis* of Cézanne) and arrive at an order whose sacraments are more abstract and less material, less symbolically vested in objects and more cerebrally induced through aesthetic processes related to the artistic medium itself. Modernism seized the spiritual privileges of post-impressionism but did away with their referential specificity. Furthermore, in aesthetically abstracting from the spirituality of its antecedents, modernism (a) retained all the cryptic prestige of the spiritual without owing any responsibility to previous spiritual expectations and (b) achieved new glamour on account of aesthetically embodying spiritual phenomena in a less material incarnation.

Modernism is a mystical form of credit for failure. One sets up an unrealizable aspiration to a 'universal language of form' which, when reached, turns out to be supremely uninformative and semantically self-defeating, for no one can apprehend the meaning in the abstraction and recognize the intention. The artist strives either (a) to produce an abstraction whose meaningless is challenged by a gestural 'auratic' presence of mark-making or (b) to produce a potentially meaningful representation which is challenged by a stressful mannerist conformity to an abstract and universalizing language of form. You either agonize your abstraction or you agonize your representation. But in this agony, there is a bizarre and entirely sacramental virtue, widely understood by all proponents of modernism and its audience. For decades, now, many generations of artists have practiced a kind of sacrifice. They have sacrificed their talent. And for that sacrifice, they are given credit as true artists, dedicated to the cult of artistic progress.

The artist who seeks to cultivate a traditional idiom (a lonely and unsustainable aspiration) has failed to sacrifice his or her talent. He or she clings to the demonstration of perceptual evocation and cannot therefore claim the virtues of artistic sacrifice. Meanwhile, the artists who have seen the need for the sacrifice gladly take the plunge and gather their strengths in all kinds of other talents—many of which are not artistic—to produce incomprehensible work with an unfamiliar address and a staunch resistance to communicative ends or celebration of unnamed ambiguities or portentous obscurities. Anyone who works in an art-school anywhere in the western world can witness the sacrifices on a daily basis. The young art student is introduced to the perceptual disciplines of drawing, by way of backdrop—like the altarpiece before the altar—in the hope of gaining or reinforcing talents; but even when this enthusiasm is served by life-drawing classes constructed in good faith by competent lecturers to yield such skills, the neophyte will soon be induced to renounce them. It is not the pressures of the lecturers but the paradigm of history. At a certain point, after having glimpsed the possibilities of engaging his or her talents, the uninitiated artist becomes convinced that it is necessary to sacrifice the emerging talent in order to serve the sacramental nature of art, that economy of symbolic actions which makes art have spiritual claims. Students face the degrading prospect that their chances in a manual representational idiom are not supported by the definition of contemporary art and the trajectory of history; their first and most innocent aspiration must be sacrificed to show faith in the progress of art. It is not necessary for teachers to purvey this message; and there is no conspiracy. The sacrifice is structurally embedded in the way that art is understood during and after modernism. The student bows the head and submits.

ENDNOTES

1. Smith's commitment to his own coinage is especially motivated by the broader aim of periodizing the twentieth-century in art-historical terms. See Smith (1998, 4–5) for the opening discussion of the formalesque, described as a "style-cycle" as distinct from a style.

2 See Crary (1999): in his analysis of works by Manet, Seurat, and Cézanne, Crary discusses each artist's inventive approach as a contribution to late nineteenth-century changes in the understanding human vision and perceptual experience.

3 Auguste Rodin, *The Walking Man*, 1900–1907, bronze, Musée Rodin, Paris.

4 See Le Normande-Romain (2004, 145–159): while Rodin's fragmentation of the figure refers to the heritage of classical antiquity, his conception of *The Walking Man* also encompasses the element of time as it relates to human movement, and as this, too, can be manipulated through the figurative form.

5 See Tompkins Lewis (2000): in her words, Cézanne was always "a painter's painter," as demonstrated by his lifelong commitment to working intensively across the spectrum of traditional genres in painting. "It was from his fellow artists that he received his first, most consistent and, with few exceptions, until the very end, his only expressions of support" (8).

6 Karl Schmidt-Rottluff, *Red Tower in the Park*, 1910, oil on canvas, Städel Museum, Frankfurt.

7 Thus, for instance, Ernst Ludwig Kirchner, *Nude Behind a Curtain (Fränzi)*, 1910, oil on canvas, Stedelijk Museum, Amsterdam.

8 Henri Matisse, *The Green Line (Portrait of Madame Matisse)*, 1905, oil and tempera on canvas, Statens Museum for Kunst, Copenhagen.

9 For Elderfield (1996), Matisse's representations of women can be viewed as a part of a strategy for self-analysis and self-representation; see this extended essay, or lecture, on the role of female models in Matisse's reflections on the creative processes of painting.

10 Staller (2001, 163–267) examines Picasso's cultural and aesthetic formation in Màlaga, arguing that the artist transformed those specific, coded languages and signs that pervaded his early life in Catholic Spain into a basis for the hermeticism of cubism.

11 Ernst Ludwig Kirchner, *Four Bathers,* 1910, oil on canvas, Von der Heydt-Museum, Wuppertal.

12 Kandinsky's essay in Russian, "On the Spiritual in Art," was first presented on the artist's behalf as a lecture in St Petersburg, in 1911. See the English edition of this philosophical, optimistic tract in Bowlt and Washton-Long (1980).

13 Schafter's (2002) monograph has the advantage of considering the theories of Ruskin, Jones, Semper and Riegl simultaneously in the one volume, in relation to the modernism of late nineteenth- and early twentieth- century central Europe. See also the monumental study *Modernism's History* by Smith (1998).

14 The probable date of this treatise is ca. 1909–1910; urging the abolition of ornament from functional or utilitarian objects and design, Loos intended the text as a public lecture: see Long (1997, 440–445).

15 On Mondrian as "the purest and most single-minded of the great pioneering abstractionists," see Golding (2000, 9–46). Abundantly illustrated, this monograph examines the breadth of meanings and pictorial truths with which abstraction was self-consciously invested by the European originators of abstract painting, and by their major American successors.

16 Piet Mondrian, *Evening; Red Tree*, 1908, oil on canvas, Haags Gemeentemuseum, The Hague; *The Gray Tree*, 1911, oil on canvas, Haags Gemeentemuseum, The Hague; *Flowering Appletree*, 1912, oil on canvas, Haags Gemeentemuseum, The Hague. A comparison of these works well demonstrates Mondrian's transformation of the natural motif into a structural motif.

17 Piet Mondrian, *Pier and Ocean 5 (Sea and Starry Sky)*, 1914, charcoal and gouache on buff paper, Museum of Modern Art, New York, is a well known example from the *Pier and Ocean* series; *Composition,* 1916, oil on canvas with wood strip, Solomon R. Guggenheim Museum, New York.

18 And even one so close to God as St John declares that 'no one has ever seen God'. *John* 1.18; see also the same text in *1 John* 4.12.

19 For example, Kazmir Malevich, *Suprematism (18th Construction)*, 1915, oil on canvas, Stedelijk Museum, Amsterdam.

20 Kazmir Malevich, *Black Square*, 1915, oil on canvas, Hermitage, St Petersburg. See the major exhibition catalogue by Drutt (2003), which takes this iconic work as a starting point for detailed documentation and reflection on the origins and development of suprematism.

21 In the history of abstract art and design, the high formality of such reductionism can be shown to develop into ornamentation: see the exhibition catalogue by Brüderlin (2001), which brings Stella's work into a different kind of conjuction with that of the earlier, European abstract painters.

22 At the same time, in her provocative book aimed at a broad readership (unconfined to those with a specialist interest in the art world), Suzi Gablik argues: "To the public at large, modern art has always implied a loss of craft, a fall from grace, a fraud, or a hoax. We may accept with good grace not understanding a foreign language or algebra, but in the case of modern art it is more likely, as Roger Fry once pointed out, that people will think, when confronted with a work they do not like and cannot understand, that it was done to insult them" (Gablik 1984, 23).

REFERENCES

Brüderlin, M., ed. 2001. *Ornament and Abstraction: The Dialogue Between Non-Western, Modern and Contemporary Art.* New Haven: Yale University Press.

Crary, J. 1999. *Suspensions of Perception: Attention, Spectacle and Modern Culture.* London and Cambridge: MIT Press.

Drutt, M. 2003. *Kazimir Malevich: Suprematism.* New York: Guggenheim Museum. [Exhibition catalogue.]

Elderfield, J. 1996. *Pleasuring Painting: Matisse's Feminine Representations.* New York: Thames & Hudson.

Gablik, S. 1984. *Has Modernism Failed?* 2nd ed. London: Thames & Hudson.

Golding, J. 2000. *Paths to the Absolute: Mondrian, Malevich, Kandinsky, Pollock, Newman, Rothko and Still.* London: Thames & Hudson.

Kandinsky. 1911. "On the Spiritual in Art". In *The Life of Vasilii Kandinsky in Russian Art: A Study of on the Spiritual in Art* (1980), edited by Bowlt, J. E.; Washton-Long, R., and translated by Bowlt, J. Russian Biography Series 4. Newtonville, Massachusetts: Oriental Research Partners.

Le Normande-Romain, A. 2004. "The Lesson of Antiquity". In *Rodin: The Zola of Sculpture*, edited by Mitchell, C. Subject/Object: New Studies in Sculpture Aldershot: Ashgate Publishing. 145–159.

Long, C. 1997. "Ornament, Crime, Myth, and Meaning". In *Architecture: Material and Imagined.* Proceedings of the 85th American Collegiate Schools of Architecture Annual Meeting. Washington. 440–445.

Schafter, D. 2002. The Order of Ornament, the Structure of Style: Theoretical Foundations of Modern Art and Architecture. Cambridge: Cambridge University Press.

Smith, B. 1998. *Modernism's History: A Study in Twentieth-Century Art and Ideas.* Sydney: UNSW Press.

Staller, N. 2001. *A Sum of Destructions: Picasso's Cultures and the Creation of Cubism.* New Haven: Yale University Press.

Tompkins Lewis, M. 2000. *Cézanne.* London: Phaidon Press.

Cite this chapter as: Nelson, Robert. 'The new and the true'. *The Spirit of Secular Art: A History of the Sacramental Roots of Contemporary Artistic Values.* Melbourne: Monash University ePress. pp. 8.1–8.18. DOI: 10.2104/ssa07008.

CHAPTER 9

IN THE NAME OF CRITIQUE

Robert Nelson

On account of its kinship with the mechanistic world of industrial progress, modernism frequently brought satire and ridicule upon itself. Let us ignore the sometimes inspired derision in which conservative art critics would exercise their wits against the new art. The more lasting satires were oblique and would come from the radical artistic quarter itself. It is possible to interpret much modern art (as the American art historian Donald Kuspit has done) as a form of parody, either of itself or of the whole idea of representation or non-representation.[1] It is possible to interpret the Picasso of synthetic cubism as a jokester, for his work does not arise out of an intellectual or spiritual obsession (as Mondrian's does) but from a kind of compulsion toward the prank, the modernized lyrical grotesque. It is hard to judge; for even allowing that Picasso sought to be humorous in a kind of abstracted burlesque, his work can still be seen as heroizing its own prowess of innovation, without its conceits being over-burdened by irony.

The satirical tradition of the twentieth century is seen more obviously with Dada. The movement has often been interpreted as a reaction to the First World War, an anarchic expression of disgust for all forms of authority. There may be some truth in this; but Dada has a critical dimension which is properly poetic, making bizarre *folie à deux* with the materialist philosophy which had informed the fabric of the industrial world and had recently gone so far as to colonize the psyche in the works of Sigmund Freud. In the performances and visual works of artists such as Francis Picabia and Marcel Duchamp, the materialistic basis of modernity would be poetically satirized as absurd.

In Picabia's painting *Machine turn quickly*, an assembly of cogs is figured in the flat idiom of mechanical drawing. The deadpan rendering of the geometric components—which do not make much sense from an engineering point of view—are offset by the absurdity of the title.[2] It is true that some people implore machines to do something when they are in a transport of enthusiasm, rage or desperation (as when you swear at your bicycle for getting a puncture); but the invocation is in vain, for the machine cannot hear; and if it did hear, by some mechanical miracle, it would not understand. Everything is inverted. The psychological engagement with the machine (though in some sense instinctual) is misplaced. Instinct gives you the subjective identification with the mechanical; but logic (that is, an objective mechanism of thought) distances you from the machine, fills you with disappointment and possibly makes you laugh that you could ever have wanted to talk to a machine.

In Picabia's *Amorous Parade*, a similarly irrational assembly of cogs, levers, counterweights and various processing units (perhaps boilers and so on) allegorizes sexual functions.[3] The title refers to a demonstrating of erotic interests, as of courtship. The theatre of instinct is rather rudely translated to a mechanism. Nothing in the erotic scenario—whatever an amorous parade is—has a cause in a spiritual or wilful dimension of the soul. Machines work in complicated ways and are analogous to humans in their interaction of separate components, all assembled to lend one another some function which the other component cannot supply. But the organic character of the human body links all corporal matters to the mind, to controlling moods, to will and feelings. Machines lack feelings and will. The reason a flywheel turns is that an armature spins it; the reason the armature pushes and pulls at the wheel is that it is driven by a piston; the reason the piston pumps is the rhythm of pressure caused by the release of steam; the reason there is steam is that there is combustion ... and so on. In the whole exegesis of the machine there is never a mention of will; for what is wilful and organically reciprocal can never be mechanical. The will of the machine entirely defaults to the person who built the machine or wanted it to function in the way that it does. And now that it has been built, it has no choice to function otherwise; nor will it ever experience any dissatisfaction, including when it grinds to a halt after being neglected by its careless operator.

The distinction between human and machine advertises the qualities of will and spirit which distinguish the organic from the mechanical. But since the writings of Freud, the distinction could not be maintained so complacently. While of course conceding that the human is inordinately more complicated than a machine, Freud nevertheless saw no reason to suppose that the psychological element of the organism is inherently spiritual, that is, non material. On the contrary, Freud imagined that all processes in the psyche ultimately have a material cause, even though we may never adequately understand it. Those dimensions of experience which we intellectually quarantine from the material world such as will and feeling probably belong to a biochemical system which behaves according to the laws of science just as much as the function of the liver or muscles. In the final analysis, all emotional phenomena may be reduced to the biochemistry of the body and its hormonal activity and neuronal relationships.

Although no biochemist, Freud effectively began the inquiry into the material nature of the psyche by identifying distinct parts within it which have a somewhat 'mechanistic' bearing on the other. Thus, the I (or ego) is conceived as a powerless centre of the psyche in which a person feels his or her identity; the ego is surrounded by three strong elements, the source of energy or drive, the voice of negation or conscience (*superego*) and the outside world. These forces lie in a difficult and stressful balance. Through the circumstances of a person's life, any of the forces is likely to have a destructive dominance in the psyche and threaten the ego with the terrible consequences of neurosis. To see the psyche in this dynamic of stresses radically lends itself to a mechanistic revaluation of the spiritual, especially when Freud further defines the three forces in materialistic terms.

The element of will (which is clearly central to the spiritual defence against determinism) is considered an energy. The energy which causes a young woman to be kind to her grandmother is the same energy that gives her the sex-drive or allows her to write a symphony: in essence it is libido, diverted one way or another in sublimations either in her control or not. Freud would not deny that the young woman has a choice; but the choice would ultimately be an expression of the libido in its balance with the other forces.

The element of conscience (which again is central to the spiritual defence against determinism) is considered as a precipitate of experiences of childhood in which the erotic urges of the child make an adjustment to the economy of parental affection. Freud famously describes this as the Œdipus complex, a drama in which the young boy wants to get rid of his father and exclusively love his mother. In the successful resolution of this complex, the boy learns to assimilate the presence of the father as a form of authority, admirable in its own right; and this new 'intellectualized' affection in the child creates the inner voice of negation or conscience. Where once the child had to be physically or verbally discouraged from impulsive actions, now he or she generates the messages autonomously. Parental fear is abstracted and internalized in a potentially crushing inner decree, capable of making the child lose all confidence and worse. Conscience is not a voice of God; it is not learned through religion nor is it some innate part of the immortal soul. It is a condition of fear abstracted through various memories and installed in the mind for the benefit or disintegration of the personality. For thus challenging the spiritual understanding of the key mystical concepts of will and conscience, Freud is even more rancorously scorned and anathematized by spiritually inclined people than is Karl Marx. No one had advanced the frontier of scientific materialism so far nor so eloquently.

Freud's influence on art has often been acknowledged, but with a common emphasis on the Surrealists and their absorption of Freud's use of dreams in penetrating the unconscious. But the profounder Freudian contribution to the history of ideas seems more interestingly interpreted by the Dadaists, especially Picabia and Duchamp. In Picabia's two works mentioned and Duchamp's famous *Large Glass: the Bride Stripped Bare by her Bachelors, Even*, the mechanistic analogies to psychological processes are interpreted literally.[4] Erotic scenarios are played out in the cipher of machines, which is very funny, since there is undoubtedly a mechanistic element in human response to stimuli; yet *au fond* we know that we are not machines and that we have will. When people behave mechanistically, we laugh, as had been noted in an uproarious little book by the French philosopher Henri Bergson, *Le rire* of 1900.[5] Bergson believed that we have laughter in order to chasten ourselves of the mechanical. Laughter enables us to identify mechanical behaviour as absurd and thus, admonished by the ridicule, we can correct it and behave with the appropriate organic rhythms of life. He thought that laughter was functional: it prevented people from lapsing into the mechanistic and losing touch with the organic intelligence of the world around them. And so, ironically, Bergson's interpretation of laughter as anti-mechanistic is itself a kind of mechanism. It is as if all metaphysical pathways lead to the absurd.

If in the nineteenth century, Nietzsche announced the death of God, the twentieth century would have to reckon with the death of metaphysics. Abstract artists from Mondrian to Rothko and Newman, would never acknowledge the crisis in which materialist philosophy had plunged metaphysics and would continue—with mixtures of delusion and pretension—to fabricate ghosts in the void. Their genre of spooky formalism is inoffensive and sometimes, as in Pollock, monumentalizes the gestural impulse, magnifying the spontaneous or automatic with memorable results. But the tradition of Dada more truthfully confronts the status of the spiritual in the century. The inner landscape has no gods, no totems, no established sacraments. But delightful paradoxes emerge in this recognition which lend themselves to aesthetic embellishment. First, the world of no spirit is absurd, for it is mechanistic. Second, the recognition of spirit is absurd, for there are no spirits but only processes which are ultimately biochemical. Third, the wilful attempt to erect a substitute spirituality—or will or psychological autonomy—is absurd, for it mechanically compensates for something which does not exist. A person can only live by having absurd faith in such things; and faith can only work if it is understood as absurd, for it has to countenance the void of spirit. And so, in a somewhat anarchic irony, the absurd reaches an extraordinary prestige and becomes the new sacramental genre of the century.

The prestigious new aesthetic is evident in Picabia and Duchamp whose absurdist works are utterly ambiguous, having no definite agenda if not the relishing of the absurd. But they are artworks, rather than statements of abstract philosophy, because they aestheticize the absurd by manufacturing more of it and apparently revelling in it. The works are garlands of lacunae, festoons of nonsense, artfully baffling over a self-consciously defective joke. And so Dada fulfils the great sacramental paradigm of art from the past. It displaces an earlier order of belief (or believed aesthetics) and installs in its place a more secular disbelieving art; but the new art finds its way to hold onto the aesthetic privileges of semantic grace and balance, and so claims the sacramental status of the older art while being infused with radical prestige for yielding up the spirit of the older art in a de-ritualized genre.[6]

Duchamp's ready-mades represent the degree-zero in artistic belief, for they mock both the concept of representation and the ideal of aesthetic beauty. Taking a bottle-rack or a shovel or a urinal and putting it in the gallery with a facetious title is funny in a peculiarly severe way.[7] The gesture of the ready-made can be interpreted in several ways, the most simplistic of which is a polemic against the institution of galleries, especially the arbitrariness by which their hallowed walls can classify anything as art. Against this naive dead-end 'nominative discourse', the deeper critical content of Duchamp's ready-mades concerns the absurdity of reproduction. Unlike paintings, say, which reproduce nature, a bottle-rack is reproduced by a machine; but the machine can only reproduce—it has no choice—and the spiritual desolation of the progenitor-machine is reflected by the fact that each new bottle-rack is an identical reproduction of the last. Reproduction is something that nature and humans do by instinct; yet the instinct does not necessarily reflect reason or will; and in the potentially endless propagation of machinery, as when the bottle-rack is churned out in multiples through the assembly line, the rationale for each item has no intention or organic growth stamped upon it which would distinguish it from any other item in the mould. The art of representation is stripped of its most fundamental aesthetic quality, the sense of intention. For Duchamp, the only artistic intention to warrant belief is an arbitrary industrial object which, in the context of the gallery, suggests that aesthetic intentionality is as absurd as mechanical reproduction.

After the Second World War, the non-formalist tradition of Dada resumes, so to speak, in conceptual art. At times it is sanctimonious and gloriously leftist in a self-referential way, deploring the capitalist ownership of art objects—hence the overwriting of art with mainstream ideology—and seeking the salvation of art in the non-material or at least non-commodity. But at its best, that is, when poetic and not merely polemical, conceptual art is absurdist, funny and sacramental. Installations of alarmingly little content are intentionally confusing and offer an intellectual titillation in the conundrum of whether or not there is an intelligible purpose. The communicative absurdity of many installations is an aesthetic, even if the artist nourishes an ambition somewhere in the project to launch polemics against dominant ideology of aesthetics. The work in itself does not fulfil the polemic nor is it intended to. It is constituted as an art work by virtue of its obliqueness to the purpose, its absurdity, its aesthetic engagement with an interpreter. It is sacramental in the same way that Dada is sacramental.

As in Dada, the artwork is dispensable: performance is sometimes considered to offer a more direct route to the critical oxymorons of art—the messages which deal with the absurdity of a prefigured intention or teleology—giving the absurd a greater immanence. Also referred to as body art or happenings, performance art sometimes appears to be a return to a corporal liturgy (especially in artists like the Viennese Hermann Nitsch, who consciously evokes archaic blood sacrifices with learned references to ancient rites, or the Chinese Zhu Yu who devoured a human foetus in 2000), but the style of many art performances is cerebral and abstracted.[8] In general, however, performance art follows the pattern of inverted spirituality noted in the other stages of the progress of western art: it renounces the spiritual economy of the established art object—what theorists called the aura of the artwork—and so displaces an earlier iconic code or symbolic tradition which encouraged belief. But the radical abolition of 'auratic' forms would leave nothing to view as artistic unless some translated manifestation of it managed to creep back into the minimalist genre. The new art without objects (post-object art) is just as auratic as the old object-based art; but it gains new prestige by seeming to make redundant the outdated symbolic status of older art, the very art whose spiritual or aesthetic interest it subsumes. The catch is, of course, that the progressive secularizing of recent traditions is predicated on absurdity—because, in the art of Dada, a believed aesthetic has already been obliterated—so that the progress of art becomes circular, rather as in the popular image of a dog chasing its tail. The artist is only interested in paradoxes: how can this manifestation relate ideas while resisting the commodified visual language for relaying ideas? How can I infuse the installation with the ideology of resistance against mainstream commodification while avowing an uncommunicative idiom? Art becomes more and more inaccessible; the essays written about it become impenetrable because they are the exegesis of aesthetic contradictions, sometimes with little to say beyond the absurd, while politicized intentions are constantly dangled in front of the work, artfully not imposing anything upon the precious ambiguity of the sacraments.

The canonically inscrutable directions of the visual arts occur against a backdrop of a new medium, a medium of infectious popular appeal which historically outstripped the public attention of any other art form, namely film. Like photography, film has all the rights of technological superiority over existing art forms and, from the time when it was widely distributed, film must have seemed poised to make all the other arts redundant. Even photography, with its seduction of verisimilitude, was surpassed by film. In a film, things do not appear to be staged (which of course they are to a heightened degree) but to happen in front of your eyes with urgency and drama. The ability to effect changes in time, to create sudden movements or expressions or mutations of mood, was unprecedented and uncanny. In its narrative continuity and sensory impact, some immaterial aspect of the film apparently passes into your being; it follows through by showing you the results of actions; the sequences and performances have a narrative or documentary destiny which is the fulfilment of the story or message; and these contingencies do not seem gratuitous, as in abstraction, but functional and necessary.

The moving image solved many of the most problematic embarrassments of photography; for just as a photograph is good for recording static or fleeting appearances but not particularly distinguished at representing narratives, film had a pre-eminence in narrative, challenged only by literature. The attempts to render narrative photographically always tended to lack credibility. You could obtain credible actors; but the characters are never given a generous histrionic space in time in which to show off their lines. Even if you made a series of instants, the actor in each one risked the character of a prop. You also then need a viewer who can 'read' this sequence, which is liable to be either obvious or obscure. In all events, the performance of the actors would be summarized by a second's exposure and this précis could result in something iconically stilted; for the medium tends to pre-empt the action and freeze it like a zoological specimen in a vitrine. Performative or theatrical photography resulted in some brilliant photographs, like those of Charles Dodgson, but we tend to marvel at the life of the actors more than the feigned protagonists of the theatrical scene.

Narrative in film seemed believable, indeed compelling in being rehearsed in one's own space, unlike, for example, the very dignified but remote medium of theatre. Perhaps for that reason, early film-makers were quick to exploit the power of the medium for horror. A monster about to attack a helpless female arouses more sympathy and fright than in any other medium because of the sensational proximity of the movement to the perspective of the viewer. But this dramatic prowess by no means mapped out the confines of the medium. Ever since, film-makers have been exploring the inexhaustible potential of the medium for memorably conveying information or sensory transport or emotional predicaments, issues of social justice, the different emphases in the consciousness of men, women and children and so on.[9] Film seems to synthesize the visual power of image-making and the argumentative power of literature. It is, effectively, a form of literature; but adds to the traditional text-based medium an unparalleled immediacy and accessibility. Never before had so many people been able to share an enthusiasm for an artwork (or a story or however we label the experience of the new medium) and talk about it, dream about it, be moved to tears, be haunted, exhort other people to see it. These qualities of public involvement can be witnessed any day of the week among almost any bunch of westernized people. Seldom does one hear anything similar of people's encounter with an artwork in the purely visual arts.

The advent of film did not have a direct influence on the other arts. For example, film did not lessen the viability of narrative in painting; for painting had long abandoned the genre in the decades of early modernism. The potential competition between media which was discussed *à propos* painting and photography did not really arise. Yes, certain people undoubtedly did consider painting an inferior technology, rapidly to be made obsolete; but for the most part, spectators simply regarded the two media as different and incomparable—which in a sense they are—and no particular challenge was felt. The fact that the public used its increasingly disposable money and leisure time to see films, and very little by way of the visual arts, did not reflect *per se* on the status of the traditional visual arts.

If anything, the advent of film confirmed the elliptical directions taken by the visual arts. It now seemed provident that painters had opted out of narrative and illusionism and had identified a direction exclusively proper to the static visual plane in which film would not be able to follow. Their prudence was not merely strategic but logical and faithful to the essence of the visual arts. When film gathered its extraordinary public momentum, artists would gain a sense of history corroborating the trajectory of modernism. The sacramental offices of painting as abstraction were somehow more mysterious as the expectations of pleasing a *vulgus* had been dispelled by the priority of film among the crowds. Everything that film had to offer which was exceptional—and no one doubted that—amounted to a checklist of qualities which the visual arts had spurned during modernism for the sake of its sacramental status. These filmic qualities could be described as communication, direct expression, the relaying of information, the representation of spaces, human interaction, moods, specific emotions, specific messages, ideological comment and protest. The visual arts had found the route to ascend to sacramental status by disowning these features (once also memorably cultivated in painting and sculpture) and rather exclusively defining the terms of modernist practice as uncommunicative. Film, as the medium of communication *par excellence*, not only represented no challenge but enhanced in its complementary art the quality of sacramental stylistic exclusivity which is the genius of modern art.

Even the extent to which film lays claim to sacramental status of its own did not change the complacency of this relationship. Films are extraordinarily keen on sacrifice. You can hardly watch a film but there will be an untoward death in its plot. The genre of suspense, for example, jealously glories in the moments before a death, stretching out the imminence of the predictable blow, so that spectators are all steeling themselves in dread anticipation; for what they await will inevitably be fulfilled, rather as in classical myth. Presumably the benefit of watching the fictive catastrophes of film lies in a cathartic process. It seems very uncharitable to interpret the nightly sacrifices of people on the big screen as merely gratifying the sadism of the viewing population; for so many people cannot all be depraved, or at least it would be too rude to recognize it.

The sacrificial economy of film is different to that of ancient theatre, in which the salient quality of the fatal hero is a superintending destiny governing that person who will be undone at someone's hand, possibly a god's. In ancient tragedy, the hero's death is understood before the play begins, for there is a prior mythical role for each hero which cannot be averted any more than his or her identity can be changed. The structure of myths involves fate, all established in a known cosmos of names, places and deities; the plot cannot be invented. The basis of film is generally different, depending for its dramatic power on the skilful invention of plots, each copiously producing heroes and anti-heroes, the number of whom seems almost beyond count. Even when mythological or well-known historical themes are treated in film, the status of the heroes loses its sense of destiny; for the handsome movie-stars induce the same suave and exciting charisma on the classical protagonists as they normally give to their contemporary roles. You have the sense that the hero's deeds are staged not for any spiritual value in the inevitable sacrifice but to entertain a relatively uninformed audience with memorable surprise actions, bodies, phrases and inventive episodes. As a medium, film is generally secular. That is not to say that film cannot successfully treat religious subjects and give them either a traditional or a new and imaginative inflexion. But the spiritual film-maker in some sense has to countenance the basically secular character of the filmic language in order to do so, a language which will easily overwrite holy conceptions with secular ones, ultimately profane and economically overdetermined with its famous and beautiful actors hitching their charisma to pious archetypes. Many filmmakers attempting to represent the life and death of Christ, for example, fail, especially in conveying the numinous; and their work is *Kitsch*. Film is inherently *machina*, not much *Deus*.

Still, what are all those deaths about? Screen-death multiplies exponentially with the advent of television. Every night in any westernized metropolis, a person can choose to watch murders in all colours, involving all kinds of motives. Most of the murders are fictitious and have to be, for real murders are not sufficiently prolific and many are needed each night. A westernized child is used to seeing more carnage in a week than the average Roman adult saw in a lifetime at the Colosseum. Even cartoons involve shootings and killings. Is this sophisticated barbarism an outlet for aggressive urges in a remissively disciplinary society? Or are the murders sacrificial in some yet unexpressed dimension?

Perhaps the questions are unnecessary. Even in archaic cultures not all deaths were sacrificial, not even all publicly staged deaths. Indeed, the sacrificial killings would have represented a small proportion, mostly involving animals. The route from sacrifice to sacrament to aesthetic is by no means the only cultural course in which death is presented or represented. The bulk-death of television seems both pre-sacrificial and artistic, without a proper sacramental element from which the viewer draws spiritual elevation or, as Christians say, is sanctified. But who would be so bold as to deny the nightly slaughter some ghostly efficacy? It would be imprudent to say anything with finality because, among other possibilities, one effect is certain: the viewer becomes insulated from the shock of violent death, accepts—at least on television—the reality of killing humans and prepares to take deep breaths with equipoise. The viewer knows that the deaths are ritual killings, that is, regardless of the narrative, they are artificial and performed by actors under the careful stewardship of numerous experts. And they know that the story hangs around the motif of a murder or murders plural. The murders are there for the pleasure of viewing a 'mystery' (a coincidental term in our discourse?) or 'suspense' and the manipulation of the murder and its circumstances is the key to an aesthetic experience. One kills people in order to have fictions. The sacrifices are performed to grant importance to acts of imagination within the medium.

Television is not quite the same as film, though clearly there is overlap and the spatial uniqueness of film is constantly threatened by films receding to DVD—sometimes even run through the computer—with their exegetical and confessional appendices which give the austere filmic genre a familiarity and humour unknown in previous generations. But from the outset, the main difference between film and television is a kind of domesticity in television, not merely in the physical location of the cathode-ray tube or liquid-crystal display in a lounge-room or family-room but the constancy, the familiar sequencing, the everyday-ness, the way that television proposes intimacy with the viewer through regular personalities who present movies, the news, the weather and so on, people who say hello and goodbye and smile at you as if they knew you. Sometimes they are called hosts. Film is structured around the idea of an artistic masterpiece which is spellbinding, whereas television—while obviously screening numerous films with the values inherent in the medium of film—tends to be structured around the idea of continuity, the eliciting of loyalty in the viewer to choose one channel over another. The television series is the best symbol of this, taking a limited bunch of actors on weekly episodes or, as with soap opera, daily episodes. Of course they encourage a following, even an addiction. Children will cry if they miss a certain program and, on certain nights of the week when popular series are screened, urban restaurants suffer a loss of patronage. The rhythms and the face of television have a diurnal complexion. The television sits in the living space with an air of belonging, commanding the domestic environment and even offering a keynote to the furniture and definition of rooms.

It is difficult to imagine that television has not affected visual relationships, the very understanding of 'viewing' and visual participation.[10] It is not necessary to go out of the house for the most thrilling and absorbing encounter; and a new forceful language of the visual (in part just a dynamic extension of graphic design) creates almost tribal attachments in the community to certain programs and personalities. On television, the normal visual world and its rhythms do not stand up very well; they need to be laundered, garnished with clichés and animated with an appropriate televisual pace. Like all media, television is highly artificial; but unlike most other media it pretends to a ubiquitous domain of experience, from the world-wide perspective of current affairs to the most intimate levels of emotional engagement in families.

Alongside television (and where in the western world can one avoid television and not be alongside it?) all other arts are apt to seem esoteric. The exception is film but only because it is televised or might be or can be enjoyed in portable format, as noted, and played at home at call. The visual arts can be televised but rather by way of reportage or art history, ironically turning the visual arts into a rather bookish genre. As with film, the visual artists are free to ignore television and most do, for very similar reasons to those that explain the marginal status of film in the sacramental consciousness of artists.

But other artists, coinciding with the early proliferation of television in the United States, tackled the theme of popular culture in works of the most tellingly equivocal kind. Pop art, as in the UK, did not particularly relate to television but popular imagery of all commercial kinds. Popular, in the modern world, means commercial. The communicative energies of capitalism were discovered in their new prowess, the faculty of infiltrating popular consciousness with the quality of newness and generating celebrity through new entitlements of exhibitionism. Television is still probably the ultimate channel of infiltration, giving to products the new prestige of the mass-market, conferring upon the object a must-have status.

In this world in which the value of objects is given a commercial representation to the widest public, a radical inversion takes place in the very notion of prestige. In the past, the value of something has stood in inverse proportion to its availability. If something is rare, it is proportionally valuable. The reason silver is more valuable than aluminium is that silver is less available than aluminium; there is consequently less supply and greater demand for silver; so the price for silver is higher than that for aluminium. But the world of media sets other values which may not have the material presence of money but which have enormous currency. Industrially reproduced products and photographically reproduced figures from film and popular music have a prestige related to the extent of their dissemination rather than their rarity. In Andy Warhol's silk-screens, objects, such as the Campbell's soup can, and stars such as Marilyn Monroe and Elvis Presley are reproduced with degraded resolution, perhaps suggesting the number of times the image has been reproduced.[11] Nobody could ever count the number of images of Marilyn Monroe. There would have been millions, most of which have perished. A given image of the voluptuous diva is effectively trash—because common—but the prototype has mythical status on account of the very process of mass-reproduction which paradoxically consigns any single image to the near-worthless.

But if this is the historical backdrop to Warhol's work, the images make no attempt to synthesize the inversion of value in modern media. Warhol's images are artfully resistant to any form of comment. All that we know is that the brand names, the stars, and certain images such as the electric chair and spectacular motor accidents are famous on account of mass-reproduction. The works do not say anything about the condition; 'equivocal' is too strong a word to use of Warhol's work, for the mechanically reproduced silk-screens do not quite equivocate between messages. They are without messages, iconographically radical but non-committal, drained, scarcely even acknowledging that there might be any distinctive messages among which a person might identify a higher virtue. Similar things can be said of other pop artists, such as Roy Lichtenstein, Tom Wesselman or Mel Ramos.

Because of its address to popular culture, pop art has sometimes been construed as an early form of postmodernism. It forsakes the hallowed goal of abstraction—which is the genius of modernism—and seeks no lofty universals, no totalizing aesthetic principles, no visual supremacy in the form of geometric planes or gestural ciphers of powerful instinct. It is an art of specific reference: it refers to well-known commodities, personalities or other popular media (such as rock music, advertisements or comic books) and it is also an inclusive art: it brings into the high aesthetic realm of large paintings the icons of contemporary life, which would have been rated vulgar by former connoisseurial standards, and it takes on cultural circumstances of an almost indiscriminate kind, linked only by fame, popularity or notoriety. For the first time, too, it confronts its audience with the equalizing force of media, in which a politician, a filmstar and a serial murderer are in some sense equated with Campbell's soup. Warhol does not have motifs; he has images, things which are already art. His work is art about the economy of images, which seems, in its self-reflexiveness, rather a postmodern discourse.

Of course, postmodernism remains to be defined (let us attend to that presently); but the term postmodernism is not necessary for a discussion of pop art. For all its lack of interest in universal aesthetics, pop art is thoroughly modernist. You could say that pop art is post-formalist but that epithet is neither remarkable nor useful. German expressionism is somehow post-formalist but it is assuredly modernist. The modernism of pop art lies in two fundamental tenets: first, its celebration of newness via stylistic novelty and, second, its semantic evasiveness. Pop art works on the old ambiguities of modernism and ultimately has nothing to say about popular culture. The acknowledgement of popular culture does not lead anywhere; when you look at one of the stars, you are not caused to remember their lines or their melodies, any more than you are induced to recall the sugary-salty savour of Campbell's soup. Warhol visits popular culture not by a phenomenological devotion but because he is addicted to its mechanisms of fame; he is fixated at the threshold where a person becomes a commodity, where he or she enters a commercial ambience mechanically geared to promoting fame exponentially for commercial reasons.[12] Relative to any person of flesh and blood, the personality emerging from such processes has a strong dimension of the absurd.

If we wanted to gild the lily, we could easily argue that Warhol's work is expressive in that much. The figures whom he represented in high-contrast and artificially coloured silk-screens are disembodied, are the product of machinery, are the bloodless wraiths of fame. But true to modernist habits, the works do not really seek to communicate; and interpreting them as an ambitious poetic critique of popular culture undermines what magic they have. Their magic is the old modernist ambiguity which is essential to the innovative displacement of subject matter by novel style. Warhol is undoubtedly seduced by the radical look of modern imagery, but especially if it can give him a new visuality on canvas. And so he extrapolates the poor resolution in a photograph of a film-star, enhances the tonal depredations of mass-printing, and enlarges the weak photographic volumes on an epic scale. Confounding the one medium with the other yields an unsettling dissonance, inducing upon the star the aura of freak, at once monstrously overwhelming yet absent, transfigured, repographically unfleshed, abstracted from normality and glorying in the medium of visual trash as the ghost of popular fame.

Credit must be given to Warhol for this idea which, once having been invented, required no imagination to rehearse any number of times with the same mechanical blandness that belongs to the very mass-produced imagery which is his subject-matter. It is a credit which must be extended to all artistic innovators, the sacraments of artistic change in which an art-form from the immediate past is secularized or taken out of its liturgical context and stripped of its faithful spiritual agency. The new art returns the spiritual content in an abstracted form and obtains the credit for universalizing what was formerly confined to the faithful. And so while taking away the liturgical context, the new art nevertheless retains the spiritual prestige and seems yet more aesthetically powerful on account of dispensing with former cultural incumbencies and making the spiritual autonomously artistic.

Warhol's work is all these things with respect to popular culture. It takes on the glamour of the famous filmstars but lifts their disembodied images into an abstracted and weird visuality which disdains any part of their popular cult. You get the thrill of the presence of Marilyn but never encounter what makes Marilyn special. Warhol takes the spooky magic but accepts no responsibilities by way of narration or cult-building. The sacramental paradigm was never more parasitic (to use Benjamin's word, cited in Chapter 1) than with Warhol; for he adds little but subtracts to achieve a new stylish universality whose very emptiness has a spiritualized aura. Warhol's pictures are extraordinarily flimsy, predictable and neutral; but art-lovers get a great buzz out of them. That is because, for all their faults, they lay claim to the sacramental and, without further skill or scruple, assume its agency in the contemporary art-lover hungry for contemporary sacraments.

The reason Warhol is not postmodern is that his work does not belong to a critique. Nor, incidentally, is it a celebration; it is a perfectly impassive vehicle of expressive neutrality, just like the work of Mondrian or Rothko. The theoretical antithesis of this abstracted tradition is postmodernism. The simplest definition of postmodernism is that it is a critique of modernism. It is unfortunate that the word postmodern suggests 'after' modern, as if postmodernism followed upon the demise of modernism. But modernism is not extinguished by postmodernism. The two are concurrent and complementary. The continuing relevance of modernism is in fact necessary to postmodernism.

Beginning with architecture in the seventies, postmodernism arose as an antagonist of modernist uniformity. Against the abstracted and universal language of form cultivated in the Bauhaus and the international style, postmodern architects, beginning with Robert Venturi, advocated an architectural iconography which communicated the distinctive identity of communities, their associations and symbols.[13] Buildings must accommodate and assert difference: they should find the popular vernacular and, rather than impose a universal language of form, buildings should reflect on the cultural roots of communities or institutions. Though perhaps not always appreciating the nuances of Venturi's writings, architects world-wide during the eighties demoted clean and uniform neutrality in favour of expressive presence, especially the accenting of doorways and windows by means of pediments, columns, arches, canopies, entablatures and other classical motifs, suitably reincarnated in contemporary industrial materials and serving very few of the ancient principles of ornament. Unlike their modernist predecessors, postmodern architects had recourse to the styles of the past; but they usually engaged the historicist spirit in a backhanded way, wilfully undermining the gravity and logic of the august tradition which they quoted by means of flimsy materials and inappropriate articulation. Architects enjoyed not only the idea of an eclectic patchwork of ancient and modern, high and vulgar—mixtures which were described by the term inclusiveness—but relished the idea that architecture could be witty, full of ingenious *contrapposto*, conceits and caprice, full of contrasting references and whimsical formal contradictions, just as it was with the architecture of Giulio Romano in the sixteenth century. All of these eccentric features contrasted radically with the humourless austerity of modernist architecture, professing an exclusiveness of form and reference in the ideal abstract geometry of line and plane.

The movement did not constitute a recovery of the past; it involved very little nostalgia and was sometimes intrinsically and knowingly cynical in its 'abuse' of the classicism which it deliberately cited in bad faith, denying the classical motifs the function and dignity proper to them. The aim was to be smart with the complexity of references where the modernists had been smart with the elimination of references. There was no question of a return to the ancestral authority of the classical tradition with its gravity and power of concertedly articulated forms and logically emphatic ornaments. By the nineties, the twisted revivalism had lost energy and architects returned, alas, to the uncommunicative buildings of modernism, which lack an address to the street and fail to accompany the pedestrian with familiar rhythms and the supportive presence of measured space. Architecture is still broadly historicist but its historical quotation centres on disruptive moments (modernism itself) and lacks the classical symbolic sympathies with human scale, proportion and articulation.

In the fine arts, the historicist temper was also felt, with a strong return to figurative painting, soon, in turn, to be chased by an equal and opposite appropriation of conceptual art. The historicism was not pursued for its own sake but in order to proffer a critique of the moral and aesthetic assumptions which underpin the styles and iconography of previous traditions. When an artist cultivated an illusionistic idiom, for example, he or she was expected to spike the homage by undermining its seriousness with non-classical or non-linear interventions, to disrupt the pictorial space or the logic of the illusion or the narrative and so on. Artists have found such strategies very easy to carry out, for they succeed when they fail, when the authority of the picture is lost, when the illusion is disappointed or deliberately mucked up. For artists with few drawing skills, the agenda of self-contradiction and paradox was a god-send.

Some artists, like the Russians Komar and Melamid and the Italian Carlo Maria Mariani, managed to bring off a bland rehearsal of illusionistic traditions while still acutely parodying the symbolic order which promoted them; but most artists, having little intrinsic faith in the project of representing space and volume by a gestural argument of perceptual intuitions, found it both physically easier and ideologically safer simply to confound their illusions with multiple layering. Thus, lumping together images of an incongruous visuality, they produce pictures which owe more to collage than to traditions of handling coherent space. The example of collage has spooked most postmodern picture-making. As pastiche became the new originality, few postmodern artists who quote older traditions have successfully avoided it.

For the rest, postmodern practice had a certain resemblance to modernist practice. Italian and German neo-expressionism may have had more references than German expressionism around 1911; but the exorbitant brushstrokes in strong colour (now on boastful large-scale canvases) look similar and speak of a similarly conceited heroism in the artist, regardless of any subtexts which may be supposed to undermine the cavalier style. Developments in the eighties were hectic and short-lived. By the end of the decade, neo-expressionism was already unpopular and neo-geo or new abstraction became a hit. But wherever postmodern art visited the forms and meanings of modernism, the result was visually difficult to distinguish from the brash antecedent which it sought to parody or, as some people said, 'ironize' or 'problematize'. As an artistic movement based so comprehensively on theory, the issue of such a tenuous separation did not escape the attention of artists and commentators.[14] But the productive effect was limited. The very embarrassment of not being able to distinguish the critique from its target was understood as a great postmodern confession of artistic complicity, an allegory, in effect, of the way in which art-historical agendas co-opt their own revisions and implicate their own critique in semiotic treachery. So long as the work could be represented as somehow confessional, somehow revealing its faults with self-reflexive rhetoric, all failures could be heralded as successes. There was never a movement which attracted so many Jesuitical apologias, busily obsessing about the extent to which the work deconstructs itself, confesses its artifice and makes a thousand *mea culpas* over drawing from a discredited past. The minor industry in writings to accompany exhibitions was—and still is—entirely necessary to establish the credibility and artistic worth of the work.

This aspect of postmodernism is unchanged. Outside the ambience of people who understand the concept of deconstruction, who read abstruse exhibition catalogues and knotty articles in forbidding magazines, new art is unintelligible and inaccessible. This, too, is regarded as good postmodernism, not because there is anything intrinsically appealing about public incomprehension but because the ultimate dependence of the artwork on texts finally discredits the myth of artistic autonomy, that is, the idea cultivated throughout modernism that the artwork should stand by itself, obtaining recognition for its own fetishistic visuality and requiring no extrinsic information, narrative or ulterior structure of language, ideology, symbol or myth. The gruelling exegeses of postmodern art are understood as countervailing the modernist conceit of radical independence from cultural givens. Art is a form of discourse. It was during modernism as well but was never recognized or acknowledged, for it served the shamanistic conceits of modernists to project the aura of total autonomy from cultural traditions. Modernism as a transcendent abstraction aspiring to universality of form and content discouraged the identification with cultural incumbencies. Postmodern visual practice, on the other hand, would reject this autonomy—larded, as it was, with numinous pomposity—and would freely signal its debt to the medium of text.

The argument is not silly but the outcome is. The failure of the artwork to communicate on its own would be understood as a candid virtue, an honest sacrifice of unearned artistic privileges. The virtue-loving critical spectator would be required to find the profound critiques within inscrutable artworks of unrewarding visual calibre, using texts of impeccable sanctimony. Sometimes it was possible to recognize a well-intentioned idea. It was seldom possible to respond directly to it, however, as the form and content did not match and were purposefully pushed out of alignment in order bravely to disrupt the former authority of the artwork and deconstruct the seamlessness of an inherited semiotic system.

Postmodernism (which in many ways is noble and profoundly intellectual) perfectly matches the sacramental paradigm which has operated throughout the progress of western visual art. It is a process of secularization: it inherits a series of forms associated with sacred ideas—as in the hallowed universality of abstraction, the transcendental aesthetic experience autonomously distilled and concentrated as artistic essence or supreme spirit—but rejects the holy implications, seeks to send them up and make polemics against their spiritual authority. In creating this artistic critique, however, the radical new secularizing art still depends on the old forms; it regurgitates them by necessity and necessarily enjoys their undeconstructed prestige. Postmodern art selfconsciously 'endgames' with complicit intentions; but the net result is to have the privileges of modernism (or any anterior tradition) without its responsibilities, without the beliefs, without the conviction of an artistic destiny to move the spectator emotionally to higher planes of consciousness. Yet because it passes off the old forms in the guise of a deconstructed and de-ritualized series of arguments, postmodern art gains the further prestige of translating the visual material of a belief-structure into aesthetic agnosticism.

The verbs associated with the postmodern project are seldom affirmative. Postmodernism is always 'interrogating', 'asking questions about' and so on. Celebration is structurally problematic, for it is not discursive or dialectical. Much of our spiritual hunger is ignored. This paradoxical exclusivity in a movement based on inclusiveness rather makes postmodernism unsustainable; because, apart from the narrowness of its communicative scope, it has little appeal among people who do not have an axe to grind with a dominant symbolic order. And even among those who are understandably disaffected with mainstream values, the resulting productions are ungiving, inscrutable and frequently boring. An art which merely interrogates is unpoetic, often making bad discourse as well as bad visuality. Art is a peculiarly bad system in which to interrogate for its whole social predication is celebratory. This leaves only one aesthetic joy for postmodernism and that is the beauty of the absurd, the same motif as that indulged by Dada.

Postmodernism as a series of inclusive ideological propositions is likely to survive as long as modernism survives; but as an energetic artistic movement, it seems to have dubious prospects. It has difficulty creating excitement and is vulnerable to all kinds of unholy impulses from popular culture. Meanwhile, a tidal-wave of modernism has crashed upon the empty discursive beaches, scattering all before it: the global enthusiasm for digital technology.

Computers had been used in banks and other bureaucracies for decades; but in the eighties, the personal computer began its exponential proliferation, entering homes as much as the workplace with new and advanced methods of handling information. During the nineties, the hardware and software improved to such an extent that millions of private domestic users could enjoy modem-access to commercial servers, linking them with global information sources on the internet.

The new technologies are unlike the old computer systems, full of arbitrary codes and reams of data inaccessible to all but computer boffins and unintelligible to all but accountants. The new technologies are based on a visual interface in which people can see options in a graphic display (often of some beauty) and physically engage with it using the gestures—admittedly somewhat rudimentary—of wrist movement and finger-pressing on a mouse or touch-pad, all of which registers visually on the screen. Looking down a constantly unfolding avenue of illustrations, the virtual traveller in a suburban lounge-room can discover information of a personally interesting kind anywhere in the world. The experience has an almost transcendental dimension, as the user overcomes incredible physical distances in an effortless slipping between icons in order to contact virtual spaces, images and texts, or 'sites' as they are better known.[15] The sites are visually configured by their proprietors to offer an interactive experience which reflects a communicative desire on their part, usually to advertise or sell goods or services. The virtual landscape of the internet is charged with expressions of desire. It runs through electrical impulses but is driven by hormones. The visual language developed for the internet tends to the biomorphic: graphic designers are engaged with an enviable talent for integrating text and abstracted image, resulting in a peculiarly synthetic sign-making idiom cultivated in advertisements on television and elsewhere. The virtual universe is a world of seduction.

Part of the seduction lies with the interactive nature of computer software. Other media have probably entertained people with greater style and poetic grace but the digital media offer the incomparable flattery of being a vision-manager in the centre of the universe—finally superseding Renaissance perspective—able to control the material flashing up on the screen with instant commands. There is no longer a 'spectator' but a user, a person dynamically empowered with choices, one who is no longer structurally passive, absorbing whatever has been patronizingly prefigured for entertainment, but an agent who decides what is to be presented. Never mind that in many cases the decisions are negligibly greater than those offered by a passive telly-watcher holding a remote control; never mind that most sites prefigure what you want to see just as patronizingly as a film does. The structure of the computer suggests the opposite: you have infinite choices, total power to manage the virtual spaces which you enter, flit out of, revisit or use as a launching pad for some other trajectory.

Part of the seduction lies in decentralization, both physical and metaphoric. The physical sense is obvious enough: the idea that you, personally, have to go to a greater metropolis to enjoy certain experiences is weakened. Information (which includes the experience of events) is infinitely transferable, linked by any number of references. One no longer needs to live in New York to know a great deal about the institutional life of the town, and even to have some interaction with it (mostly as a consumer). But the metaphoric sense is equally compelling: your engagement with a medium no longer has a centre in the intention of the creator; there is no longer an artistic master narrative which you have to follow—as with books or films—but an infinitely fragmented series of visual and textual vignettes linked by inviting choices. It is the medium of nomadic attention; it offers a perpetually empowered distraction in the wandering of interest, in which instructions to proceed down a linear path must be made sufficiently enticing in order to attract a following. The sense of authorship, the confidence in a single narrator, is largely absent, unless you get hooked on a game. You visit things as if they merely inhabit a periphery, lacking an authorial presence until invested by the grace of your attention.

And then there are less personal and more universal metaphors. Part of the seduction of the digital network lies in the metaphoric embrace of the new technological system itself, progressively acting less and less like a machine and more and more like a neuronal system, a global organism that pulses with a live expression of physical and mental interaction. Since they were invented, computers have been invested with the fantasy of replacing the brain or making the brain redundant. Now the empire of such fantasies is global, presenting a world-brain, trafficking all significant exchange of information and even material in the form of money. Nearly all money—except the few dollars in your pocket—is digital. So all economic and intellectual aspects of the world are not only represented in the digital environment but they actually occur through it, exist within it and can no longer exist without it.

Since the twenties, modernism has been obsessed with the machine and the organism. Many aspects of modern art have been devoted to making the organic seem more mechanical, just as many aspects of modern design have been devoted to making the mechanical more organic. With computers, the modern vision is fulfilled; for at last we have a machine which, regardless of its appearance, acts like an organism with intelligence and promises to make organic processes happen without biological fallibility. Of course, the extent to which computers replicate the simplest neuronal activity of the body is negligible; but nobody is discouraged from entertaining the fantasy. What computers really offer is the promise of a mythical future in which anything will be possible.

Like photography and film and television before it, digital technology does not replace the established arts like painting and sculpture, and presents no challenge to them. If anything, it acts as a convenient vehicle—just as photography did with painting—by creating virtual galleries which are carefully constructed to preserve the high prestige of the manually created object and spaces. There is no threat to the classical media for two reasons: first, the digital medium is unsuited to registering a gestural language and abstracts from the corporal with a certain technological remoteness. Second, the fine arts have long been addressing a tiny elite of art-lovers, unconcerned with dominant media such as television. Painting and sculpture have plenty of conceits upon which to survive and in most senses retain the proprietorship of artistic prestige. But that is not to say that the fine arts will not use computers prolifically, especially in projects which involve the trafficking of information.

The signs, however, indicate directions which fulfil the sacramental paradigm encountered so often in the past, and not the least in the disruptive movements of the twentieth century. Where the fine arts deal with the digital or the televisual it is by way of strategic complication, an aesthetic of resistance, which the average user will never appreciate. The media are configured by capital to provide easy access; when the artist uses the digital media, the digital works become either abstruse, deconstructive, absurdist or satirical. The artist takes a medium already laden with metaphoric conceits—conceits suggesting the digital substitution of spirit, an autonomous neuronal activity beyond the body but abstracting the bodies and energies of the world community—and sends it up, confounds its agency and makes fun of its supposed universality and futuristic pretensions. But in conducting such interventions, the new art does not shun the high prestige of the new media of which it offers a critique; on the contrary, it accepts all the glamour of the spiritualized machine and retains it while secularizing the content as satire. Through the deconstructive jokes and opaque critiques, the naïve mystique of the digital is enhanced by embracing a witty knowingness. If the new digital art did not contain this secular sacramental element, it would not be recognized as poetic or artistic at all but simply another manifestation of information technology. The artistic part is the sacramental part. It was ever thus; and whatever progress the hectic pace of digital innovation may bring, it will not change the definition of art, established from archaic patterns and translated into the age of critique with the same structures to translate belief and spirit into a de-ritualized aesthetic.

ENDNOTES

1 Kuspit (2000a). First published in 1993, this forceful essay addresses the assumptions inherent to definitions of modern art, taking a psychoanalytic approach. See also Kuspit's (2000b) collection, which witnesses painting as the foremost medium amongst the array of artistic practices competing for attention under the rubrics of modernism and post-modernism.

2 Francis Picabia, *Machine tournez vite (Machine Turn Quickly)*, ca. 1916–1918, gouache and metallic paint on paper, laid down on canvas, National Gallery of Art, Washington.

3 *Amorous Parade*, 1917, oil on cardboard, collection of Mr and Mrs Morton G. Neumann, Chicago.

4 Marcel Duchamp, *The Bride Stripped Bare by her Bachelors, Even* (widely known more simply as *The Large Glass*), 1915–1923, oil and lead foil between glass, Philadelphia Museum of Art, Philadelphia. Moffitt (2003, 169–224) pursues the content and signification of *The Large Glass* in terms of Duchamp's spirited fascination with esoteric literatures and alchemy.

5 Bergson (1911). The material of *Le Rire* was first published in 1900, in a series of articles in the *Revue de Paris*.

6 On relationships between Dada and the twentieth-century history of American modernism, see Naumann et al. (1996). This exhaustively documented exhibition catalogue amounts to a celebration of Dada activity, in all its irruptive yet auratic variety, as translated to America, and furthered by its encounter with the tumultuous context of 1920s New York.

7 Marcel Duchamp, *Bottle Dryer (Bottle Rack)*, 1914 (lost original), readymade, galvanized iron bottle rack; *In Advance of a Broken Arm*, 1915 (lost original), readymade, wood and galvanized iron snow-shovel; *The Fountain by R. Mutt*, 1917 (lost original), readymade, porcelain urinal with black paint. The *Bottle Dryer* of 1914 is usually described as the first 'pure' or 'unassisted' readymade.

8 *The Art of Destruction: Writings of the Vienna Actionists* (Green 1999) documents the self-consciously 'extremist' and radicalizing work of the four artists known as the Vienna Actionists: Hermann Nitsch, Günter Brus, Otto Muehl, and Rudolf Schwarzkogler, during the period of particular notoriety in Europe's post-war art scene, 1962–1974.

9 Film was well placed to explore the richness of Freud's inquiries. On historical and cultural parallels between the technologies of cinema and psychoanalysis, see Kaplan, (1998, 152–164). Hence, for example, "... Hollywood very quickly gravitated to a popularized version of Freud's theories in the post-World War II period, when, as a result of war traumas demanding psychoanalytic treatment, Freud's theories were circulated even more widely than before. Freudian ideas seemed to offer the authority of 'science' for the stories the cinema was already telling ... Producers saw the relationship between the dreams of their audiences and the 'dreams' Hollywood put forth on the screen" (158).

10 See Farmer (2000). This catalogue of the eponymous exhibition on work about, using, and demonstrating the influence of television by artists in America and western Europe who engaged directly with the mass media (as distinct from other contemporaries preoccupied by the more exclusive, aesthetic values of abstract expressionism).

11 For immediate background to Warhol's 1962 silk-screened images of Campbell's Soup cans, and of Marilyn Monroe, see Watson (2003, 79–83).

12 On Warhol as no less than "an enduring brand" now, see the introductory comments in Watson (2003: xi): "It is just as if Andy Warhol never went away. He was simply transformed into a tote bag, or a gender studies dissertation, or a reality TV show, or a thirty-seven cent postage stamp."

13 See Venturi (1966) for a defence of stylistic inclusiveness and diversity. See also Venturi, et al. (1972): together these two titles can be called Venturi's key contribution to theorising architectural postmodernism.

14 One of the most beautiful expositions of the art and art theory of the 1980s is the Australian Rex Butler, *An Uncertain Smile*, Artspace, Sydney 1996. In many ways the creative response to the period in writing is the memorable part. See also the bafflingly eloquent Edward Colless (also Australian), *The Error of My Ways*, IMA, Brisbane 1995, for which Butler provides an insightful introduction.

15 Beardon and Malmborg (2002) provide articulate perspectives on digital art as a field of practice still emerging and reaching for definitions, which convey the positive potential typically ascribed to virtuality and to digital technologies. This volume draws together twenty-seven influential articles originally published in the journal *Digital Creativity*.

REFERENCES

Beardon C.; Malmborg, L., eds. 2002. *Digital Creativity: A Reader*. Innovations in Art and Design. Lisse: Taylor & Francis.

Bergson, H. 1911. *Laughter: An Essay on the Meaning of the Comic*, translated by Brereton, C.; Rothwell, F. New York: MacMillan.

Farmer, J. A., ed. 2000. *The New Frontier: Art and Television, 1960–65*. Austin, Texas: Austin Museum of Art. [Exhibition Catalogue.]

Green, M. 1999. *The Art of Destruction: Writings of the Vienna Actionists*, translated and edited by Atlas Arkhive 7. London: Atlas Press.

Kaplan, E. A. 1998. "Freud, Film, and Culture". In *Freud: Conflict and Culture*, edited by Roth, M. S. New York: Knopf. 152–164.

Kuspit, D. 2000a. *The Dialectic of Decadence: Between Advance and Decline in Art*. Aesthetics Today. New York: Allworth Press.

Kuspit, D. 2000b. *The Rebirth of Painting in the Late Twentieth Century*. New York: Cambridge University Press.

Moffitt, J. F. 2003. "Duchamp in New York with Esoteric Patrons and the Large Glass, 1915–1923". In *Alchemist of the Avant-garde: The Case of Marcel Duchamp*. SUNY Series in Western Esoteric Traditions. Albany: State University of New York Press. 169–224.

Naumann, F. M.; Venn, B.; Antliff, A. 1996. *Making Mischief: Dada Invades New York*. New York: Whitney Museum of American Art.

Venturi, R. 1966. *Complexity and Contradiction in Architecture*. New York: Museum of Modern Art in Association with the Graham Foundation for Advanced Studies in the Fine Arts. Distributed By Doubleday & Company.

Venturi, R.; Scott Brown, D.; Izenour, S. 1972. *Learning from Las Vegas: The Forgotten Symbolism of Architectural Form*. Cambridge, Massachusetts: MIT Press.

Watson, S. 2003. *Factory Made: Warhol and the Sixties*. New York: Pantheon Books.

Cite this chapter as: Nelson, Robert. 'In the name of critique'. *The Spirit of Secular Art: A History of the Sacramental Roots of Contemporary Artistic Values*. Melbourne: Monash University ePress. pp. 9.1–9.18. DOI: 10.2104/ssa07009.

CHAPTER 10

GLOBALIZATION OF THE INDIGENOUS SPIRIT

Robert Nelson

Throughout the years of postmodern irony, relativism, parody, complicity and subversion, the western art market became hungrier than ever for authenticity. Artists emerging from academies were unable or unwilling to furnish cultural authenticity; because, at its best, their work was a handsome critique of distasteful ideologies. An art professing genuine enthusiasm, such as all pre-industrial cultures enjoyed, was apparently no longer feasible. Cultural sophistication now denied the art lover the innocence of art; and it was no longer even possible to enjoy the naïve aesthetic joy of the old masters, for they, too, were to be read through socio-political analyses ranging from the skeptical to the caustic, dwelling on the chauvinist scandals of patriarchy and their artistic reflection in paintings and sculptures. Among art lovers desperate to vest their affection in objects which hang on walls, there was only one striking solution: the art of Indigenous people who—unless belonging to urbanized communities—had no interest in postmodern manipulation of cultural history. This may explain a part of the remarkable international success enjoyed by the art of Indigenous people.

Indigenous art is quintessentially regional. Its character is identified with the local community in which it is produced. Perhaps in no community is this adherence to a locality so pronounced as in Australian Aboriginal painting, in which iconographic rights and meaning are tied to the land. In spite of this, Aboriginal art is now absorbed into a globalized art market, in which its aesthetic status—if not its original or intended meaning—is understood to be culturally transferable, available to an international audience where it is promoted with a simultaneous air of ancient spirituality and modernist formalism. Even when enjoying a critical reception in Frankfurt, Paris or Melbourne, it is evaluated through inscrutable mixtures of localized awareness of the Dreaming and the aesthetics of abstraction, with all the connotations of universality which would paradoxically negate the deeper attachment to country and theogony which explains the gestation of the work.

The entry of Aboriginal art in the globalized art scene (as in major international art fairs and exhibitions like the Documenta or the Venice Biennale and the marketing of auction houses like Christies and Sotheby's) is artistically and ideologically fraught.[1] The global reception has undoubtedly had an impact on current visual production, which naturally mutates according to historical circumstances. The new international fortunes have benefits and drawbacks, from the symbolic to the economic.[2]

Although the ethnological and aesthetic appropriation of Indigenous artefacts in European culture is old and has been studied in the critical discourses of orientalism and western imperialism, the dilemmas confronting Aboriginal art in the global context are far from exhausted in the literature and in practice. The aesthetic virtues recognized by the international community are not necessarily those that belong with the spirit and intention of the artists. There is scope for recognition but also falsification. Questions abound as to what creates the aesthetic prestige in the urban international art-loving community. Indigenous artefacts (*e.g.* Oceanic, American or African) do not, of themselves, have immediate or automatic prestige. The large production of trinkets and attire available world-wide is associated with tourism and attracts little attention in a gallery environment. This is true, for example, of Aboriginal boomerangs. These are not normally understood to possess the same kind of cultural authenticity and formal grandeur contained in paintings based on the Dreaming or interpreting ritual markings pictorially extrapolated from their use in sacred ceremony.

The directions taken by Aboriginal art (coincidental or strategic) have been extraordinarily felicitous in reconciling Indigenous spirituality and European aesthetics. The translation of desert idioms and subject matter into paint on canvas—subsequently stretched and presented with all the conventions of contemporary art—is a signal development, as is the use of primary and secondary colours in acrylic.[3] It has yielded contemporary art of the highest order; and to this extent, no explanations beyond the claim to quality need be considered. In the following chapter, the discussion of Aboriginal art is restricted to tribal Aboriginal art. The powerful artistic achievements of urban Indigenous artists, such as Gordon Hookey, Richard Bell or Destiny Deacon, is not devalued by not being included here. It demands a separate discussion, and one which is strongly related to the post-structural critique of western scientific and cultural assumptions. This discussion is concerned with the spiritual traditions of the Aboriginal people and the sacred status of their art.

Prior to the settlement of Europeans on the Australian continent in 1788, the native inhabitants had maintained cultural practices for many millennia. Some archaeologists suggest that the religious ceremonies and art can be dated to 40,000 BC or even earlier. The most ancient rock paintings in caves show a style similar to the manner in which bark paintings are executed today in Arnhem Land, the top coastal region of the Northern Territory. This is not to deny some evolution in the history of Aboriginal art; but the ritual basis which produced the figures and patterns umpteen millennia ago was undoubtedly very close to the ceremonial practices which Europeans encountered while colonizing the country.[4]

At least on an institutional level, the colonizing Europeans did not recognize any spiritual or cultural claim which the Indigenous peoples had in any of their art or rites. The country was described in quaint Latin as nobody's land (*terra nullius*), a term which unhappily reflects the perception of Indigenous people as non-existent and without rights. European settlement was a catastrophe for the Aborigines. In some parts, such as the southerly island of Tasmania, the Aborigines were systematically slaughtered to the point of near extinction. Influenza and various forms of genocide also largely eliminated the native population around the fertile cooler South-East of the continent, the most rapidly developing parts in which still today much of the population (and consequently commercial and bureaucratic power) resides. This is the part which contains the two largest metropoles, Sydney and Melbourne, with tall office towers, opulent leafy suburbs and well-defined industrial belts. The great European motif of centralization spread far into the country, with the devastation of scrub-lands and forests for organized farming and a reticulation of roads connecting a hierarchy of towns and cities. The industrial development of the more fertile zones was extremely rapid, as was the expulsion of Aboriginal people from any terrain considered worthy of industrial exploitation.

Comparatively little is known of the art of the Southern Aboriginal populations; for at the time of the most energetic European conquest, the Aborigines—or Koories as they are known in the South—were not in the habit of painting or sculpting with durable materials; and little respect for the apparently ephemeral creations prevailed among the settlers, anxious to beat off any adversity and establish their economic security.[5] In fact so little remains of Koori cultural practices that scholars of Aboriginal art normally focus their attention on the areas of Australia in which a continuous rapport with the Dreaming and its sacred culture are still conspicuous. These are the Kimberley Ranges in Western Australia, certain important parts of the huge Desert regions (mainly in the Northern Territory and South Australia), the North of Queensland and the Torres Straight Islands, as well as Arnhem Land, mentioned before. On the international scene, Aboriginal art and culture have a presence inversely proportional to the European presence in the populous cities.

Scholars have noted that some fascination with Aboriginal culture began early. The general European population of the nineteenth century was undoubtedly incurious and racist; but writers talking about the identity of Australians in the twentieth century frequently sought to appropriate some of the ancient magic of the Indigenous peoples.[6] The sympathy for Aboriginal culture (and particularly art) has escalated exponentially in the last decades of the century, to the point that cultural commentators and artists in the European tradition sometimes admit to a sense of impotence before the awesome spiritual purpose of Aboriginal art. It is difficult to find any contemporary western equivalent for the formal invention and high aesthetic deliberateness of Aboriginal art.

Aboriginal art is rich in variety. An expert has no difficulty distinguishing between the regions mentioned above. Arnhem Land art is characterized by the celebrated X-ray style for depicting creatures, as well as flat paint for certain spirits known as Mimi. Cross-hatching (*rarrk*) is a common element of Arnhem Land depictions.[7] Desert art is characterized by the absence of a profile view of figures; it tends to be topographical in conceiving a bird's-eye view of sites in which episodes take place.[8] Patterns built up with dots is as common in Desert art as cross-hatching is in Arnhem Land. But although art-lovers can show off their connoisseurship by distinguishing between the regions in this way, Aboriginal artists are not primarily motivated by stylistic interests. Many of the motifs which today are sometimes mistaken as stylistic design-tropes were used in painting the body for ceremonial purposes and have ritual significance, often of a secret nature.

Commentators seem to agree that the basis of all tribal Aboriginal art is religious.[9] The *Leitmotiv* is a period of creation and forming of the land and its creatures, known by the English term 'the Dreaming'. During the Dreaming, ancestral spirits roved across the land, interacting with the land and its inhabitants. The travels of the ancestral spirits are responsible for the natural appearance of the land, but also for the spiritual quality of certain localities. Sites are imbued with the character of the ancestral spirits or with the episodes which marked their transit at such sites. The land is pervaded by the magical presence of the ancestor spirits; it is part of a narrative cosmology which gives natural features a spiritual meaning.[10]

The presence of the ancestor spirits is not mythological, which is a misleading term. The word *myth* refers to stories which are no longer believed, dead religion, even if they may have been believed in the past. Aboriginal people profoundly identify with the reality of the Dreaming: it is the central and commanding religious truth and there is nothing mythological about it. Anthropologists still use the word 'mythological' with unwitting colonial condescension. Alas, it is inappropriate as applied to the beliefs of Indigenous people. The sense in which the Dreaming is religious and not merely mythological brings us to the heart of Aboriginal culture. The ancestor spirits are not abstractions, like Plato's *theos* who is the intellectual embodiment and principle of all ideas at their most essential and supreme, almost a god of abstraction. The ancestor beings have a narrative identity and one does not contemplate them in the abstract, achieving spiritual enlightenment by the mere act of attempting to comprehend the purity of the highest spiritual condition. Aboriginal religion is not based on the extrapolation of spirit. It is based on the human and geographical memory of episodes, conveyed for thousands of generations by tribal elders and reflected in the logic of the land. The ancestor beings in some sense abide all around; they remain in the investment which their contact inherently yielded in a given location. Geography, in the Aboriginal cosmology, is a universe of vestiges. The spirits in some sense perpetually haunt the land but they do not manifest their presence in their entirety; they are immanent but lack the narrative actuality which they demonstrated during the Dreaming. Access to the reality of the Dreaming is the central theme of Aboriginal spirituality.

Hence the role of art and ritual. Ancient rituals are enacted in order to activate the ancestral beings. The purpose of ritual is to bring the reality of the Dreaming into consciousness, so that the ancestral spirits can move, as it were, from the immanence of physical geography to the wilful energy of autonomous divinity. To activate the divinities of the Dreaming requires an inspirational force in the participants who are specifically authorized figuratively to relay the Dreamings by traditional performances. Rituals re-enact certain episodes from the Dreaming and invoke the archetypical reality of events of high consequence in the Dreaming, ancient encounters between beings and terrain which left a physical legacy, inscribed in the land or within the shape of creatures. The rituals call upon the divine to re-enter the realm of contemporary experience and visit the 'communicating' members of the tribe with a poignant manifestation of spiritual power. In this way, Aborigines constantly maintain a contact with the ancestral spirits; they enjoy a personal franchise with a creative cosmology, in turn linking them to the physical realities of the land and its creatures.

Art has a similar function to ritual. It invokes the ancestral beings by re-enacting divine episodes. Aboriginal art is not pre-eminently iconic. It tends to be about dynamic relationships between beings in a certain narrative context. It is not predicated on the Graeco-Roman (later Christian or even Buddhist) idea of setting up an image which receives veneration, as if acting by divine proxy. As in Aboriginal ritual, the art positively activates the ancestral beings; it brings them up, so to speak, from a kind of dormant background to a keen and direct clairvoyance. Though the subject matter is necessarily traditional and formulaic, its rehearsal must be inspirational in activating the divinities.

Part of the difference between Indigenous and western outlooks can be expressed in the appearance of Aboriginal art, which is usually (though not always) schematic. It serves the fundamental cosmology very little to show spirits in a naturalistic way; for the optical incumbencies of illusionism presuppose a series of distinctions between protagonists and their surrounding space. Illusionism is obsessed with how far into the middle-distance any given figure in the foreground may reach. It is consumed by the posture of people, the carriage of their head and spine, the movement of their hands and their facial expression. Western painting which has long cultivated the arts of illusionism is intensely analytical in processing visual information, following the analytical temper of scientific and philosophical inquiry. To a western spectator, the logical separation of figures from the planes of their spatial context is axiomatic. But in Aboriginal art, the dichotomy of 'figure' and 'space' seems less compelling. Of course, up to a point, there is necessarily a binary relationship between a figure and the surroundings; but the art is conceived around a mystical interaction between beings—and often beings and land—which occurred during the Dreaming through a non-dialectical transfusion of powers. The events of the Dreaming are not easy to conceive as so many dramas upon a stage, as when westernized spectators view actors strutting and negotiating their way on an ideal platform set up to face an audience. Aboriginal art is not about spectacle and has no theatrical correlates, least of all in tribal ceremony.

The western theatrical economy of spectator and performer assumes (a) a fictively determined stage which represents a certain place and (b) an autonomous actor, able to parade the scripted performance in an arbitrary number of square metres anywhere in the world. Like western painting, western theatre—and consequently film and television—contemplates the world through a universal window. The art of representation through this window is about conjuring illusions, suspending disbelief, evoking the drama by replicating a life-like series of actions in a credible space. Nothing could be further removed from the genius of Aboriginal art and ritual than this universal and transferable vantage point. Aboriginal art is not staged so that the spectator may see. There is a prior understanding among the initiated by which they can already see. The artistic gesture (typically involving dance, music and body-painting) is conceived by way of invocation. It is intended to activate the spirits, to bring their agency to a benign involvement with the participants. Art is a process of sharing in the being of the divinities rather than observing their form from outside.

From a western perspective, the artistic rehearsal of the Dreaming is also functional, associated with empirical survival-skills in a harsh country. It may not occur to a traditional Aborigine to separate the sacred aspect of the Dreaming from the practical or functional aspect; for the two are intermeshed. The Dreaming concerns the formation of the land; it narrates the history of places and identifies characteristic features, such as water-holes or edible plants, by the events which took place there or which even created a given feature. In a somewhat undifferentiated landscape, the task of learning the whereabouts and use of certain features is a prerequisite for survival. The knowledge of the dry regions is not necessarily complicated but it is unthinkably extensive, like the vastness of the land itself. An individual may intimately know about thousands of hectares, within which he or she will be able to recall the precise location of countless and diverse vital natural amenities. The intimacy of this knowledge is gained through the Dreaming. Nobody would keep an abstract list or encyclopaedia, not even in the mind, for the abstraction of such systems would place the information in a relatively meaningless and arbitrary structure. The stories of the ancestor spirits are a more sophisticated 'retrieval system' than lists and encyclopaedias, for they not only embody the practical information in a way which conveys the sacred history of the land but they install the knowledge in a peculiarly embodied, memorable and meaningful form.

The narratives are learned through the body in dance, song, music and in body-painting. The rehearsal of the stories through the body is absolutely sacramental. In holy ceremonies, the actions of the Dreaming are performed through corporal gestures, each one acting as a kind of landmark around which sacred information is meaningfully located in a kind of analogue pattern, an inevitable unfolding which denotes places, ancestor spirits and humans. Traditional information is assimilated by corporal re-enactments which 'institutionalize' the authority of the stories; and through the somatic rehearsal of the stories and the rhythmic processes of dance and song (which instal the vast material in memory), the communicating participant also intellectually refers the authority of the stories to the factual reality of the land. The land and its creatures remain the great repository of stories, the tangible memory of holy events which resulted in the life-giving forms of the country. It is incorrect to think of Aboriginal ceremonies as didactic—say by analogy to the catechism—for they are true sacraments, perhaps the most essential that ever were.

In its origins (and still in tribal practice), Aboriginal art is inseparable from the sacramental status of such ceremonies. There are—and probably always were—certain motifs which could be used by artists without a deeply sacred basis, such as the patterns placed on boomerangs or other implements, of no conspicuous link to an identifiable part of the Dreaming. But the Dreaming is very encompassing and it would be imprudent to dismiss holy connotations wherever the Aboriginal artist decides that an object deserves decoration. The distinction between the decorative arts (meaning applied ornament) and the fine arts (meaning autonomous figures) does not exist in Aboriginal consciousness, just as it did not exist throughout most of western cultural history. The application of Aboriginal ornaments without a narrative role is nevertheless a sign of a holy link between the object and the Dreaming. But even allowing for some margin of uncertainty, the great bulk of Aboriginal production is not only a reflection of the dreaming but a visual prompt for activating the spirits of the Dreaming, in a manner analogous to the activation of spirits in the ceremonies.

The history of Aboriginal art is difficult to write without concentrating on the work of recent decades. The standard histories concentrate on the seventies, eighties and nineties for a number of reasons. First, production during the European take-over prior to these dates was encouraged very unevenly and was undoubtedly widely scorned among European settlers as any kind of artistic counterpart to the art of western galleries. Second, the production of artefacts in tribal societies was not structured around an idea of preservation and, with the exception of certain rock paintings which are in some sense 'maintained' by tradition, many works were often conceived as being ephemeral and dispensable, in spite of being labour-intensive. The basis of this 'disposability' may have been body-painting, which is appropriate for a given ceremony but has no aspirations to transcend the event in a permanent form. Third, such objects as may have survived would often have fallen into the hands of particularly uncaring people. But fourth—and perhaps the strongest reason: the production of Aboriginal work seems to have escalated exponentially since (a) the recognition of Aboriginal art among western collectors who are interested in it for aesthetic rather than anthropological qualities and (b) the encouragement by western educators, dealers and collectors, for Aborigines to produce art for an uninitiated secular audience, using durable, consistent and easily workable industrial materials, particularly, of course, synthetic polymer paints and canvas.

Aboriginal art today is extraordinarily prolific. An example is Balgo art, emanating from a number of communities on the north-eastern edge of the Great Sandy Desert in Western Australia. Some 500 acrylic paintings on canvas are sent out with invoices each year. But the sheer quantity of production is perhaps the least impressive aspect. The more striking part is the prolific character of the imagination, revealed in copious inventions based on traditional motifs, patterns and, of course, subject matter. Although we know little about the pre-colonial art of the Aborigines (for who could count the number of body-paintings in a given year?) it is nevertheless difficult to imagine such a brilliant efflorescence as we have today.

Nearly all aspects of western contact with Aboriginal culture seem to have been corrosive, resulting in the annihilation of much of the Aboriginal patrimony, not to mention the people themselves. The one outstanding exception—and that only in recent times—is art. Contact with a western market, bureaucratic infrastructure and art materials appears not only to have achieved the conspicuous external promotion of the ancient traditions but also to have invigorated them internally. The even spread of a canvas enables the artist to express an episode from the Dreaming with great freedom, uninhibited by the constraints of scale, texture or curvature on rocks or bodies. In effect, the other-worldly narrative character of Aboriginal art seems to thrive upon the abstract ground of a blank western canvas. Even decorated sculpture—which ought to take its cue from the logic of ornamental markings of the features of the body—seems to enjoy the abstracted spaces of a white gallery in which ensembles of sculpted figures can move between a kind of plastic autonomy and a ceremonial interaction which re-enacts the marking of place somewhere else.

The success of Aboriginal art is a source of joy to the wider Australian community. It is a warm story of cultural jealousies breaking down on both sides of a social divide. On the one hand, western artists do not begrudge Aboriginal artists the high prestige and international public acclaim to which western artists (in spite of training at art school) have no access. On the other hand, Aboriginal artists show a willingness to proffer sacred material—or at the very least material with sacred connotations—to a secular audience, trusting, it seems, that the western connoisseurs receive the artistic precipitate of their patrimony without profaning it. Debates among tribal elders in the seventies concerning the sharing of the Dreaming with the uninitiated were generally resolved in favour of interchange; but certain sacred themes were deemed too holy and demanded secrecy. Of these, of course, non-indigneous scrutineers have no knowledge and it seems impious to inquire. The non-Aboriginal community is more than satisfied with the spiritual generosity of the Aboriginal community and artists. The history of westernization upon Australia has given Aborigines every reason to be unforgiving and rancorous. In spite of this, their work is without bitterness or acrimony.

The magic of Aboriginal art derives from a number of sources. First, there is a fine aesthetic quality in the often complicated configurations. They have a symmetry which, however, is almost never obvious but seems to proceed from an intuitive sense of order. The term 'design' is sometimes invoked but the work does not submit to a drafted order. Second, Aboriginal art has a sacred link with the Dreaming; for the motifs, as handsome as they may be, are by no means merely decorative: the motifs are meaningful and connect places cosmologically with creator spirits in episodes passed down for untold thousands of years. Third, recent Aboriginal art, while still acting as a repository of such prestigious traditions, is also a symbol of a new and highly productive franchise between an archaic sacramental consciousness and a dynamic globalized cultural market.[11] The art is consequently a cheerful sign of novel cross-cultural vigour in which the ancient prospers through the paradoxical spiritual dependency of the industrial culture. Aboriginal art is a historical marvel, (a) maintaining a vast stock of knowledge for countless thousands of years of isolation in Australia, (b) surviving the sudden assault of western colonization and (c) growing in unprecedented volume and formal richness, with incomparable prestige in the western art scene in metropolitan Australia and beyond.

On another level, the success of Aboriginal art has been to allow itself to subscribe to the sacramental paradigm noted throughout the previous chapters. First, Aboriginal art presents itself with a powerful basis in an awesome sacred knowledge, totally essentialist, ritualistic and holy: it is not just sacred in its references but in its efficacy. Second, Aboriginal art graciously lets itself be presented in a secular context, in the first instance simply to communicate the dignity of the culture but thereafter to be relished as imaginative aesthetic wonders, without presupposing that the spectator has any awareness of the spiritual content. Third, the content abides, not because western spectators know what it is but simply that they know that it is there; it is inherent, though now inherently in the background. And finally Aboriginal art wins extra prestige for reconciling the sacred with the secular, for bringing what is specifically sacred in a small community to a universal platform in which its secularized spookiness may be assimilated from any spiritual or non-spiritual perspective.

There is nothing at all wrong with this sequence. In any event, it is a historical inevitability. The Aboriginal artist and the westernized spectator have a necessary and laudable desire to effect a cultural meeting, analogous to the reconciliation so long hoped for. They both make generous concessions. The Aboriginal artist gives up some of the exclusiveness of the tradition and allows the artistic manifestations of an essentially religious order to enter a secular and relativist forum. Meanwhile, the westernized spectator gives up expectations to see straight-forward perspectival or decorative pictures and accepts the visuality of a more or less alien tradition. But in all this, there are two concessions that cannot be made, no matter how tolerant or generously disposed is the mutual spiritual embassy. The first is that for all their scholarly diligence and good will, western spectators are unable to comprehend the deeper ritual significance of the Aboriginal artworks in their rapport with the Dreaming, for they lack tribal initiation, language and education, which includes a first-hand 'corporal-narrative' knowledge of geography. The second unwitting article of western inflexibility is the definition of art. When it enters the western gallery, the Aboriginal artwork is co-opted into an argument of abstraction, the abstraction of spirit from a ritualistic function to a hypothetical aesthetic universality, precisely free of the liturgical contingencies of the time and place and unique cultural circumstances which may have instigated it. The role of art has been decided in Europe for the last two and a half millennia. Aboriginal art, though hugely anterior, cannot change the structure; for it has already just qualified as 'art', with the colossal privileges of western spirituality installed in its new predication. Once Aboriginal artefacts are art, they obey—so to speak—the pattern of abstraction of spirit which, it seems, they are most constructed to avoid.[12]

Aboriginal art is deeply attached to a ritualistic function and, of course, it consequently makes little sense to detach Aboriginal art from the role of physically enacting or 'embodying' directly meaningful narratives with their specific poignancy in the Dreaming. No one would ever force the issue. No one is requiring Aboriginal art to submit to an alien paradigm. There is no compulsion; there is only ubiquitous esteem for cultural difference and indeed encouragement for the strongest statement of Indigenous spirituality. But the new structure in which Aboriginal art nevertheless graciously finds itself is overwritten with western authority. Artistic authority in the west is achieved by traducing the liturgical and establishing artistic autonomy for the secularized form of sacred origin. But the genius of western assimilation conceals its sovereign authority with subtle appropriations of the spiritual economy which it has replaced. The high prestige of Aboriginal art owes everything to its spiritual origins. Western artistic institutions do not demand the annulment of these origins; on the contrary, the tribal origins are recognized and celebrated as the basis of the artistic power of the works. It is just that the final credentials of Aboriginal art which warrant its promotion as high art entail the further stage of transcendence by means of aesthetic excellence and autonomous visuality.

Western culture is obsessively competitive. We like to rank everything. In art, we establish prizes (as for athletes) and, even if we do not, curatorial recognition and the market create a *de facto* hierarchy which everyone but the naïve knows about. Some artists 'get to the top' while others never approach such heights. We love cultural champions, people who have 'broken through' with innovation, that quality most hypostasized through the styles of modern art. These social motifs are alien to Aboriginal culture, in which the making of art—as with all ritual energies—has always been a matter of partnerships, collaboration and the selfless maintenance of age-old traditions. But Aboriginal art cannot enter western culture without enduring competition, the invidious taxonomy of struggle, which separates genius from plodder. High fliers are in no time identified and promoted. Names are attached to works with jealous scrupulosity and, of course, there is always talk of fakes. Aboriginal art is not difficult to copy or fudge or 'rip-off', as Australian vernacular puts it with appropriate violence. Paintings by the most illustrious artists are normally sold complete with certificates and photographic authentication showing the artist holding the painting in a desert location.

It may be that in Indigenous society, prior to the advent of the Europeans, certain members of a tribe were somehow distinguished as particularly competent with activating the spirits of the Dreamings in a visual form. But it is unlikely that this facility would have been understood as an artistic gift in the sense of visual talent which we recognize in western culture. A gift—that is, faculties developed in an individual—would be less important in tribal society than the privilege institutionally vested in a person of a certain status. The pre-eminence of the person would be associated with ancestral rights to the story, a form of proprietorship granted by specific patterns of patrilineal and matrilineal descent. One has the status of 'master', as it were, not on account of making art well but having the authority within the community to invoke the story. Cleverness in art does not confer authority; rather, the authority enables the art: it permits the expression of a story whose proprietorship is strictly guarded. Least of all would an artist gain authority by staging some kind of radical redefinition of traditional forms or breaking through the barriers of convention.

Against the grain of the traditional social order, western culture induces a canon of distinction. It has little understanding of the Indigenously holy; it only knows that holiness *ought to be there* and that will suffice. Meanwhile, what it wants from tribal culture is what it sought from modernism: innovation, novelty, radical solutions, an air of abstraction and the aesthetic for its own sake, bolstered, paradoxically, by the condiment of cryptic knowledge (as in modernism), that unapproachable awesome cachet of the tribally sacred. This scheme of priorities is tactfully suppressed but in its historical trajectory is structurally irrepressible. It may also explain certain aspects of the spectacular Aboriginal Renaissance which seem distinctively imaginative, outgoing, monumental, gesturally spontaneous and artistically bold. Part of the reason for the great fame of the late Emily Kame Kngwarreye is probably related to the hidden scheme of priorities which has informed western progress from antiquity.[13]

Kngwarreye's paintings are by no means the only work which could serve as an example of the artistic freedoms of recent Aboriginal art, especially by women. We could look equally at the work of other women from Utopia, such as Minnie Pwerle, Kathleen Petyarre, Ada Bird

Petyarre or Lorna Fencer Naparrula.[14] The work of such women displays a rhapsodic quality, with the traditional Aboriginal tropes—such as sequences of dots or stripes—apparently loosened from a strict totemic or narrative role. In tribal society, there had always been a distinction between the visual work of men and that of women. It belonged to the gender of patriarchal authority to represent the great stories of the Dreaming while women (depending on the regional context) tended to confine themselves to domestic themes or so-called women's designs (*awelye* or *yawulyu*) applied to the limbs and breasts in ceremonies. An almost archetypical gender difference emerges: in subject matter, the work of men embodies powerful links with ancestral divinity and, in style, is circumscribed by a kind of discipline, not always formally rigorous but always functioning with a sense of definition of place and episode. The subject matter of women, on the other hand, does concern the divine but via less heroic manifestations of the sacred or via another ceremony (in which body-painting is integral). Women's art involves another layer of artistic intercession; it is 'once removed' from direct involvement with the Dreaming; it is once removed from the authoritative activation of the divine and dwells more on the communal participation in liturgies. In style, it is relatively unconstrained, free-flowing and visually musical.

Kngwarreye began painting canvases late in life (in her mid seventies) though she would have participated in body-paintings for many decades prior to her recourse to western art materials and the convention of the regular two-dimensional canvas. When approaching the rigid geometry of the rectangle, Aboriginal artists seldom respect the supreme co-ordinates of top/bottom, left/right, but lay the canvas on the ground and either turn it around as they work or move their position at the edge in order to treat the canvas 'democratically', without an abstract attachment of any edge to an imagined horizon. But in Kngwarreye's works, the lack of specific orientation is further accentuated by the free spread of dots or lines, often aligning themselves with a certain directional energy but not one which privileges a given orientation.

In her early works, Kngwarreye filled her canvases with a gentle hail-storm of dabs, taking the traditional Aboriginal dot-motif to a more monumental patch, a quantum which does not so readily submit to the logic of a pattern. And indeed the pattern among the differently coloured patches is often gained and lost as you look. The painting is animated by your perceptual intelligence oscillating between a sense of the structured and the random. The effect is aesthetically enchanting. But the experience is more than merely aesthetic in a formalist sense. The distribution of dabs equally oscillates on an iconographic or cultural level, for in one instant you recognize a sonorous pattern of an abstract or universal nature and, in the next instant, the traces of an almost heraldic ornamental regime, setting out tracks of traditional formulae in an inspired routine of marking the body or retracing ancient stories through their danced-corporal inscription on the body. The combination of the two is scintillating, as the force of ancestral body-designs retains an awesome magic in the background, while the sweet pitter-patter of dabs yields rhapsodically to a sense of cultural permeability.

In Kngwarreye's later paintings, forceful marks are laid out on canvas in a strongly binary argument of strokes, forming a highly directional ensemble which seem both vigorous and intimate at the same time. These works transpose on a grand gestural scale the body markings of tribal ritual, extrapolated with a great sense of urgency from the tender site of the body to the austere rectangle in which the gestures paradoxically resonate with the artistic heroism of western abstract painting.[15] It is as if the aspiration of western artists to arrogate to their work a sanguine 'primitive' unpremeditated spiritual transcendence has finally been fulfilled, with the difference that the gestural prowess in Kngwarreye is genuinely tribal rather than intellectually artificial. So there is multiple magic in Kngwarreye's art. The work can be proffered in the western art scene as a kind of abstraction—which in a sense it is, for it exorbitantly extrapolates from ornamental traditions—but it equally retains an intimate link with a symbolic order, the very quality lost in the secularization which explains the progress of modern art in its march toward abstraction. Finally, the controlled manic energy of Kngwarreye's paintings, heaving the intricate body-ornament into a monumental form, on an abstract rectangular ground with totemic frontality, is a sign of the infiltration of western ambitions in the traditional mind. Prior to the opportunities of western resources, the 'exorbitance' of Kngwarreye's extrapolations would not have been possible. One way or another, Kngwarreye fits in with the paradigm of the highest western artistic prestige. She monumentalizes upon the canvas an inspirational transcendence of traditional forms and meanings, gathering potent symbols, and apparently freeing them from their ancestral limitations through a grand aesthetic simplicity. And even though, from a western point of view, a precise spiritual meaning is deferred in favour of a general aesthetic response, a definite spiritual root remains in the art to testify to a supreme religious authority, unquestioned, unfathomable, and only contactable through the intuitive sympathy which the art excites. In one sense, it is easy to consider that women like Emily Kame Kngwarreye, Minnie Pwerle or Lorna Fencer are the ultimate modern artists.

The sacramental status of Aboriginal art generally is underwritten by other historical factors which are less positive though of crucial importance to the post-colonial world. The belated esteem for Aboriginal art seems to compensate for two centuries of oppression, not just of Aboriginal people in Australia but Indigenous people wherever they (and their ancestral cultures) have been extirpated by western powers around the globe. The whole of the Euro-American world knows and understands the plight of Aborigines in Australia which, in any case, is analogous to the plight of other Indigenous peoples. There are few secrets in the Antipodes, for the paradigm of the colonization does not originate in Australia but in Europe; and it is to the grand old world of rapacious empires that all ethnographic scandals must be referred. It is difficult for westernized people not to consider the past with a sense of guilt, even though their ancestors may not have been involved in killings, neglect or ruthless exploitation. You either belong to the industrial culture or not; and if you do, you have inherited the benefit of the violent displacement or destruction of Indigenous cultures.

Undoubtedly there is a certain melancholy which suffuses the perception of Aboriginal art, a knowledge of the eternal loss of the living presence of whole nations. Australians sometimes experience this on a daily basis, as they are haunted by the vestiges of place names. In Melbourne, for example, there are perhaps only 12,000 Koories: they were 'relocated' last century. Melbourne is widely held to be the most European of the Australian metropoles; but its suburbs and localities nevertheless enshrine the traces of tribal memory. Thus, among a preponderance of names such as Kew and Canterbury, one also encounters names such as Banyule, Dandenong, Darebin, Derrimut, Kananook, Karingal, Kooyong, Langwarrin, Maribyrnong, Moorabin, Mordialloc, Murrumbeena, South Yarra, Wantirna, Warrandyte and Werribee. There is no correlation of these names to class. The Aboriginal names seem to have been retained as if by chance. It is difficult to find out the history of such places or even the meanings of the names.[16] Australian townspeople are often unable to perceive contemporary Aborigines as more than the urban dispossessed, as if degraded reliqua of an unimaginably ancient nomadic culture, sacrificed to our own during the southern deforestation.

The motif of sacrifice (ethnocide) is now ever-present in the conscience of the art world. If ever it recedes from contemporary awareness, there are urban Aboriginal artists who remind the art-loving public of the cultural effacement wrought by European settlement, not to 'rub in' the disgrace but to explore the underlying paradigms of intolerance which once seemed to excuse the banishment of Aborigines from their own land. Artists such as Richard Bell have satirically monumentalized the racism of the uneducated, while Gordon Bennett has tackled the sophisticated methods of systematic western image-making and epistemology, locating the historical maltreatment and slaughter of Aborigines in an obsessive network of linear control and definition. In Bennett's paintings, stereotypically stylized dark figures are fixed within grids and scientific co-ordinates; their plight is apparently orchestrated by the famously objective tools of classification and order, for these intellectual and visual systems easily lend themselves to chauvinistic applications and probably have certain assumptions of cultural supremacy embedded in their very value-free appearance. The genius of drawing up maps consistent with geometric principles is compared to drawing up perspectives conforming with optical principles; and these are compared to drawing up spaces according to universal geometric modernist principles. They are all implicated in a form of intellectual totalitarianism, aggressively establishing an imaginative regime which makes the nomadic Aborigine anomalous, disempowered, obsolete.

The appreciation of Aboriginal art by westernized people is undoubtedly genuine and warm. But there is always a dimension of atonement. To partake and even deeply to sympathize on an aesthetic level is to receive remission for ancestral European sins which have never been expiated. Our enjoyment of Aboriginal art, no matter how profound, is probably never complete without the superintendence of the Judeo-Christian spiritual economy, that trade in spiritual debits and credits that still makes us scrupulously neurotic and which causes us to make sacrifices or to hatch sacramental abstractions of them to vouch for our well-being.[17]

European rituals subsume the appreciation of Aboriginal art and it is illogical for non-Aborigines to study Aboriginal art without simultaneously studying their motives within western culture, the western assumptions which they bring to the encounter and the benefits of doing so within the economy of western culture. If this process leaves little scope for innocently viewing the autonomy of the Aboriginal symbolic order, it is tragic; but the story of the engagement of the Indigenous with the western is inherently tragic, and its artistic interpretative reflection can hardly be expected to avoid that sense of tragedy, least of all when it hopes for cathartic relief.

Aesthetic experience is not exactly sly but it conscripts all contrary motifs to flatter the comprehension and magnanimity of the spectator. The aesthetic 'moment' in the psyche is fundamentally generous and wilfully imputes wonder to whatever it focuses upon; it does not try to be devious but it nevertheless constitutes a personal cosmology which is capable of reconciling all illogical combinations of ideas provided that the individual identity of the aesthete is reinforced. Nowhere is this seen with greater sharpness than in the marvellous esteem for Aboriginal art. It has high credibility in its formal originality derived from immediate contact with a spiritual order; but it gains extra artistic prestige and currency by transcending that order. Aboriginal art comes from a backdrop of austere and grave elders, law, ritual punishments and so on; it is deeply invested with priestly ancestral authority; but in the whitefella economy this backdrop is only enjoyed as a western mystery, sublimely archaic and formidably inaccessible. The greatest impact is made by artists whose work parallels the aesthetic transcendence of time and place (the absolute opposite of Aboriginal tradition) which forged abstraction in the western modernist tradition. Among non-Aborigines, Aboriginal art is most keenly felt as a religious experience when it is locked inside a Judeo-Christian economy of guilt and expiation; it most poignantly registers as a spiritual phenomenon when it works in the conscience in ways that have questionable links with the Dreaming. The interest in Aboriginal art is best understood among non-Aborigines by appreciating the place that its reception has in western spirituality.

But if western spectators enjoy it and Aboriginal artists are gratified by the interest of their patrons, there is little to complain about. Aboriginal art deserves all its praises. Furthermore, there is already a system long established from ancient times in Europe for coping with all cultural contradictions in art: it is the sacramental order, unabashedly flexible enough to make harmonious spiritual sense of any secular attrition anywhere in the globe.

ENDNOTES

1 Belting (2003, 62–73). A now well-known example of the challenges to the institutional vocabulary and frameworks of art history posed by Aboriginal art arose in relation to the 1989 exhibition "Magiciens de la terre," at the Centre Georges Pompidou, Paris; see 67–68. See also the catalogue of the major exhibition presented at Torino's Palazzo Bricherasio in 2001 (Green 2001, 21–33).

2 Myers (2002) is an intricate, localized study of the cultural, art-historical and other issues arising from the international 'transformation' of the acrylic paintings produced by the Pintupi people since the 1970s.

3 See the authoritative text by McCulloch (2001), as well as the monumental collaborative text by McCulloch et al. (2006), one third of which is devoted to Aboriginal art.

4 See Chaloupka (1993). During a period of forty years, Chaloupka has documented over 3,000 rock art sites in the Arnhem Land plateau, endeavoring to trace and construct a chronological order of styles.

5 G. Harradine and K. Kruger, eds., *This is Koorie Art* (Melbourne, 2000), is the catalogue from an unprecedented exhibition that showcased items from the unique collection of over 5,000 Koorie historical objects, artefacts, and contemporary works by Koorie artists and craftspeople preserved by Melbourne's Koorie Heritage Trust Inc.

6 See McLean (1998).

7 On training young bark painters today in the correct use of techniques inherited from rock art, including the crosshatching, see Garge (2004, 107–111). This volume is the catalogue of a far-reaching exhibition of the work and practice of Kuninjku artists from Aboriginal communities west of Maningrida in the Northern Territory, from the nineteenth century onwards.

8 Corbally Stourton (1996). This is a vibrantly illustrated history of the Papunya Tula or Western Desert art movement.

9 See Wally Caruana's (1990) thesis that Aboriginal art "is inherently connected to the religious domain", p. 7.

10 See Hume (2002).

11 For a deeper view of the Aboriginal art market, see Healy (2006).

12 Unless we see Aboriginal art as knowing appropriating or co-opting western conventions.

[13] See Isaacs et al. (1998), an exhibition catalogue which represents the artist's work and its reception from a variety of art-historical and more personal perspectives.

[14] See, for example, Nicholls and North (2001).

[15] "While Abstract Expressionism explains the existence of an aesthetic which allows for the appreciation of Kngwarreye's painting in a principally non-Indigenous market, it fails to account for the way in which her particular form of abstract painting emerged from the hand and mind of an elderly woman in a desert community in Australia" (Sayers 2001, 206). Sayers's inclusive survey of traditions in Australian Art considers dynamics of interaction between the work of Aboriginal and non-Aboriginal artists, linking these especially through the theme of the landscape.

[16] See Hercus et al. (2002): the research presented in this collection of papers does not relate specifically to the south-eastern Australia, but demonstrates what little can be recovered about the historical networks of Indigenous placenames for other parts of the continent.

[17] See Smith (2000, 10–21), who refers to "the national account, the economy of debt-creation and requital, which weaves the textures of Australian life. This density of the past in the present is as vivid for Australians as the memory of the Industrial Revolution is for the English. It is an intensely reflexive counterpoising of action, inaction, guilt and payback, yet subject to a complex forgetting. Historian Henry Reynolds has called it 'this whispering in our hearts'" (11).

REFERENCES

Belting, H. 2003. "Global Art and Minorities: A New Geography of Art History". In *Art History After Modernism*, translated by Saltzwedel, C.; Cohen, M. Chicago: University Of Chicago Press. 62–73.

Caruana, W. 1990. *Aboriginal Art*. London: Thames & Hudson.

Chaloupka, G. 1993. *Journey in Time. The World's Longest Continuing Art Tradition: The 50,000-year Story of the Australian Aboriginal Rock Art of Arnhem Land*. Sydney: Reed Books.

Corbally Stourton, P. 1996. *Songlines and Dreamings. Contemporary Australian Aboriginal Painting: The First Quarter-century of Papunya Tula*, edited by Corbally Stourton, N. London: Lund Humphries Publishers.

Garge, M. 2004. "Growing Up in a Painted Landscape". In *Crossing Country: The Alchemy of Western Arnhem Land Art*, edited by Perkins, H. Sydney: THNH. 107–111.

Green, C. 2001. "The Global Significance of Western Desert Painting". In *Aborigena*, edited by Bonito Oliva, A. Milan: Electa. 21–33.

Harradine G.; Kruger, K. eds. 2000. *This is Koorie Art*. Melbourne: Koori Heritage Trust.

Healy, J. 2006. "A Fragile Thing: Marketing of Remote Area Aboriginal Art". Doctoral dissertation. Melbourne: The University of Melbourne.

Hercus, L.; Hodges, F.; Simpson, J. eds. 2002. *The Land is a Map: Placenames of Indigenous Origin in Australia*. Canberra: Pandanus Books, Research School of Pacific and Asian Studies, Australian National University in association with Pacific Linguistics.

Hume, L. 2002. *Ancestral Power: The Dreaming, Consciousness, and Aborignial Australians*. Melbourne: Melbourne University Press.

Isaacs J.; Holt, D.; Holt, J.; Ryan, J.; Smith , T. 1998. *Emily Kngwarreye: Paintings*. Sydney: Craftsman House.

McCulloch, A.; McCulloch, S.; McCulloch Child, E. 2006. *The New McCulloch's Encyclopedia of Australian Art*. Melbourne: Miegunyah Press.

McCulloch, S. 2001. *Contemporary Aboriginal Art: A Guide to the Rebirth of an Ancient Culture*. Sydney: Allen & Unwin.

McLean, I. 1998. *White Aborigines*. Cambridge: Cambridge University Press.

Myers, F. R. 2002. *Painting Culture: The Making of an Aboriginal High Art*. Objects/Histories Critical Perspectives on Art, Material Culture, and Representation. London: Duke University Press.

Nicholls, C.; North, I. 2001. *Kathleen Petyarre: Genius of Place*. Kent Town, South Australia: Wakefield Press.

Sayers, A. 2001. *Australian Art*. Oxford History of Art. Oxford: Oxford University Press.

Smith, T. 2000. "Australia's Anxiety". In *History and Memory in the Art of Gordon Bennett*. Birmingham: Ikon Gallery.10–21. [Exhibition catalogue.]

Cite this chapter as: Nelson, Robert. 'Globalization of the Indigenous spirit'. *The Spirit of Secular Art: A History of the Sacramental Roots of Contemporary Artistic Values*. Melbourne: Monash University ePress. pp. 10.1–10.15. DOI: 10.2104/ssa07010.

CHAPTER 11

CONCLUSION

Robert Nelson

On the basis of the sacramental paradigm, you could theoretically predict the next movement in the history of western art. All you need do is identify the dimension of current practice which lays claim to some abstracted sacredness—or which entails a belief in the spiritual efficacy of art—and you can be sure that in short order a movement will arise which will (a) extrapolate from its forms, (b) reject its involvement with spiritual belief, (c) nevertheless enjoy the prestige of the disowned spirituality and (d) gain extra artistic credit for carrying an unsustainable belief into a critical new abstracted aesthetic which requires fewer ties with spiritual institutions. Since archaic times, western art has generally conformed to this paradigm and, given the continuing trajectory of western reason, there are grounds to believe that for the foreseeable future it *must* conform to the paradigm. Art is structurally located as an activity which abstracts from a spiritual order and yields an aesthetically disembodied spirituality in a post-liturgical community. It lifts the spiritual from institutional authority to individual disposability. Of course it is possible that art in the future may have a different role; but not all visual production attains the title of art even today, and it is possible that the visual production of the future which does not conform to the sacramental paradigm may also not be called art. We reserve the title of art for the abstraction of the cultish. In western societies, art is intrinsically an activity which negotiates between a constantly evolving ritualistic spiritual authority and a constantly evolving skepticism, forever critically reviewing the cultural predication of a previous aesthetic, and facilitating a spiritual movement from institutional authority to private fancy. In the celebrated cases in which art assumes the political role of resistance to dominant ideology, the same pattern is manifest, even if a little more ambiguous and structurally introverted.

There is a question, however, of the value of the art which fulfils the sacramental paradigm. In some epochs, the results form a succession of masterpieces while in other epochs, the adherence to the same paradigm yields aesthetically questionable visions. The paradigm yields brilliance and embarrassment; it explains the inspiration of one epoch but could equally help identify the destitution of another. It may be that there are no values intrinsic to the structure of art. The paradigm, after all, is a process, not a result. Values cannot automatically be ascribed to its outcomes, else all art would be granted equal and unilateral credit. But given that the paradigm is central to artistic vision, can it be used for distinguishing good art from mediocre art?

There is no rule but sometimes the art of greatest merit is produced when artists sympathetically appreciate the archaic spiritual order which centuries of secular progress have obscured from contemporary view. Artists who understand that art is ritualistic in origins and cultish in its historical structure are perhaps more likely to clinch the vital concept of the next secular sacrament in their own epoch. When art is produced in the consciousness of its sacramental pregnancy, there may be something genuine and profound about the next appropriations of sacred privileges. It is not an issue of being respectful toward the surpassed; it is an issue of integrity, an honesty and awareness about engaging a spiritual status whose spiritual authority one disavows.

Consciousness of the archaic religious background to art and its progressive abstraction in the aesthetic also discourages in artists the arbitrary innovation, the changes in style which have no justification other than a desire for distinctiveness, which amounts to the distinctiveness of the gimmick. For stylistic advancement to assume cultural profundity, it is less important to symbolize the newness of contemporary life than to revise the understanding of sacredness which has been inherited from remote millennia.

But I am not a soothsayer. Artists are commonly exhorted to think of the future rather than the past when working out their vision. This advice is part of a great positivistic enthusiasm which probably sustains many artists but it also has its limitations: it flatters the vanity of those conceited enough to trust their clairvoyance and who believe that they can always be prophetic innovators. Yet the past has laid all the terms of spiritual investment in art; and significant developments in art seem to be those which renegotiate the stressful dialectic relationship between the sacred and art. It seems unlikely to me that art will ever exist without a sacramental structure in its aesthetic underpinnings.

There is a danger, on the other hand, that artists could exaggerate the cultish element of art and reify it in a way which disappoints the sacramentally abstracting virtues of aesthetics. In particular, the awareness of archaic rituals surviving in contemporary art could prompt an unproductive enthusiasm in the practice of sacrifice. For decades, the high-priest of this excitement is the eloquent Austrian performance artist Hermann Nitsch. His practice draws heavily upon the prestige of archaic sacrifices and refers to recent aesthetic history by way of justification.

> You know that in my theatre, beasts are eviscerated, initially sheep, later oxen. Even in Trakl, the butchering of a beast is rehearsed and in Kokoschka there is a celebrated picture in which an almost-living wether is painted together with a hyacinth, a turtle and a water-newt. Hoffmannsthal derives all lyric poetry from the sacrifice of a ram. In an early work there is a discussion in which the fact of substituting a human offering with an animal offering is compared to the way that actual sensory experience is replaced by language (Jocks 1998, 163a).

With regard to the violence of spent entrails, this artist represents no danger at all. Nitsch stage-manages his rationale with Viennese grace in a properly sacramental aesthetic. It is true that he tears the guts out of animals but they were dead already and, above all, the evocation of sacrifice is theatrical and not propitiatory: there is no god and no cult of traditional authority which is not entirely artificial. And so while Nitsch hacks up animal flesh with an air of ancient ritual, he in fact (a) only mimics a religious liturgy for dramatic effect, (b) draws upon the brutal prestige of archaic sacrifices while acknowledging none of their responsibilities to divinity, (c) draws upon the recent aesthetic tradition which refers to blood sacrifices and (d) obtains credit for transferring the raw spirituality of prehistoric cultures to an avant-garde transgressive art-form which is universal in all westernized urban agnostic cultures.

But under this comedy, there is in fact a real sacrifice which Nitsch has made long since, as so many promising artists have done upon graduating from art academies the world over for almost a century. As we contemplated with the history of modernism, Nitsch has sacrificed his talent. He can perform sanguine allegories and critiques of cultural meanings; he can use talents such as philosophical judgement to identify issues and can engage his wits to conflate a contribution to history by representing elementary ideas in an unsynthesized visual or performative idiom;

but he can never allow his artistic talents to become vested in a celebratory manifestation. And Nitsch is by no means the most modest artist. For the rest, the outlook for talented artists is grim. The international altar of deconstruction is hungry for youth to lay their talents upon the icy slab; the sting of the avant-garde blade is brief and then there is surely a promise of a great artistic life beyond, the *outre-tombe* of talent which is the fame of artistic progress.

The sacrificial nature of contemporary art is full of ironies, balancing bitterness and humour in a marvellous parade of clever installations. The artist, having sacrificed his or her talents that were cultivated since childhood (especially identified by parents and teachers through drawing and painting), is inclined to create forbiddingly unintelligible works for the general community; the arts community is inclined to stand in awe at the dedication of the artist, witnessing the entrails of talent, so to speak, seen on the wall, the floor or the monitor; and the public, if not totally alienated, is intimidated and confused by the spread of spectacles, from outlandish and exorbitant installations by dedicated fanatics to minimal works of ascetic severity. In Germany and Australia, for example, there has been a spate of installations and videos dealing with the everyday. The spectator is treated to a display of young people demonstrating their lackadaisical coolness, their glamorous insouciance, their passive subjection to fashions, lifestyles, popular music and sympathy for advertising. The air of compliance with a dominant capitalist economy may be disheartening for many spectators, expecting revolutionary sentiment from artists, a spirit of resistance that characterizes the art of modernity from Romanticism onward. But maybe the scandal is predictable, for the young artists concerned are wilfully sacrificial, willing irrational indifference upon their destiny as artists rather than the high calling of social critic or visionary.

Rightly or wrongly, none of this makes me feel at all pessimistic. Artists generally do what artists must. The results are sometimes perplexing and apparently meaningless, all of which deserves to be interrogated with due curiosity. Sometimes, unfortunately, there is an unhelpful mixture of complacency and mystification which, when embraced or promoted in the personality-cults of a local art-scene, requires a web of insincerity to make artificial integuments for the symbolic coherence of the art. But although you can from time to time identify symbolic scandals in the arts press, the present embarrassments of art do not toll the end but signal the enduringly logical and formidable agony central to the development of western art. In essence, it is the clash between a dialectical progressive mindset and a sacramental backdrop that still gives art its claim to spirituality.

REFERENCES

Jocks, H. N. 1998. "Hermann Nitsch: Über Blut, Fleisch und Gedärme in Kunst und Literatur". *Kunstforum International* 140: 163a.

Cite this chapter as: Nelson, Robert. 'Conclusion'. *The Spirit of Secular Art: A History of the Sacramental Roots of Contemporary Artistic Values.* Melbourne: Monash University ePress. pp. 11.1–11.3. DOI: 10.2104/ssa07011.

REFERENCES

Adams, S. 1997. "British Art and Restoration France". In *The Barbizon School and the Origins of Impressionism*. London: Phaidon. 48–52.

Anrich, G. 1894. *Das antike Mysterienwesen in seinem Einfluss auf das Christentum*. Goettingen: Vandenhoeck & Ruprecht.

Aquinas, T. *Summa Theologiae* 3.61.a1. Rome: Forzani et S. Giovanni Bardi. 1927 edn.

d'Argencourt, L., in collaboration with Walker, M. S. 1984. *William Bouguereau, 1825–1905*. Montreal: Montreal Museum Of Fine Arts. [Exhibition catalogue.]

Armstrong, C. 2002. "A New Manner in Painting: Emile Zola on Manet". In *Manet Manette*. New Haven: Yale University Press. 31–47.

Aronberg Lavin, M. 2002. *Piero della Francesca*. London: Thames & Hudson.

Auchincloss, L. 1996. *La Gloire: The Roman Empire of Corneille and Racine*. Columbia, South Carolina: University of South Carolina Press.

Augustine. *Epistulae* 138.7.

Barber, C. 2002. *Figure and Likeness: On the Limits of Representation in Byzantine Iconoclasm*. Princeton, New Jersey: Princeton University Press.

Barolsky, P. 2003. "The Finger of God". In *Michelangelo and the Finger of God*. Athens, Georgia: University of Georgia, Georgia Museum. 29–55.

Bataille, G. 1970. "L'anus solaire". In *Œvres Complètes,* vol. 1, *Premiers Écrits 1922–1940*. Paris. 79–86.

Beardon C.; Malmborg, L., eds. 2002. *Digital Creativity: A Reader*. Innovations in Art and Design. Lisse: Taylor & Francis.

Beldon Scott, J. 1991. *Images of Nepotism: The Painted Ceilings of Palazzo Barberini*. Princeton, New Jersey: Princeton University Press.

Belting, H. 2003. *Art History After Modernism*, translated by Saltzwedel, Caroline; Cohen; Mitch; Northcott, Kenneth. Chicago: University of Chicago Press.

Belting, H. 2003. "Global Art and Minorities: A New Geography of Art History". In *Art History After Modernism*, translated by Saltzwedel, C.; Cohen, M. Chicago: University Of Chicago Press. 62–73.

Belting, H. 1994. *Likeness and Presence: A History of the Image Before the era of Art,* translated by Jephcott, Edmund. Chicago: University of Chicago Press.

Belting, H. 1987. *The End of the History of Art?* translated by Wood, Christopher S. Chicago: University of Chicago Press.

Benjamin, W. 1931. *The Work of Art in the Age of Mechanical Reproduction*. [*Das Kunstwerk im Zeitalter seiner technischen Reproduzierbarkeit*]. Suhrkamp Verlag, Frankfurt am Main, 1981 edn.

Bergson, H. 1911. *Laughter: An Essay on the Meaning of the Comic*, translated by Brereton, C.; Rothwell, F. New York: MacMillan.

Boardman, J. 2002. *The Archaeology of Nostalgia: How the Greeks re-created their Mythical Past*. London: Thames & Hudson.

Borsook, E.; Superbi Gioffredi, F., eds. 1994. *Italian Altarpieces 1250–1550*. Oxford: Clarendon Press.

Boyd White, J. 2001. "The Depth of Meaning in Vermeer". In *The Edge of Meaning*. Chicago: University of Chicago Press. 257–288.

Brown, J.; Garrido, C. 1998. *Velázquez: The Technique of Genius*. New Haven: Yale University Press.

Brüderlin, M., ed. 2001. *Ornament and Abstraction: The Dialogue Between Non-Western, Modern and Contemporary Art*. New Haven: Yale University Press.

Bunbury, A. 2004. *From Paris With Love: The Graphic Arts in France 1880s–1950s*. Melbourne: National Gallery of Victoria. [Exhibition catalogue.]

Butler, R. 2002. "Bright shadows: Art, Aboriginality, and aura". *The South Atlantic Quarterly* 101 (3) Summer: 501–518.

Cafritz, R. 1989. "Rococo Restoration of the Venetian Landscapes and Watteau's Creation of the Fête Galante". In *Places of Delight. The Pastoral Landscape*, edited by Cafritz, R.; Gowing, L.; Rosand, D. Washington: Weidenfeld and Nicolson. 149–181.

Caruana, W. 1990. *Aboriginal Art*. London: Thames & Hudson.

Cast, D. 1988. "Humanism and Art". In *Renaissance Humanism*, vol. 3, *Humanism and the Disciplines*, edited by Rabil, A. J., Jr. Philadelphia: University of Pennsylvania Press. 412–449.

Chaloupka, G. 1993. *Journey in Time. The World's Longest Continuing Art Tradition: The 50,000-year Story of the Australian Aboriginal Rock Art of Arnhem Land*. Sydney: Reed Books.

Childs, E. C. 1999. "The Photographic Muse". In *The Artist and the Camera- Degas to Picasso*, edited by Kosinski, D. New Haven: Yale University Press. 25–33. [Exhibition catalogue.]

Clement, R. T. 1996. *Four French Symbolists: A Sourcebook on Pierre Puvis de Chavannes, Gustave Moreau, Odilon Redon, and Maurice Denis*. Art Reference Collection 20. Westport, Connecticut: Greenwood Press.

Corbally Stourton, P. 1996. *Songlines and Dreamings. Contemporary Australian Aboriginal Painting: The First Quarter-century of Papunya Tula*, edited by Corbally Stourton, N. London: Lund Humphries Publishers.

Cox, J.; Ford, C. 2003. *Julia Margaret Cameron: The Complete Photographs*. Los Angeles: Getty Trust Publications, J. Paul Getty Museum.

Crary, J. 1999. *Suspensions of Perception: Attention, Spectacle and Modern Culture*. London and Cambridge: MIT Press.

Crawford, W. 1979. *The Keepers of Light; A History and Working Guide to Early Photographic Processes*. Dobbs Ferry, New York: Morgan and Morgan.

Cumont, F. 1902. *Les mystères de Mithra*. Paris; Brussels: H. Lamertin. 1913 edn.

Danto, A. 2003. *The Abuse of Beauty: Aesthetics and the Concept of Art*. Chicago: Open Court.

Danto, A. 1997. *After the End of Art: Contemporary Art and the Pale of History* Princeton, New Jersey: Princeton University Press.

Denny, D. 1972. "Sánchez Cotán, 'Still Life with Carrots and Cardoon'". *Pantheon* 30: 48–53.

Denziger, H. 1932. *Enchiridion symbolorum*. 18th edn. Fribourg: Herder & Co.

Diderot, D. 1995. *Diderot on Art*, edited and translated by Goodman, T. 2 vols. New Haven: Yale University Press.

Dieterich, A. 1903. *Eine Mithrasliturgie*. Leipzig: B. G. Teubner.

Drutt, M. 2003. *Kazimir Malevich: Suprematism*. New York: Guggenheim Museum. [Exhibition catalogue.]

Dunkerton, J. 1999. "North and South: Painting Techniques in Venice". In *Renaissance Venice and the North: Crosscurrents in the Time of Dürer, Bellini and Titian*, edited by B. Aikema, B.; Brown, B. L. London: Thames & Hudson. 93–103. [Exhibition catalogue.]

Eco, U. 1986. "Living in the New Middle Ages". In *Travels in Hyperreality: Essays*, translated by Weaver, W. San Diego: Harcourt Brace Jovanovich. 81–82.

Elderfield, J. 1996. *Pleasuring Painting: Matisse's Feminine Representations*. New York: Thames & Hudson.

Elkins, J. 2004. *On the Strange Place of Religion in Contemporary Art*: New York: Routledge.

Elkins, J. 1997. *The Object Stares Back: On the Nature of Seeing*. San Diego: Harcourt Brace.

Elsner, J. 1988. "Image and Iconoclasm in Byzantium". *Art History* 11: 471–491.

Farmer, J. A., ed. 2000. *The New Frontier: Art and Television, 1960–65*. Austin, Texas: Austin Museum of Art. [Exhibition Catalogue.]

Ferroni, G. 1980. "La 'Sofonisba': Un Classicismo senza Conflitto". In *Convegno di Studi su Giangorgio Trissino*, edited by Pozza, N. Vicenza: Accademia Olimpica. 111–138.

Focillon, H. 1948/1989. *The Life of Forms in Art*, translated by Hogan C. B.; Kubler. G. New York: [Publisher unknown].

Franzelin, J. 1899. *De ss. Eucharistiae sacramento et sacrificio*. Rome. S.C. de Propaganda Fide.

Freedberg, D. 1992. *Disfiguring: Art, Architecture, Religion*. Chicago: University of Chicago Press.

Freedberg, D. 1989. *The Power of Images: Studies in the History and Theory of Response*. Chicago: University of Chicago Press.

Frugoni, C. 1998. *Pietro and Ambrogio Lorenzetti*, translated by Pelletti, L. Antella, Florence: Scala.

Gablik, S. 1984. *Has Modernism Failed?* 2nd ed. London: Thames & Hudson.

Gamwell, L., ed. 2000. *Dreams 1900–2000: Science, Art, and the Unconscious Mind*. Cornell Studies in the History of Psychiatry. Binghamton: Cornell University Press.

Garb, T. 1998. "Modelling the Male Body: Physical Culture, Photography and the Classical Ideal". In *Bodies of Modernity: Figure and Flesh in Fin-de-Siècle France*. London: Thames & Hudson Ltd. 54–79.

Garge, M. 2004. "Growing up in a Painted Landscape". In *Crossing Country: The Alchemy of Western Arnhem Land Art*, edited by Perkins, H. Sydney: THNH. 107–111.

Gavuzzo-Stewart, S. 1999. *Nelle Carceri di G. B. Piranesi*, Italian Perspectives 2. Leeds: Northern Universities Press.

Goffen, R. 1997. *Titian's Women*. New Haven: Yale University Press.

Golding, J. 2000. *Paths to the Absolute: Mondrian, Malevich, Kandinsky, Pollock, Newman, Rothko and Still*. London: Thames & Hudson.

Graf, F. 1993. "Myth, Sanctuary, and Festival". In *Greek Mythology: An Introduction*, translated by. Marier, T. London: Johns Hopkins University Press.

Green, C. 2001. "The Global Significance of Western Desert Painting". In *Aborigena*, edited by Bonito Oliva, A. Milan: Electa. 21–33.

Green, M. 1999. *The Art of Destruction: Writings of the Vienna Actionists*, translated and edited by Atlas Arkhive 7. London: Atlas Press.

Green, T. 2000. *Nicolas Poussin Paints the Seven Sacraments Twice: An Interpretation of Figures, Symbols and Hieroglyphs, Together with a Running Commentary on the Paintings, the Drawings and the Artist's Letters*. Watchet: Paravail.

Grimaldo Grigsby, D. 2002. *Extremities: Painting Empire in Post-Revolutionary France*. New Haven: Yale University Press. 165–235.

Hacking, I. 1992. "The Self-Vindication of the Laboratory Sciences". In *Science as Practice and Culture*, edited by Pickering, A. Chicago: University of Chicago Press. 29–64.

Harradine G.; Kruger, K. eds. 2000. *This is Koorie Art*. Melbourne: Koori Heritage Trust.

Healy, J. 2006. "A Fragile Thing: Marketing of Remote Area Aboriginal Art". Doctoral dissertation. Melbourne: The University of Melbourne.

Hepding, H. 1903. *Attis, seine Mythen und sein Kult*. Giessen. In *Religionsgeschichtliche Versuche*, vol. 1, by Dieterich, A.; Wuensch, R. Giessen: Ricker.

Hercus, L.; Hodges, F.; Simpson, J. eds. 2002. *The Land is a Map: Placenames of Indigenous Origin in Australia*. Canberra: Pandanus Books, Research School of Pacific and Asian Studies, Australian National University in association with Pacific Linguistics.

Hills, P. 1999. *Venetian Colour: Marble, Mosaic, Painting and Glass 1250–1550*. New Haven: Yale University Press.

Hoeniger, C. 1995. "The Reframing of Gothic Altarpieces During the Renaissance". In *The Renovation of Paintings in Tuscany, 1250–1500*. Cambridge: Cambridge University Press. 101–126.

Hughes, R. 2003. *Goya*. London: Harvill.

Hume, L. 2002. *Ancestral Power: The Dreaming, Consciousness, and Aborignial Australians*. Melbourne: Melbourne University Press.

Isaacs J.; Holt, D.; Holt, J.; Ryan, J.; Smith , T. 1998. *Emily Kngwarreye: Paintings*. Sydney: Craftsman House.

Jobert, B. 1998. *Delacroix*, translated by Grabar, T.; Bonfante-Warren, A. Princeton, New Jersey: Princeton University Press. 78–88.

Jocks, H. N. 1998. "Hermann Nitsch: Über Blut, Fleisch und Gedärme in Kunst und Literatur". *Kunstforum International* 140: 163a.

Jordan, W. B. 1985. *Spanish Still Life in the Golden Age 1600–1650*. (Fort Worth, Texas: Kyoto. [Exhibition catalogue.]

Junquera, J. 2003. *The Black Paintings of Goya*, translated by Evans, G. London: Scala Publishers Ltd.

Kandinsky. 1911. "On the Spiritual in Art". In *The Life of Vasilii Kandinsky in Russian Art: A Study of on the Spiritual in Art* (1980), edited by Bowlt, J. E.; Washton-Long, R., and translated by Bowlt, J. Russian Biography Series 4. Newtonville, Massachusetts: Oriental Research Partners.

Kantorowicz, G. 1992. *The Inner Nature of Greek Art*, translated by Benson, J. L. New York: New Rochelle. 123–135.

Kaplan, E. A. 1998. "Freud, Film, and Culture". In *Freud: Conflict and Culture*, edited by Roth, M. S. New York: Knopf. 152–164.

Koch, H. 1900. *Pseudo-Dionysius Areopagita in seinen Beziehungen zum Neuplatonismus und Mysterienwesen*. Mainz: [Publisher unknown].

Kosinski, D. M. 1988. "Gustave Courbet's The Sleepers: The Lesbian Image in Nineteenth-Century French Art and Literature". *Artibus et Historiae* 18: 187–199.

Kuspit, D. 2000a. *The Dialectic of Decadence: Between Advance and Decline in Art.* Aesthetics Today. New York: Allworth Press.

Kuspit, D. 2000b. *The Rebirth of Painting in the Late Twentieth Century.* New York: Cambridge University Press.

Ladner, G. 1953. "The Concept of the Image in the Greek Fathers and the Byzantine Iconoclastic Controversy". *Dumbarton Oaks Papers* 7. Dumbarton Oaks.

Leis, H.; D'Amato, J. L. 2005. "Para una teoría de las prácticas del ambientalismo". *Theomai*, First semester, no. 11.

Long, C. 1997. "Ornament, Crime, Myth, and Meaning". In *Architecture: Material and Imagined.* Proceedings of the 85th American Collegiate Schools of Architecture Annual Meeting. Washington. 440–445.

Maginnis, H. B. J. 1997. *Painting in the Age of Giotto: A Historical Reevaluation.* University Park, Pennsylvania: Pennsylvania State University Press.

Marlais, M. A. 1992. *Conservative Echoes in Fin-de-Siècle Parisian Art Criticism.* University Park, Pennsylvania: Pennsylvania State University Press.

Marsh, A. 1993. *Body and Self: Performance Art in Australia 1969–92.* Melbourne: Oxford University Press.

Martineau, J., ed. 1992. *Andrea Mantegna.* London: Royal Academy of Arts. [Exhibition catalogue.]

McCauley, E. A. 1994. "Braquehais and the Photographic Nude". In *Industrial Madness: Commercial Photography in Paris, 1848–1871.* New Haven: Yale University Press. 105–194.

McCulloch, A.; McCulloch, S.; McCulloch Child, E. 2006. *The New McCulloch's Encyclopedia of Australian Art.* Melbourne: Miegunyah Press.

McCulloch, S. 2001. *Contemporary Aboriginal Art: A Guide to the Rebirth of an Ancient Culture.* Sydney: Allen & Unwin.

McLean, I. 1998. *White Aborigines.* Cambridge: Cambridge University Press.

Meixner, L. L. 1995. "Courbet, Corot, and Democratic Poetics". In *French Realist Painting and the Critique of American Society, 1865–1900.* Cambridge: Cambridge University Press. 142–193.

Mérot, A. 1995. *French Painting in the Seventeenth Century*, translated by Beamish, C. New Haven: Yale University Press.

Migne, J. P. 1844–64. *Patrologiae Cursus Completus. Series Latina.* Paris: Garnier.

Moffitt, J. F. 2003. "Duchamp in New York with Esoteric Patrons and the Large Glass, 1915–1923". In *Alchemist of the Avant-garde: The Case of Marcel Duchamp.* SUNY Series in Western Esoteric Traditions. Albany: State University of New York Press. 169–224.

Moorhead, J. 1986. "Byzantine Iconoclasm as a Problem in Art History". *Parergon* n.s. 4: 1–18.

Morand, K. 1991. *Claus Sluter: Artist at the Court of Burgundy.* London: Austin.

Morgan, D. 2005. *The Sacred Gaze: Religious Visual Culture in Theory and Practice.* Berkeley: University of California Press.

Morgan, D. 1999. *Visual Piety: A History and Theory of Popular Religious Images*. Berkeley: University of California Press.

Morrison, V. 1997. "The lion and the horse series". In *The Art of George Stubbs*. Sydney: Sandstone Books. 108–116.

Myers, F. R. 2002. *Painting Culture: The Making of an Aboriginal High Art*. Objects/Histories Critical Perspectives on Art, Material Culture, and Representation. London: Duke University Press.

Nagel, A. 2000. *Michelangelo and the Reform of Art*. Cambridge: Cambridge University Press.

Naumann, F. M.; Venn, B.; Antliff, A. 1996. *Making Mischief: Dada Invades New York*. New York: Whitney Museum of American Art.

Nelson, R. 2007. "Brilliant Fantasy Worlds Capture Travesties in Motion". *The Age*. 30 May, p. 17.

Nelson, R. 2006. "Agonised voice of scream and howl". *The Age*. 31 May, p. 24.

Nelson, R. 2006. "Manhattan's Trashy Treasures". *The Age*. 4 October, p. 24.

Nelson, R. 2006. "Belligerence that silences the viewer". *The Age*. 25 January, p. 18.

Nelson, R. 2003. "Don't Try This at Home". *The Age*, A3. 15 October, p. 7.

Newberry, T.; Bisacca, G.; Kanter, L. B. 1990. *Italian Renaissance Frames*. New York: Metropolitan Museum of Art. Distributed by H.N. Abrams, c1990.)

Nicholls, C.; North, I. 2001. *Kathleen Petyarre: Genius of Place*. Kent Town, South Australia: Wakefield Press.

Nicholson, K. 1990. *Turner's Classical Landscapes: Myth and Meaning*. Princeton, New Jersey: Princeton University Press.

Nickel, D. R. 2002. "Ducks That Lie in Tempests". In *Dreaming in Pictures: The Photography of Lewis Carroll*. New Haven: Yale University Press. 55–72.

Le Normande-Romain, A. 2004. "The Lesson of Antiquity". In *Rodin: The Zola of Sculpture*, edited by Mitchell, C. Subject/Object: New Studies in Sculpture Aldershot: Ashgate Publishing. 145–159.

North, M.; Ormrod, D., eds. 1998. *Art Markets in Europe 1400–1800*. Aldershot: Ashgate Publishing Limited.

Olson, T. P. 2002. *Poussin and France: Painting, Humanism and the Politics of Style*. New Haven: Yale University Press.

Ovid. 1959. *Fasti* 5.193–220. Loeb classical library. English translation by Sir James Frazer. London; Cambridge, Mass. : Heinemann; Harvard University Press.

Pesch, C. 1908. *De sacramentis, praelectiones dogmaticae*. Fribourg: Herder & Co.

Pieri, M., ed. 1995. *Il Barocco. Marino e la Poesia del Seicento*, Cento Libri per Mille Anni. Rome: Ist. Poligrafico e Zecca dello Stato-Archivi di Stato.

Plax, J. A. 2000. *Watteau and the Cultural Politics of Eighteenth-Century France*. Cambridge: Cambridge University Press.

Pocock, G. 1980. *Boileau and the Nature of Neo-Classicism*, Major European Authors Series. Cambridge: Cambridge University.

Pohlmann, U. 1996. "Alma-Tadema and Photography". In *Sir Lawrence Alma-Tadema 1836–1912*, edited by Becker E., et al. New York: Rizzoli. 111–124.

Posner, D. M. 1999. *The Performance of Nobility in Early Modern European Literature*, Cambridge Studies in Renaissance Literature and Culture 33. Cambridge: Cambridge University Press.

Puttfarken, T. 2000. *The Discovery of Pictorial Composition: Theories of Visual Order in Painting 1400–1800*. New Haven: Yale University Press.

Rice, S. 1988. "Souvenirs". *Art in America* 76: 156–171.

Robertson, M. 1993. "What is 'Hellenistic' about 'Hellenistic' Art?" In *Hellenistic History and Culture*, edited by Green, P. Hellenistic History and Culture, 9. Berkeley: University of California Press.

Rodner, W. S. 1997. *J. M. W. Turner, Romantic Painter of the Industrial Revolution*. Berkeley: University of California Press.

De Sanctis, F. 1970. *Storia della letteratura italiana*, edited by Lanza, M. T., 7th ed. Milan: Feltrinelli.

Sayers, A. 2001. *Australian Art*. Oxford History of Art. Oxford: Oxford University Press.

Schafter, D. 2002. The Order of Ornament, the Structure of Style: Theoretical Foundations of Modern Art and Architecture. Cambridge: Cambridge University Press.

da Silva, J. A. 2005. "A reforma 'Eucarística' do Concílio Vaticano II, vista dentro do contexto histórico geral da liturgia". National Conference of Brazilian Bishops. São Paulo.

Smith, A. 1977. *An inquiry into the nature and causes of the wealth of nations*. Chicago. University Of Chicago Press (first published London: W. Strahan and T. Cadell, 1776).

Smith, B. 1998. *Modernism's History: A Study in Twentieth-Century Art and Ideas*. Sydney: UNSW Press.

Smith, R. R. R. 2002. "The Use of Images: Visual History and Ancient History". In *Classics in Progress: Essays on Ancient Greece and Rome*, edited by Wiseman, T. P. Oxford: Oxford University Press.

Smith, T. 2000. "Australia's Anxiety". In *History and Memory in the Art of Gordon Bennett*. Birmingham: Ikon Gallery.10–21. [Exhibition catalogue.]

Snow-Smith, J. 1993. *The Primavera of Sandro Botticelli: A Neoplatonic Interpretation*. New York: Peter Lang Publishing.

Spivey, N. 1996. "Revealing Aphrodite". In *Understanding Greek Sculpture: Ancient Meanings, Modern Readings*. New York: Thames & Hudson.

Staller, N. 2001. *A Sum of Destructions: Picasso's Cultures and the Creation of Cubism*. New Haven: Yale University Press.

Stewart, A. F. 1997. *Art, Desire and the Body in Ancient Greece*. Cambridge: Cambridge University Press.

Tarn Steiner, D. 2001. *Images in Mind: Statues in Archaic and Classical Greek Literature and Thought*. Princeton, New Jersey: Princeton University Press.

Taylor, M. C. 1992. *Disfiguring: Art, Architecture, Religion*. Chicago: University of Chicago Press.

Taylor, M. C. 1984. *Erring: A Postmodern A/Theology*. Chicago: University of Chicago Press.

Tompkins Lewis, M. 2000. *Cézanne*. London: Phaidon Press.

Trinkaus, C. 1999. "Renaissance Ideas and the Idea of the Renaissance". In *Renaissance Transformations of Late Medieval Thought*, Variorum Collection Studies Series. Aldershot: Ashgate Publishing. 667–684.

Troup, C. 1998. *The Image as Body: Reflections on Language and Art Restoration through Neri di Bicci's Le Ricordanze 1453–75*. Melbourne: Monash Publications in History, Department of History, Monash University.

Vasari, G. 1979 edn. *Lives of the Most Eminent Painters, Sculptors, and Architects*. New York: Abrams.

Venning, B. 2003. *Turner*. London: Phaidon.

Venturi, R. 1966. *Complexity and Contradiction in Architecture*. New York: Museum of Modern Art in Association with the Graham Foundation for Advanced Studies in the Fine Arts. Distributed By Doubleday & Company.

Venturi, R.; Scott Brown, D.; Izenour, S. 1972. *Learning from Las Vegas: The Forgotten Symbolism of Architectural Form*. Cambridge, Massachusetts: MIT Press.

Verdon, T. 2002. "The Spiritual World of Piero's Art". In *The Cambridge Companion to Piero della Francesca*, edited by Wood, J. M. Cambridge: Cambridge University Press 30–50.

Veyne, P. 1983. *Les Grecs ont-ils cru à leurs mythes?* Paris: Éditions du Seuil.

Watson, S. 2003. *Factory Made: Warhol and the Sixties*. New York: Pantheon Books.

Weis, A. 1992. *The Hanging Marsyas and its Copies: Roman Innovations in a Hellenistic Sculptural Tradition*. Rome: Bretschneider.

West, S. 2004. *Portraiture*. Oxford History of Art. Oxford: Oxford University Press.

Wheelock, A. K., Jr. 1995. *Vermeer and the Art of Painting*. New Haven: Yale University Press.

White, J. 1993. *Art and Architecture in Italy 1250–1400*, 3rd ed. New Haven and London: Pelican History of Art.

Wiles, D. *Tragedy in Athens: Performance Space and Theatrical Meaning*. Cambridge: Cambridge University Press.

Williamson, P. 1995. *Gothic Sculpture 1140–1400*. New Haven: Yale University Press.

Wilson, C. 1992. *The Gothic Cathedral: The Architecture of the Great Church*, 2nd edn. London: Thames & Hudson.

Wind, E. 1980. *Pagan Mysteries in the Renaissance*. Oxford: Oxford University Press (first published Faber & Faber 1958).

Wixom, W. D. "Byzantine Art and the Latin West". In *The Glory of Byzantium: Art and Culture of the Middle Byzantine Era A.D. 843–1261*, edited by Evans, H. C.; Wixom, W. D. New York: The Metropolitan Museum of Art. 435–507.

Woodford, S. 2003. *Images of Myths in Classical Antiquity*. Cambridge: Cambridge University Press.

Zola, E. 1867. "Une nouvelle manière en peinture: Edouard Manet". *Revue du dix-neuvième siècle*, 1 January.